GERALD E. SWANSON, M.D.
9601 UPTON ROAD
MINNEAPOLIS MN 55431
TELE: 881-6869

CONDENSED HISTORY
OF
MEEKER COUNTY

1855 - 1939

PRICE $3.00

COMPILED AND PUBLISHED BY

FRANK B. LAMSON
LITCHFIELD, MINNESOTA

BROWN PRINTING COMPANY

DEDICATION

This history of Meeker County, 1855 - 1939, is dedicated to Jesse V. Branham, Senior and Junior, who were among the outstanding heroes of 1862 and to those other sturdy pioneers who were their associates in the years of that period of danger with its hardships and privations. These noble men and women laid the foundation for the marvelous development that followed in their wake. . . . .

THE PIONEER

The sinking sun is shedding gold,
  Upon a picture rare and grand,
There is a pioneer of old,
  Harvesting his grain by hand.
He grips the cradle in his hands,
  And moves with steady even stride,
Then stops to bind with golden strands,
  Of straw, the grain which is his pride.
And from his brow he's wiping sweat,
  The evidence of honest toil,
Here is reward ne'er to forget,
  The first fruits of the virgin soil.
I pause with reverence in my heart,
  And from my eyes the tear drops start
When I recall the pioneer souls,
  And how they struggled toward their
    goals.

They tasted danger and despair
  And untold hardships had to bear.
Oh, they were challenged to supreme
  Self sacrifice and faith and hope,
They were men who kept a dream
  Though oft with grim fact forced to
    cope.

* * * * * *

A tribute, then, to pioneers,
  Who, facing dangers, knew no fears:
And, may their courage thrill us still,
  Their strength of character and will.
Their spirit, like a torch at night,
  Must burn in us with radiance bright.

— Virginia Miller, Grove City, Minn.

Selected from a brochure published by her father, A. A. Miller, as a tribute to his pioneer father.

JESSE BRANHAM, SENIOR

No student of Meeker County History will fail to regard Jesse V. Branham, Senior and Junior as conspicuous heroes of the perilous period of the Indian outbreak of 1862. They were natives respectively of Kentucky and Indiana and established their homes in 1857 in Litchfield township. When they learned of the massacre at Acton, they were the guiding spirits of the neighboring settlers in finding a safe refuge for the women and children.

The senior Branham was sixty years of age when, at the height of the panic, he rode from Forest City to St. Paul, a distance of one hundred miles by blazed trail, to secure military assistance, arms, and ammunition for the beleaguered settlers. He later joined his family at Minneapolis where he remained until all danger had passed and the following spring returned to Forest City and two years later took possession of his homestead where he resumed his farming operations. In 1874 he took up his residence in the village of Litchfield. He was county treasurer of Meeker County 1864-1870.

He died July 30, 1893.

Mary Butler Branham, his wife, died June 12, 1888.

JESSE V. BRANHAM, JUNIOR

Jesse V. Branham, Jr., was born in Jennings County, Indiana, July 8, 1834. He was 28 years of age at the time of the Indian outbreak and had established his home in section 35, Litchfield town. On Sunday, August 17, 1862, word having reached him of the Baker-Jones massacre at Acton, he and his brother proceeded toward Acton to confirm these reports but meeting parties enroute who had come from the Baker home, he returned to his family and having rallied all his neighbors, they found a temporary refuge in the George C. Whitcomb home. Early Monday morning he piloted them to Forest City and from there, a few days later, escorted the women and children for some distance through the "Big Woods" to secure shelter at Clearwater, Wright County. He then returned to Kingston where he conferred with the settlers in formulating plans for the construction of the Kingston stockade. (See chapter relating to the Battle of Acton.)

Mr. Branham was a millwright by trade and during the winter of 1863-4 operated the water power mill at Greenleaf. He served as County Auditor 1866 to 1871. He was the first town clerk of Ness town. He drew the bill providing for the county seat contest, and gave Litchfield its name.

He died August 11, 1914. Mary Stark Branham, his wife, died Januray 23, 1915. Children: Hiram S., Alice (Mrs. W. R. Burns), Delaney E., Louise (Mrs. Peter Rodange), and Thomas F.

THE FOREST CITY MILL

1865 - 1914

This mill was erected by Hines and Kimball and at the time of its dismantling was operated by Albert DeLong.

THE MANANNAH MILL

1869 - 1923

The illustration is contributed by Elmer W. Parsons in remembrance of his father, Henry Parsons, who operated the mill, 1907-1910.

EDEN VALLEY HIGH SCHOOL
(Erected in 1927)

LITCHFIELD HIGH SCHOOL
(Erected in 1930)

— MEEKER COUNTY —

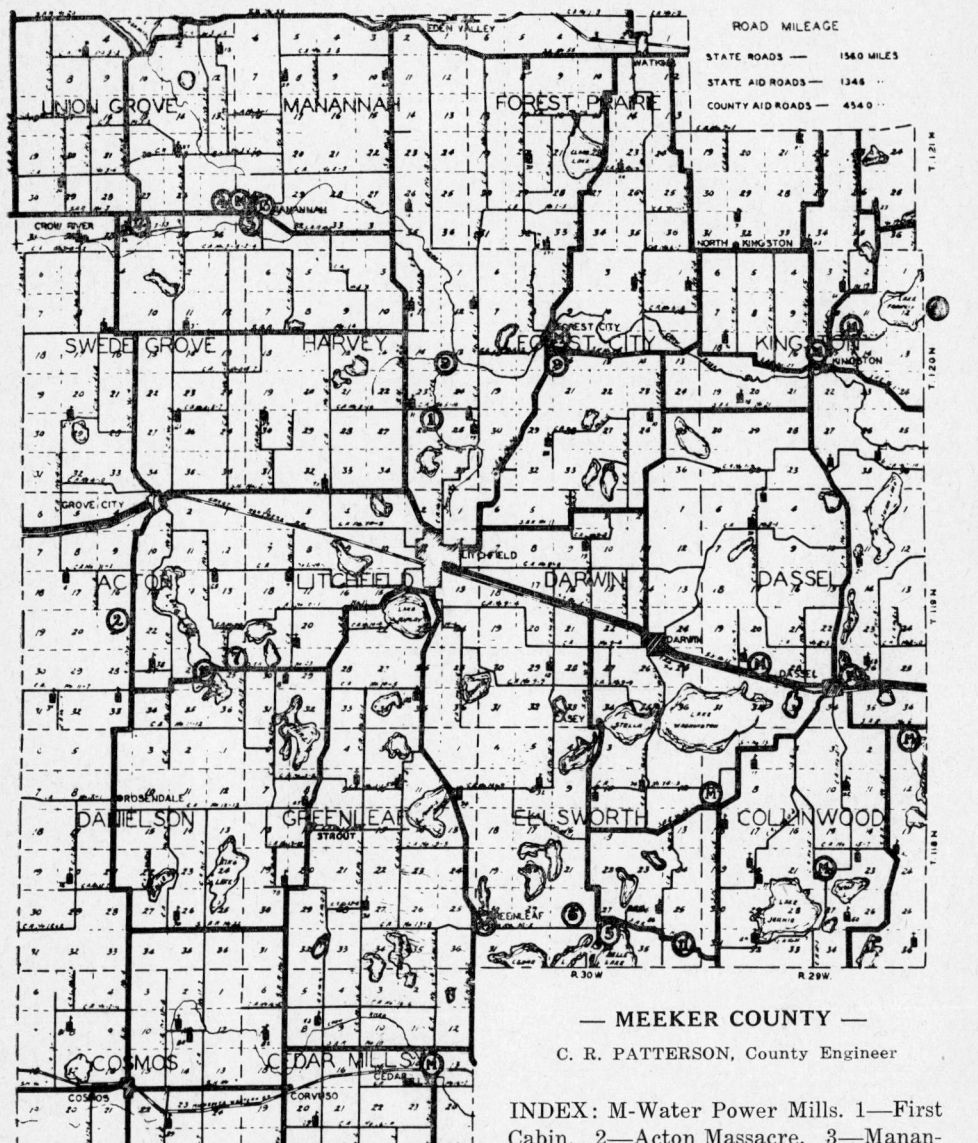

C. R. PATTERSON, County Engineer

INDEX: M-Water Power Mills. 1—First Cabin. 2—Acton Massacre. 3—Manannah Massacre. 4—Manannah Cemetery. The killing of Caleb Sanborn (5), Daniel Cross (6), Andrew Olson (7), James McGannon (8). 9—Forest City Stockade. 10—Kelly's Bluff. 11—Little Crow Meets Death. 12—Burr Oak Cemetery. 13—Manannah (Old townsite).

FOREWORD

In compiling a condensed history of Meeker County it has been the purpose of the writer to cover the high lights of pioneer days and outline the development of the county's resources during the passing years. The stories and facts presented in this volume have been carefully and patiently verified.

Readers may rest assured that the aim has been to select such matter as is authoritative, interesting and instructive. The sources of authority for the information given are the files of Meeker County newspapers, A. C. Smith's History of Meeker County (1877), Album of Meeker County History (1888), Folwell's History of Minnesota, Historical pamphlets published by M. P. Satterlee and personal interviews of the few remaining citizens whose residence extends to the period previous to the coming of the railroad.

Location and Early History

Meeker County is situated in almost the exact center of the southern half of Minnesota. The length of Meeker County from north to south is 30 miles and its greatest width is 24 miles. It is bounded by the following counties: on the north by Stearns, east by Wright, south by McLeod and Renville and west by Kandiyohi. It includes seventeen and one-half congressional townships. The greater portion of the county consisted of rolling prairie covered with brush and light timber, while a considerable area was heavily timbered.

The surface is well watered by numerous lakes and streams. The principal stream is the Crow River with its tributaries which, in pioneer days, furnished a moderate degree of transportation and reliable water power. These streams were followed by the early settlers who established their settlements at chosen points along the Crow River.

From the date of the first settlement in 1856 until the coming of the St. Paul and Pacific railroad (The Great Northern) in 1869 constitutes what may properly be termed the pioneer period in the development of the county. The principal crops during this term of years were small grains, corn and vegetables while most of the settlers gradually acquired sufficient live stock and poultry to meet in part the necessities of life. Wild game and fish were plentiful which was a great boon to the pioneers until they became more firmly established.

Meeker County was created by the seventh territorial legislature February 23, 1856 at which time it embraced all of its present territory except the towns of Cedar Mills and Cosmos which were then a part of Renville County. The county was named in honor of Hon. B. B. Meeker of St. Anthony. The Governor appointed Thomas H. Skinner, John W. Huy, and Dr. Frederick Ripley commissioners. Their first meeting was held at Skinner's home in Forest City, May 5, 1856. Dr. Ripley was not present at this meeting. He was frozen to death in a blizzard March 3, 1856 on the shores of the lake that bears his name. Very little business was transacted at this meeting; M. G. Moore was appointed register of deeds and clerk of the board and Abijah Bemis, sheriff. The county, as a whole, constituted the only election precinct. No further meetings of the board were held until January 5, 1857. At a meeting held January 4, 1858 the school tax collected in 1857 amounting to $102.80 was apportioned as follows: District No. 1, Kingston (32 pupils) received $26.88; District 2, Forest City (55 pupils) $46.20; District 3, Manannah (35 pupils) $29.40; District 4, Acton, made no returns and did not share in this division of funds.

At the meeting held April 5, 1858 the territory of the county was organized into eight towns. The county at this time embraced Townships 118, 119, 120, and 121 of Range 33 west which were at a later period annexed to Kandiyohi County and did not include the towns of Cosmos and Cedar Mills which were included in the boundaries of Renville County.

The territory embraced in the present boundaries of the county was divided as follows: Kingston included Dassel; Forest City embraced Forest Prairie and the east half of Harvey; Manannah included Union Grove, north half of Swede Grove and west half of Harvey; Rice City embraced the towns of Collinwood, Darwin and Ellsworth; Ness was the name given to the towns of Litchfield and Greenleaf and Acton embraced the towns of Danielson, and the south half of Swede Grove. These constituted the political divisions of the county until the influx of settlers following the close of the Civil War and the coming of the railroad when the boundaries of the several towns were subjected to changes in territory and name as they exist at present. The assessed valuation of Meeker County in 1858 totaled $181,571 divided as follows: real estate, $131,871; personal property, $49,700. During the years 1856 to 1869 the trading centers of the county in order of importance were Forest City, the county seat and the location until 1862 of the U. S. Land Office; Kingston, the first milling center; Greenleaf; Manannah; and Collinwood. The importance of these centers was largely due to their picturesque location and the fact that they were the flour and feed mill centers that served the settlers of that period and a considerable area of country not included in Meeker County. The coming of the railroad in 1869 was a great event. Numerous surveys were made and all of these above centers of trade were deeply interested and great hopes were entertained by all these townsites that the preferred survey would give them the supremacy. It is the contention of the settlers in all of these centers with the exception of Greenleaf that it was due to the individual settlers owning the desired acreage for right of way and other railroad purposes asking excessive prices for their land that none of these townsites failed to connect and lost their former supremacy. The village of Litchfield had been platted in June 1869 and at the election of November 2 of that year the paramount issue was the proposed removal of the county seat from Forest City to Litchfield. The total vote of the county was 929 and Litchfield won by a majority of 89 votes. A change of 45 votes would have given Forest City the victory. The coming of the iron horse over its established location had wrecked all future hopes for the then existing leadership of the well established townsites of Kingston, Forest City, Collinwood, and Manannah. These townsites have no system of transportation and no postoffices. Kingston is the only inland townsite that retains any part of its former supremacy.

THE FIRST SETTLERS

In the spring of 1855 John Huy, Benjamin Brown and a man named Mackenzie polled their way up Crow River in search of pine timber as employees of a lumber firm. They were unsuccessful in their search and returned to St. Anthony to report their failure. John Huy then organized an exploring party among whom were Rudolph Schultz, D. M. Hanson and Thomas H. Skinner and in the fall reached the junction of Crow River and creeks entering the same and then followed the course of the creek connecting Lake Ripley with the Crow River and constructed a cabin in section 25, town of Harvey, where they planned to establish a townsite which they named Kar-i-shon (the Indian name for crow.) Huy and Skinner spent the winter in their crude shack and in the spring of 1856 they explored the Crow River and discovered in sections 17 and 20, town of Forest City what they regarded as a more favorable site for a village. They abandoned their cabin and erected a claim shanty and named their changed location Forest City. Upon their chosen claim arose the village of that name which for a period of 12 years was the seat of county government. John Huy lived here until the summer of 1862 when he left the county, having previously preempted the north east quarter of section 19, Forest City town, and in 1888 he was a resident of California.

John Huy and Thomas H. Skinner were members of the first board of county commissioners. Skinner died in Milwaukee August 20, 1863 and was buried in St. Albans, Maine, the home of his boyhood. Rudolph Schultz became a permanent resident in section 26, Harvey town.

EARLY BIRTHS

The Album of History published in 1888 names Sarah Jane Dougherty, daughter of Thomas Dougherty, born in a covered wagon in Forest City, July 15, 1856 as the first white child born in Meeker County. The same history lists the birth of William Cates, son of Mark Cates, of Kingston, to have occurred July 6, 1856. In the biographical section the statement is made that Mark Cates went to Maine for his bride and returned with her to the Kingston home this same year. The biography does not give the date of marriage. The census of 1870, (John Blackwell, enumerator) under date of August 10, 1870, gives Will Cates' age as 12 which would seem to indicate that he was born July 6, 1858 or two years later than is recorded in the history of 1888.

Walter Salisbury, son of J. B. Salisbury, was born in Kingston town October 26, 1856, which is in harmony with the census record.

Ole Halverson, son of Henry Halverson, was born in Litchfield town December 11, 1856, which is also in harmony with the census record.

FIRST HOMESTEADERS

The following is a list of the first homesteaders in each of the townships of Meeker County. The first settlers in the county acquired their lands under the preemption law whereby they purchased the land direct from the government at $1.25 per acre. The homestead law did not become effective until January 1, 1863.

D. E. after each name and description represents the date of entry.

Acton—Paul Paulson. Lot 3, Sec. 10. D. E. March 10, 1863.

Cedar Mills—Daniel McGraw. SE¼ SW¼, NW¼ SE¼, S½ SE¼, Sec. 4. D.E. March 10, 1863.

Collinwood—Thomas J. Hutchins. N½ NW¼, Sec. 8. D.E. July 7, 1864.

Cosmos—Daniel Hoyt. NW¼, Sec. 20. D.E. May 9, 1864.

Danielson—Andrew Christopherson. SW¼, Sec. 2. D.E. Sept 17, 1863. Nils Danielson. NE¼, Sec. 2. D.E. Nov. 28, 1863.

Darwin—John Pieffer, SE¼ SW¼, Sec. 4. D.E. Jan. 1, 1863.

Dassel—William Cunningham. SW¼ NW¼, Lot 3, Sec. 2. D.E. Mar. 23, 1865.

Ellsworth—John C. Kruger. NE¼ NW¼, S½ NW¼, Sec. 8. D.E. June 1, 1863.

Forest City—Michael Flynn. Lot 2, Sec. 34. D.E. Jan. 1, 1863.

Forest Prairie—Robert K. Beecham. E½ NW¼, SW¼ NW¼, Sec. 18. D.E. June 23, 1871.

Greenleaf—Michael Ryan. SE¼, Sec. 20. D.E. Feb. 23, 1863.

Harvey—Rudolph Schultz. SW¼ NE¼, Sec. 26. D.E. Feb. 26, 1863.

Kingston—Benjamin F. Dorman. W½ NW¼, Sec. 20. D.E. Feb. 24, 1863.

Litchfield—Nels Klemenson. Lots 1, 2, Sec. 6. D.E. Jan. 5, 1863.

Manannah—Augustus B. Wood. Lots 11 and 12, Sec. 6. D.E. Dec. 12, 1869.

Swede Grove—Nels Halverson. Lot 3, NE¼ SE¼, Sec. 32. D.E. Aug. 3, 1863.

Union Grove—Andrew Hamilton. S½ SE¼, SE¼ SW¼, and NW¼ SE¼, Sec. 14. D.E. March 23, 1869.

When the pioneer settlers of Meeker county gained title to their land they acquired the same directly or indirectly from the government, either by preemption by which they paid $1.25 per acre to the government direct; by homestead after the passage of the homestead law which took effect January 1, 1863; by purchase of land in the odd numbered sections from the railroad company, or by purchase of school lands in sections 16 and 36 from the state. There were two other ways by which they secured lands in the early days, one by which they surrendered land warrants and the other by what is designated in the county register's office as S.H.B.S.

CITIZENSHIP

The population of Meeker County at the time of the first census in 1860 was 928 and 61 per cent of this number were native born Americans. The larger portion of this number were from New York and New England with an almost equal number from Kentucky and Virginia. There was a scattering population of Irish and Scandinavians.

The most populous settlements were found in the towns traversed by the Crow River, Kingston, Forest City, and Manannah. There was a goodly number of settlers in Greenleaf, Ellsworth, Swede Grove, and Acton and scattered settlers in other portions of the county.

The population of the county at the present time is quite cosmopolitan consisting of Americans of Scandinavian, German, Irish, and Finnish descent with a lesser number of the descendants of Colonial ancestry.

When the census of 1885 was taken the population of the county was 17,389 of which 11,588 were native born whose nationality could not be definitely determined but it is safe to say that they were very largely the descendants of those of foreign birth in proportion to the number of foreign born residents of the county at this time. The tide of emigration in 1885 had become nominal. The division of foreign born numbered at this time 5,801 divided as follows: Sweden, 3,311; Germany, 776; Norway, 664; Ireland, 273; Denmark, 268; Canada, 247; Finland, 167; and other countries, 95.

Mixed marriages were very uncommon in pioneer days. The first case of the blending of nationalities was the marriage of William H. Wilcox, a native of Ohio, and Ellen Peterson, a native of Sweden and a sister of Peter E. Hanson, an eminent citizen of Meeker County. This marriage was solemnized November 9, 1867.

The years have rolled by and among those of the third generation of the early settlers there has been an ever increasing mixture of nationalities which has improved the strain of blood that permeates the present generation. This mixture of nationalities produced a Lindberg and others who occupy high places in our country's development. Nationality distinctions have become well nigh obliterated in Meeker County. The English language has come into general use and nothing remains to designate the ancestral origin except the surnames of its citizens and the hyphenated names applied to some of our church organizations. There are a few segregated groups of Americans of foreign birth in the county among which the most numerous is a settlement of Finnish people in the town of Kingston. They have clung rather closely to their language and foreign customs and ways of living but the third generation of this group have adopted American customs and ways of living and have led their classmates in scholarship in many of our high schools and colleges. One of the most interesting of their old country institutions found in all communities of Finnish descent is The Sauna or Finnish steam bath.

SAUNA — FINNISH STEAM BATH

Even a brief sketch that, for lack of space, touches merely the high spots of the history of a Finnish people, would be very incomplete without some mention of the centuries old Finnish institution—the Sauna (Finnish steam bath). That small, smoke darkened building was almost a very part of the lives of the early Finnish people. It is today, with various elaborations of construction and convenience, a very necessary institution in the lives of the descendants of the early Finns. The building proper of the early day sauna is about 10x16 feet square, divided into two rooms. One room with benches or seats around the wall is the dressing room; the other, with a pile of stones heaped over a central fireplace (kiuas) in one corner of the room, a wide platform (lava) about 4 feet below the ceiling with steps leading up to it, is the steaming and washing room. On the lava (platform) are generally kept a supply of oak or cedar bough fans (vihtat) which are soaked in water and then steamed over the hot stones before being used.

In taking the sauna, the bathers ascend to a seat on the "lava", dash cold water on the hot stones to form steam, which is thus maintained at any desired temperature. When the steam soaked air gets quite hot, then the "vihtat" or fans come into use. The hot steamed air is fanned against the body with vigorous slapping motions of the "vihtat" (this fanning and slapping action of the skin helps to open the innumerable small pores of the skin and causes profuse sweating.) The steaming is followed by the customary thorough soaping, followed by a warm to hot rinse, which is sometimes sopped off with a cool or cold rinse to close the pores and stop the perspiration. Then a leisurely drying with a towel in the dressing room with a vigorous rubbing of the skin with the towel finishes that which to all outward appearances is all that there is to a "sauna" — except the effects. What these effects are may readily be experienced by any one who wishes to do so by taking the sauna bath.

CROW RIVER BRIDGE

The first bridge across Crow river was built at the present location of the bridge in the Kingston townsite in 1861. It was built at a contract price of $285, by M. P. Littlefield.

LOST IN A BLIZZARD

When the Dassel-Hutchinson mail carrier became lost in the blinding blizzard of January, 1873, he wound up in Litchfield instead of Hutchinson. He was docked a day's pay which was later returned to him thru the efforts of Senators Alex Ramsey and William Windom. In this blizzard Daniel Hoyt of Cosmos, Mike Condon and Mike Flynn, of Forest City, were frozen to death.

DEATH OF DR. RIPLEY

In March 1856 Dr. Frederick Noah Ripley of Shakopee and John McClelland of Glencoe were employed by Bell and Chapman to go to Cedar City, near Cedar Mills, about nine miles from Hutchinson and 13 miles from Litchfield, and there construct a log house as a temporary hotel and stopping place for newcomers and others who might conclude to settle or engage in business at the new townsite. The snow was rapidly disappearing when they started and the weather was mild. The indications were that spring was near at hand. They left from Glencoe after changing their moccasins to boots, with supplies of food sufficient to last only ten days at which time their employers promised them additional supplies. Upon their arrival they built a temporary shelter with a few logs in which to live while engaged in building the hotel and supplied cover for only the portion of the shanty under which they had their bed. A few days following their arrival a fierce snowstorm prevailed and the weather changed to bitter cold. They remained there fifteen days until all their food, except a pound of dried apples and a quart of rice, was exhausted and no one appeared with additional supplies. At the expiration of that time they started for Forest City.

It was a delightful morning when they started. A slight breeze prevailed, the air was warm and balmy and the snow was melting rapidly. Shortly after they had started the wind increased in velocity and they were enveloped by a terrible blizzard. They were compelled to establish their camp in ill sheltered quarters and having neither food nor blankets (due to their intention of making the trip of eighteen miles the same day) they suffered intensely.

They had matches with them and when night approached they started a fire. The next day they traveled until nearly noon when they discovered that they were lost and their matches had become damp and would not burn. They undertook to return to the shanty which they had left and hoped that their fire had not burned out but the fire was dead and they spent the rest of the night stamping on the ashes to keep from freezing. When morning came they resumed their tramp and were about seven miles from the shanty when the doctor became exhausted from exposure, cold, and hunger and said he could go no farther. McClelland urged him to make another effort but the doctor gave up entirely.

Sometime after leaving the doctor and while crossing the north fork of the Crow River, McClelland broke through the ice near an airhole and extricated himself with difficulty. His wet feet soon swelled so that he had to cut off his boots and he walked the rest of the way through the snow in his stockings. He succeeded in building a good fire but when his feet had been placed before the fire for a few minutes they became in such a condition that he was unable to walk. He remained in the uncompleted shanty for eighteen days before relief came. During the whole time he was able to build the fire but four times. His entire food supply during those eighteen days, after three days on the road without any kind of food, consisted of the remnants of dried apples and rice. He was brought to Glencoe and from thence to Shakopee where both of his legs were amputated, one five and the other eight inches below the knee. Dr. Ripley's remains were found two months after the last separation about half a mile from the place where he was last seen alive, his hat hanging on a bush near by and a bottle partly filled with chloroform by his side. Lake Ripley gets its name from this circumstance.

In the spring of 1856 after the snow went off the skull and other portions of Dr. Ripley, which had evidently been dragged by wolves, were found on the prairie and he was buried near the place of his death. His body was reinterred and is now buried in the Masonic lot of the Ripley cemetery.

Miss Katy Gibson, who was the first teacher in the log school house at Glencoe was the doctor's affianced bride at the time of his death. She visited Glencoe not long after his remains were found and was deeply grieved.

PIONEER SOURCES OF INCOME

GINSENG

In pioneer days the digging of ginseng was an important factor and many of our early settlers were saved from extreme want by the sale of the roots of this plant which abounded in the shady rich soil throughout the greater portion of the county. The market for this product was in China where it is regarded as a sacred medicine that possesses the requsite curative powers for all the ills of humanity. The light yellow root is used by the Chinese for every conceivable domestic and medicinal purpose and specimens resembling the human body often command their weight in gold because of supposed occult virtue. Reputable physicians contend that the roots have no pronounced medical qualities. In 1858 the price of the roots was 52 cents a pound, but in 1902 the roots brought as high as $8 per pound. Greenbury Cheney of Dassel, now an inmate of the Masonic Home, Savage, Minnesota, was regarded as the champion ginseng digger in Meeker county. It is claimed that he holds the record of digging 100 pounds in one day.

CORDWOOD, TIES AND HOOP POLES

With the coming of the railroad in 1869 and as late as 1890 one of the main sources of income was the marketing of cordwood, ties and hoop poles. Cordwood sold from 50 cents to $3 per cord (128 cubic feet), ties 15 to 35 cents each and hoop poles $6 to $9 per thousand. The average cut of wood per man was one cord, 500 hoop poles constituted a good day's cut. Every vacant space in the railroad villages of Meeker County was filled with ranks of wood. It is recorded of the late Senator Magnus Johnson that the marketing of wood was his main source of income in 1893 when he located in Section 17 in the town of Kingston. He hauled the wood to Litchfield, a distance of 14 miles and sold the same as low as $1.35 a cord.

TRAPPING AND HUNTING

The trapping and hunting of fur bearing animals, muskrats, mink, fox, skunk, and wolves was engaged in quite generally. The streams and lakes abounded in fish and there was no closed season for ducks and other wild game.

WATER POWER MILLS

The water power mills of pioneer days were a Godsend to the early settlers and contributed in a superlative degree to the development of the county. The flour mill at Kingston was the first flour mill put in operation west of Minneapolis. The construction of the mill began in 1856 and was completed in 1858. Previous to its operation the settlers were obliged to transport their flour from St. Paul, usually by ox team but we are credibly informed that there were settlers who conveyed flour on their backs. The Kingston mill was used as a fortress during the Indian outbreak.

In addition to the Kingston mill which had a daily capacity of 60 barrels the following is a list of the water power mills of the entire county:

NAME OF MILL	LOCATION	CAPACITY IN BARRELS
Forest City	Forest City	125
Manannah	Manannah	75
Washington	Dassel Town	50
Greenleaf	Greenleaf Village	80
Cedar Mills	Cedar Mills	80
Jewetts	Collinwood Town	40
Carvills	East Kingston	50
Collinwood	Collinwood Townsite	40

PIONEER SAW MILLS

Water power saw mills were operated in Manannah, Forest City and Dassel town, East Kingston and at Lake Jennie in Collinwood town.

— Steam Power Mills —

A steam power saw mill was operated in Dassel in the seventies and early eighties. Steam power flour mills were put in operation in the early seventies at Litchfield and Grove City. At the present time there is not one permanent flour or saw mill in operation in the entire county.

CHILDHOOD MEMORIES

By Sarah Jane Dougherty

The first white child born in Meeker County

I am proud of the acknowledged fact that I am the first white child born in Meeker County. I was born in a covered wagon in the townsite of Forest City July 15,1856 while my parents were enroute to the township of Harvey where they later established their permanent home.

Crow river in the years of my childhood was a beautiful stream with its smooth mossy banks, whose waters teemed with fish, and its well trod trails made by deer that came down to the river to quench their thirst.

The pioneers of Meeker county were not showered with wealth but they were happy and full of hope for the future and they fought a noble fight in overcoming the trials, disappointments and hardships of the early years. They were ever faithful to God and country.

Many memories of the past come to me. When I was an infant I was taken captive by the Indians and held for some time. My father ransomed me by giving the Indians all the provisions he had in the house. The Indian outbreak was the greatest adventure of my childhood. I well remember the early dawn of a Monday morning in the month of August 1862 when our weeping mother called us children from our beds and whispered in our ears, "Oh children get up and dress quickly, don't talk, keep still, be very quiet for the Indians are down in the lower grove." The lower grove was our playground. We had no toys but I remember my most cherished possession was a little piece of broken china.

Our task of dressing was mournful. Why did mother cry? We did not fear the Indians. They had made us gifts of moccasins and beautiful beads. Our anxiety was somewhat relieved when we mounted the hay rack and we were told to be quiet, that we are going to Forest City. The family consisted of father, mother, and nine children. Hark! A call of warning came. It was from uncle. "Make haste, and leave at once. Go to Forest City and I will meet you at Schultz's Creek." We had traveled only a short distance when a party of horsemen (two Tait brothers, Joe Harris, Mark Piper and Thomas Wheeler) approached us. They had come from Acton where the massacre of the Baker and Jones families had taken place the previous day. They accompanied us to Forest City where my father joined the home guards.

Those days bring to my mind saddening memories as I recall the distress of many settlers as they were compelled to leave their homes and personal effects they had labored so hard to secure. The hardships of pioneer life were somewhat relieved by the coming of the railway. There was joy and real happiness when the first train arrived in Litchfield. It was a more exciting event to the adults than the sight in later years of the first airplanes. In closing my letter to you, Mr. Lamson, I wish to add this message which I trust you will give space in your history:

"Dear Meeker County citizens, friends and neighbors, I know the time will soon come when I will be called to surrender my body to the earth and my soul to our Creator. It is my wish that I be laid to rest in that little graveyard near my old home with the soil of Meeker County resting lightly on my brow."

"I have lived every day of my eighty-three years in the state of Minnesota. I have never lived any other place. I have surely enjoyed myself in this state."

BOYHOOD MEMORIES

By W. R. Salisbury

First white boy born in Meeker County, living 1939
in Village of Eden Valley

My boyhood home was located in Sections 18 and 19 Kingston town on the south side of Crow River, about midway between the townsites of Forest City and Kingston. The old log cabin in which I was born October 26, 1856 stood on a high bluff overlooking a wooded tract of land bordering the river.

The tenth of November 1860 came on a Saturday. About ten o'clock I muffled up my ears and throat in a red woolen scarf and went outdoors. I glanced down the trail leading westward and noticed a mounted Indian warrior who was soon followed by others in single file to the number of about one hundred. They were armed with guns, knives, and tomahawks. They were followed by their squaws leading ponies hitched to two long poles and at the rear these poles were fastened together by cross pieces bound with raw hide thongs. In addition to drawing these crude vehicles which were loaded with tents, provisions, and papooses, each pony was laden with household utensils, rugs of bear and buffalo skins, and clothing.

After fording the river they made their camp directly across from our home. The giant maples furnished an excellent wind break and the river furnished them with water and fish were plentiful. At sundown their teepees were erected and the camp activities had ceased.

These Indians belonged to Little Crow's band of Sioux that claimed the southern part of the state while the northern part was claimed by the Chippewas and the division line between the two tribes was only a few miles north of our home.

It was early in December that Dad and I visited the camp on a calm cold winter evening. With the aid of a plank to cross the open water in the river we made our crossing and reached the camp in safety which consisted of two parallel rows of tepees with an open lane between them about fifty feet in width.

We finally came to a large tepee which we entered without ceremony and found it occupied by the chief, his squaw and a number of young children of varying ages. The chief was reclining on a buffalo skin robe beside an open fire in the center of the enclosed walls of the tepee. His squaw was sitting close to the fire to take advantage of the light and was attaching colored beads to a pair of deerskin moccasins. I noticed one little girl about six years of age whose dress, leggings and moccasins were all made of nice clean buckskin, highly ornamented with beadwork. She looked very attractive.

The chief acknowledged our presence with the single word, How! and passed his pipe to Dad who took a few puffs and passed it back to the chief. The tents soon filled with warriors who, in passably good English, recited their hunting adventures.

After awhile the chief engaged in chuckles of laughter and turning to Dad said, "Young paleface like Indian. How you like him marry young squaw?" Dad expressed his willingness. The chief called the little squaw and placing her right hand in mine mumbled a few words in the Sioux language and when he had finished pushed us together and we both fell rolling on the floor. This action created boisterous merriment on the part of those present who clapped their hands and laughed heartily. I was glad to get home and be put to bed.

Our nearest white neighbors were Uncle LaRue Prunette, his wife, Aunt Sarah, and their four children, (one-half mile west) and Uncle Joe, and Aunt Mary Weymer, (one-fourth mile east). They lived in log cab.ns facing the river. Uncle LaRue was a descendant of the French Huguenots. He was intensely religious and had Bible readings and prayers each morning before commencing the day's tasks. He shaved twice each week and never sat down to his meals without donning his tie and dress coat. These habits were unusual among the pioneers and he was the subject of sneering remarks by his neighbors.

He must have been pretty much of a dude but for all that he was a good sport. He had a fine little twenty guage muzzle loading shot gun with German silver mountings engraved with stag and running hounds.

I recall that on one occasion he killed two Canada geese in one shot and another time brought down six pigeons with one discharge of this fowling piece.

There was no closed season for game which was plentiful during the entire year, including deer, partridges, prairie chickens, and in the fall and spring, ducks and geese. Great flocks of pigeons (now extinct) came in large numbers during the months of May, June, and September and remained until the weather became cold when they left for the southland.

A few months previous to the beginning of the Civil War the entire settlement was in a state of feverish excitement. Nearly all the men in the township of Kingston had voted the republican ticket at the presidential election of 1860.

During the winter of 1860 and 1861 Indians would make almost daily visits to our home to trade game for salt and bread. They traded a buffalo hide for our dog and later father and I visited the Indian camp, when the Indians were preparing their meal. When we were about to return home the chief insisted we remain until the meat was cooked and take supper with him. He said, "You know dog you trade me? Him no good dog. Him make ——— good meat. Him cook in pot." We did not wait for supper that evening.

Early in March the Indians broke camp but in the fall they returned and set up their winter camp. They were not as friendly as formerly and about one week later the signal drums began to beat and the warriors came running from the woods and we later learned that they had pursued and scalped two Chippewas whom they regarded as s⁻ies. They celebrated this event with a frightful medley of war whoops, the beating of drums, and the confused cries of women and children, which continued for about twenty-four hours. The Indians departed during the night.

The Indians never again pitched their camp in this location nor did they again maintain friendly relations with the settlers of Kingston town. We heard of lawless acts of these heretofore friendly Indians and Uncle Joe warned the people of our neighborhood that it would not be long before the Indians would take the war path against the whites but his prophecy was not taken very seriously.

On the day following the Acton Massacre the news reached us of this event and the settlers began drawing together in the Kingston and Forest City townsites. At Kingston they built a stockade enclosing the mill.

We and our neighbors remained in our homes until we became satisfied that the danger was acute. We had not long to wait. One morning Daniel Flynn, a lad about 15 years of age came on horseback from Forest City and shouted that the Indians were coming and warned us to lose no time in seeking safety. An awful sensation of fear gripped me and I came near fainting. Mother urged me to summon father who was working in a field some distance from the house. I had to cross a deep ravine, heavily timbered and as I ran I imagined that the Indians were all about me and I saw visions of scalping knives and tomahawks. I reached Dad and delivered my message and we hurriedly returned to the house. Uncle Joe arrived and took the leadership. We hitched our team to the hayrack and went to Uncle Rue's to load their belongings and were joined by them, thence to our home to secure needed supplies and clothing and stopped on our way at Uncle Joe's to finish our load where the women and children mounted the rack and with Aunt Sarah as the driver whom Uncle Joe charged to drive like ——. We were on our way. We arrived at the Kingston mill in safety. We took refuge in a house near the mill. I had recovered from my fright. In fact, all fear left me as soon as Uncle Joe became our leader. I thought my Dad was some man but he never swore while Uncle Joe could rip out an unlimited supply of swear words.

Uncle Joe called a mass meeting that evening and then retired to read "The Camp Fires of Napoleon."

At the meeting that evening all the men were present. Uncle Joe presided and addressed the gathering and presented plans for defense which were adopted and offered to act as captain. This offer was unanimously rejected in a thunderous NO! The assembled settlers, who recognized his ability as a leader could not forget that he was an uncompromising democrat.

The Kingston Home Guards were organized and Dad (J. B. Salisbury) was elected captain due to his having served in the Mexican War where he had attained the rank of major. There were forty-three enlistments.

There was much drilling and guards were posted and scouts patrolled the roads and river. The women and children kept to their homes during the day but all were sheltered in the mill at night.

One fine morning I heard the inspiring music of fife and drum and a company of United States Infantry came down the Kingston hill and set up their tents on vacant lots. I learned they were to remain until all danger from the Indian attack had ceased. This relieved the home guards and they were disbanded.

Dad made arrangements for the family to leave for Iowa until the Indians had been driven from the state. He then returned to the old homestead and sold the live stock and then enlisted in the U. S. Army where he served until the close of the war.

THE INDIAN OUTBREAK

The most tragic events in the history of our state were the Indian troubles of 1862.

The Sioux tribe had for many years been regarded as firm friends of the whites but unfair and dishonest treatment by government officials in the distribution of annuities and the breaking of treaty agreements had antagonized the Indians to the point that they determined in their councils that they would wage a war of extermination of the whites and regain the lands ceded to the whites by treaty. The leader of the Sioux tribe at this time was Little Crow, second only to Tecumseh in leadership. "He formed his plans with care worthy of a great general by means of a secret organization known as the "Soldiers' Lodge." The first of September had been set as the date for a general uprising and a simultaneous attack on all the varied settlements.

Bishop Whipple who is generally regarded as the most reliable historian of the events leading to and culminating in the Indian uprising is recorded as follows:

"The Sioux had been our friends and for more than a quarter of a century had boasted that they had never taken the life of a white man. Our wretched Indian system was at its worst. It left wild men without government or personal rights of property and by its almshouse system at every agency was training up savage paupers."

Thanked the Judge

The first person to receive a penitentiary sentence in Meeker county was a man named Roberts in 1869. His sentence of 22 months was regarded by the prisoner as expressing great leniency on the part of Judge Vanderburgh and he thanked the Judge and invited him to visit him in his cell at Stillwater.

PIONEER TRANSPORTATION

This yoke of oxen is not typical of the ox teams of pioneer days which due to the marshy prairies and meadows were well nourished and never presented the scrawny appearance of those shown in the illustration. This yoke was owned by two city bred brothers, who lived near Grove City.

No. 1, THE APPROACH.
No. 3, THE MASSACRE.
No. 2, CABIN AS NOW STANDS.
No. 4, THE TRIAL OF GUNS.

"FIRST BLOOD."
ILLUSTRATION CONTRIBUTED BY WILLMAR TRIBUNE

This illustration reproduced after consulting pioneers who were familiar with the premises and setting of this historic event, which precipitated the massacre of 1862, is belived to be a correct picture of the same but it is stated by reliable parties that there were no horses attached to the covered wagon.

THE ACTON MASSACRE

About 11 o'clock in the forenoon of Sunday, August 17, 1862, six Indians from the Lower Agency approached the house of Robinson Jones (SW¼ of NE¼ of Section 21) town of Acton. Jones kept a frontier tavern stocked with staple groceries and the usual supply of whisky, traded for furs and engaged in farming. The Indians demanded whisky which was refused them and they became boisterous. The Indians left after a time and Jones went to the cabin house of his near neighbor Baker who lived about three-quarters of a mile distant. He left his niece, Clara Wilson, in charge of the house with a little boy, half brother of Clara and an adopted son of Mr. Jones (about two years of age) lying on the bed.

When Jones reached the Baker cabin four of the Indians arrived shortly afterward and began bantering Jones, Baker and Viranus Webster, an emigrant journeying westward, to shoot at a mark which was after a period of some minutes agreed to and several minutes of this sport carried forth. None of the three men reloaded their rifles, but the savages, while standing in the doorway recharged their pieces. While they were standing there, one of the savages raised his gun and discharged its leaden contents into the body of Jones. Another savage leveled his gun at Mrs. H. Baker; her husband, Howard Baker, sprang in front of her and received the bullet intended for his wife. Almost at the same instant two more shots rang out and Webster and Mrs. Ann Baker fell to the ground, mortally wounded. Mrs. Howard Baker, with her infant child in her arms, tried to make her escape through a window and fell into the cellar which saved her life. After this dastardly attack the Indians returned to the Jones cabin and killed Clara Davis Wilson. They did not discover the little child or enter the house. They then left the premises in the direction of the Beaver Creek settlement and the Lower Agency.

Mrs. Howard Baker, unhurt by her fall into the cellar, remained until the savages had left when she emerged from her hiding place and before leaving the house encountered an Irishman named Cox, a presumed spy of the Indians and reputed to be crazy. She entreated him to go with her to the settlement and carry the baby which he refused to do saying that "The men are not dead but drunk and in falling down had bumped their noses which made them bleed." Mrs. Webster and Mrs. Baker and the child started for Forest City stopping at the home of their nearest neighbor, John Blackwell, but found the house had been abandoned. The two women proceeded on their way and reached the house of Andrew Olson, who had a blacksmith shop on his place. From there they proceeded to Forest City, some 16 miles from the scene of the massacre. When they reached Forest City they found that Ole Ingeman had reached there at 6 o'clock and spread the alarm among the settlers.

The news of the fiendish butchery spread rapidly throughout the county and groups of settlers from near by settlements visited the scene of the tragedy. The two year old adopted child of Robinson Jones and the grandchild of Mrs. Mary Ann Baker was found lying in safety on the bed and smiled into the faces of his rescuers. The babe bore the name of Robinson J. Cotton and was placed in the care of T. C. Jewett, of Forest City, who later secured his adoption by Mr. and Mrs. Charles H. Ellis of Otsego, Wright County, Minnesota, where he remained until maturity.

The morning of the 19th sixty or more settlers gathered at the Baker home and held an inquest and the bodies of the five victims were buried in the Ness Norwegian Lutheran Church cemetery in Litchfield Township.

Following these events the settlers were panic stricken and hurried their women folks and children to points of safety to escape the ravages of the Indians. Forest City was one of the main points of refuge. From this point safety was sought by many who proceeded to better protected settlements along the Mississippi river. Many of Meeker County's brave settlers remained at Forest City to maintain this settlement as a point of refuge.

The state has erected a monument to mark the grave on which appear the following inscriptions: South Side—In memory of the first five victims of the great Indian Massacre in 1862 and buried here in one grave. West Side—Robinson, Jones, Viranus Webster, Howard Baker, Ann Baker, Clara D. Wilson. East Side—First Blood. North Side—Erected by the State in 1878 under the direction of Meeker County Old Settlers Association.

A monument has also been erected at the point where the massacre took place on the SW¼ of the NE¼ of Section 21, Acton Town, 3 miles south of Grove City on State Highway No. 4, and on a side road leading west a distance of one-fourth mile. The Baker homestead is now owned by George Paulson, Jr.

DANIEL N. DANIELSON

Daniel N. Danielson, son of Nels Danielson in whose honor the town of Danielson was named, is now 85 years of age and was nine years old at the time of the Acton Massacre. He has a very retentive memory and distinctly recalls the events of that period which were frequently recited by his father when he was present.

Mr. Danielson questions the accuracy of the foregoing record in several particulars. He furnishes the following story relating to the murder of the Jones-Baker families:

"When Jones, accompanied by the Indians reached the Baker home there was a trading of guns between the whites and the Indians previous to their shooting match. At the conclusion of this sport, the whites did not reload their guns but the Indians recharged their fire arms and without warning fired a bullet into the body of Howard Baker who was seated beside his wife on a bench in the house. He arose from his seat and shouted, Run! which command they proceeded to obey. Mrs. Baker fell thru a trap door into the cellar, Webster and Mrs. Ann Baker-Jones were the next victims and were shot in the doorway in their effort to escape. Jones had proceeded a short distance from the house and was killed near the corn crib. The Indians hurriedly left the premises and proceeded to the Jones cabin and killed Clara Davis Wilson. Mrs. Webster was seated in a covered wagon but for some unaccountable reason was not molested." In tracing the flight of Mrs. Webster and Mrs. Howard Baker and child to Forest City, Mr. Danielson contends that after leaving Andrew (Nels) Olson's blacksmith shop they proceeded to Iver Jackson's home, one-half mile distant from Olson's and from this point the alarm was given which resulted in the gathering of the settlers at the scene of the tragedy the night of its occurrence.

BIG EAGLE'S STORY

Chief Big Eagle (Folwell's History of Minnesota, Vol. 2, pages 415 and 416) is responsible for the following statement of events leading up to and culminating in the Acton Massacre. They (the four Indians) came to a settler's fence and there they found a hen's nest with some eggs in it. One of them took the eggs when another said: 'Don't take them, for they belong to a white man and we may get into trouble!' The other was angry —dashed them to the ground and replied: 'You are a coward. You are afraid of the white man. You are afraid to take even an egg from him, though you are half starved. Yes, you are a coward and I will tell everybody so." The other replied: 'I am not a coward. I am not afraid of the white man, and to show you that I am not I will go to the house and shoot him. Are you brave enough to go with me?' The one who had called him a coward said: 'Yes, I will go with you and we will see who is the braver of us two.' Their two companions then said: 'We will go with you and we will be brave too.' They all went to the house of the white man.

HISTORICAL IMPORT

The historical import of the Indian uprising of 1862 which began with the Indian massacre at Acton, August 17 of that year and terminated with the hanging of 38 Indians at Mankato has been lost sight of due to the overshadowing of this event by the Civil War in progress at that time but historical research reveals the fact that:—

"The terrible, bloody and fiendish outbreak of the Sioux Indians of Minnesota in 1862 stands out in American History as the most destructive of human life of any of the many Indian wars occurring in the western hemisphere. A recent historian tells us that: 'More white people perished in that savage slaughter than in all the other massacres perpetrated on the American continent. Add the number of white victims of the Indian wars of New England during the colonial period to the list of those perished in

Wyoming and Cherry Valleys and to the pioneers who were killed in the early white occupation of the middle west and the south, and the aggregate falls short of the number of people in Minnesota who were slain by the Sioux in less than one week in that memorable month of August 1862."

"To the above I will add that the number so slaughtered far exceeds the total of all the Minnesota soldiers killed in battle or died of wounds during the Civil and Indian Wars."

BATTLE OF ACTON

The following account of the Battle of Acton referred to by some of our historians as the Battle of Kelly's Bluff, has been a subject of both criticisim and praise of Captain Strout in command of the force engaged in conflict with the Indians under the leadership of Little Crow. The following account of the engagement is a condensed story derived from the record written by M. P. Satterlee and in the judgment of the writer is quite authentic.

Captain Strout's command was composed of about 20 newly enlisted, undrilled soldiers and the remainder of the force were civilians. The Indians outnumbered them in a ratio of four to one.

Following the Acton massacre of August 17, 1862 Captain Strout and his men were ordered to proceed to the relief of Meeker and McLeod County citizens and on Tuesday, August 26, were assembled on the Nicollet side of Bridge Square in Minneapolis. They were equipped with discarded smooth bore Austrian muskets and insufficient wagons but the Captain was empowered with authority to impress teams into service.

The march through the wilderness began and night stops were made at the following points in their march to Forest City: northern part of Brooklyn township; Monticello, and Clearwater, Wright County. They reached Forest City Friday, August 29, and the following day they left for Hutchinson by way of Greenleaf and Cedar Mills and reached Hutchinson on Saturday, where they camped on the grounds surrounding the church. They were now fairly supplied with horses and wagons. They had encountered no Indians on their hundred mile march. On Sunday they arrived at Glencoe where information reached them that prompted their speedy return to Forest City and on Monday the entire force, somewhat increased in numbers, were enroute for Cedar Mills.

Tuesday, September 3, Capt. Strout's force made a leisurely march to Acton and spent a portion of the time in repairing a slough crossing, which was very fortunate as will be shown in the events that follow. They established their camp that night at the Jones place about three-fourths of a mile distant from the Baker place, the scene of the Acton massacre. The Jones place was surrounded by timber and the tents were set in the yard.

This chosen camp has occasioned severe criticism of Capt. Strout despite the fact that no damage resulted therefrom. The Sioux (in their varied engagements with the whites) were open ground fighters. They would cloak their heads and bodies with prairie grass which has prompted the frequently repeated statement: "The Indians seemed to rise out of the ground."

On this same Tuesday, September 3, Capt. Whitcomb and a squad of Forest City Home guards were stationed at Hokan Peterson's place, section 4, Litchfield town, about 10 miles southwest of Forest City, watching for Indians in the vicinity of the Acton woods when suddenly about 150 Indians seemingly "rose out of the ground" a few rods distant. The guards made a hurried retreat to Forest City where they met one of Strout's scouts who informed them of the location of their camp at Acton.

It was evident that a surprise attack on Strout's force was contemplated by the Indians and volunteers were called for to warn Strout of his danger, an extremely hazardous mission and one requiring the highest degree of heroism. Three brave men stepped forward, Jesse V. Branham, Jr., Thomas G. Holmes, and Albert H. Sperry.

The squad was placed in command of Branham. They went east several miles, passing between Litchfield and Darwin, thence southwest passing between Round and Minnebelle lakes far down into Greenleaf town, thence northwest to Evenson Lake where they struck the Henderson-Pembina Trail. At the outlet of this lake they hunted on hands and knees until they located Strout's trail leading to Acton.

They traveled on the grass to deaden the sound of the horses' hoofs and finally reached the Acton woods. They located the Indian camp at the Baker place by the savage barking of dogs but were not molested. They reached Strout's camp and delivered their warning message.

A council of war was called and it was decided not to break camp until daylight altho some favored an immediate retreat. During the remaining hours of the night every possible preparation was made for the assured conflict on the morrow. Instructions were given, in case of attack, to hug the ground and fight for self preservation. Their instructions were no doubt prompted by the fact that due to what would seem almost criminal carelessness on the part of those charged with the issuance of ammunition, the greater part of the bullets furnished were of the wrong calibre which reduced their supply to only 20 rounds per man.

Strout's force broke camp in the early morning. Branham was assigned the duty of leading the line of retreat with A. H. DeLong acting as an advance Scout. It was their plan to follow the route chosen the night before to Forest City. They followed the prairie with Long Lake on their left. They sighted Indians and word was sent Strout to prepare to fight and his men were spread in wide open order. The scouts and Indians exchanged shots.

The beginning of the general engagement which followed was heralded by Indian signals, the waving of blankets and the blood curdling war whoops of the savages. The mounted Indians attacked from the rear. Lieutenant Kinney was ordered to charge them with a squad of 20 men, whereupon the Indians attempted to encircle the command. At this point, the ground was low and the losses were severe.

Scout Branham, the outstanding head of the retreat was shot through the lungs and Alva Getchell and George W. Gedeon were killed. Strout soon had matters under control. He divided his force into four squads which he placed at the front, rear, left, and right of the wagon train and they soon spread out driving the red skins back and the left guard kept the Indians from getting between them and the shore of Long Lake while the remaining squads drove the Indians back until they reached higher ground. At Kelly's Bluff (the present site of the Hope Lake Creamery) it was decided to go to Hutchinson. At this point Edwin Stone was killed. There was a hurried retreat, wounded men were placed in the wagons and the dead were left behind. (When the bodies were recovered and buried a few days later they had been horribly mutilated.)

At the marsh crossing, repaired the previous day, the Indians pressed them hard and captured one team and two wagons. It is claimed they would have captured and killed his entire command had it not been for previous repairs.

Scout DeLong ran the gauntlet in safety to secure reinforcements from Hutchinson and met the company a short distance from that village.

That night the wounded were lodged in the hotel. The following morning the Indians attacked the village, but all the settlers found safety within the walls of the stockade.

The result of this engagement caused Little Crow's discouragement. It was his fourth and last battle which he personally conducted. Jesse V. Branham, Jr., whose life was despaired of, was given the best of care by the local physician and the women of Hutchinson. The wound was cleansed by drawing a silk handkerchief entirely through the wound and his recovery was regarded as miraculous.

— CHRONOLOGY —

August 18, 1862, Massacre at Lower Agency; Massacre of white settlers, men, women and children from Birch Coolie to Beaver Creek; Attack on New Ulm; Battle at Lower Agency Ferry. August 20, Attack on Fort Ridgely, followed by a renewed attack, August 22, September 1, Battle of Birch Coolie, September 23, Battle of Wood Lake. November 5, 321 Indians tried and found guilty, 303 recommended to be hung. Clemency was extended by President Lincoln and 38 were hung at Mankato Friday, December 26. February 16, 1863, all existing treaties with the Indians were abrogated and annulled and all laws and rights of occupancy, and all annuities and claims then existing in favor of the Indians were declared forfeited.

For a detailed record of the events referred to consult Folwell's History of Minnesota found in all public libraries within the state.

LOCATING THE ACTON MONUMENT
Reproduced From Photo Taken by John T. Mullen

Gathering in the shade of the tree to which was fastened the target in the trial of marksmanship between Jones, Robinson and Baker and their Indian visitors preceding the murder are the illustrious group of pioneers who visited the scene of the massacre and assisted in the burial of the victims.

From left to right, Albert Delong, Even Evenson, Henry McGannon, Nels Hanson and Nels Elofson. They met in August 1909 and the Acton monument was erected the same year.

HEROES OF THE INDIAN OUTBREAK
Meeker County

At the beginning of the Indian outbreak Forest City was nearly a deserted village. Only thirteen men and three women were left of its population. These brave men and heroic women, who had determined to make a stand in defense of their homes and who, by their gallant and spirited action, stayed the tide of arson and murder, and saved the balance of the state as far as the Mississippi River from the fiendish cruelty of the relentless Sioux were: J. B. Atkinson, Thomas Grayson, Milton Gorton, William Fowler, James M. Harvey, T. C. Jewett, George S. Sholes, Dr. Thomas H. Skinner, A. C. Smith, Henry L. Smith, Judson A. Stanton, Sylvester and Hamlet Stevens and Mesdames Howard Baker, T. C. Jewett and G. C. Whitcomb. They were later joined by many others.

Their names should be perpetuated in the pages of history, with those of the noble band of Spartans under Leonidas, at the pass of Thermopylae, who devoted themselves to the salvation of their country.—Meeker County Album of History, 1888.

THE ACTON MONUMENT
Contributed by Hutchinson Leader

This monument is located three miles south and one-fourth mile west of Grove City following state road No. 4.

THE INSCRIPTION READS AS FOLLOWS:

EAST SIDE: This marks the spot where the first blood was shed in the Sioux Indian outbreak, August 17, 1862.

SOUTH SIDE: Erected by the state of Minnesota on the 47th anniversary, August 17, 1909.

WEST SIDE: Victims, Robinson Jones, Ann Baker-Jones, Howard Baker, Viranus Webster, Clara D. Wilson.

NORTH SIDE: Bodies of these victims buried in Ness cemetery.

ATTACK ON THE FOREST CITY STOCKADE

The stockade and its surrounding buildings were located in the SE¼ of SE¼ of Section 17, Forest City town, on land owned (1939) by Andrew Lingren.

The stockade furnished security to hundreds of citizens of Meeker County during the Indian Massacre of 1862. It was hurriedly constructed September 3rd, by the entire force of Home Guards and citizens. It was in the form of a parallelogram and was made of a double row of logs on end planted about three feet in the ground and projecting upward about ten feet. Bastions on the corners and numerous loop holes through the timbers afforded ample means for sweeping down its assailants and gave shelter to the marksmen from the bullets of the savages.

The entire population with the Home Guards established themselves in the J. B. Atkinson Hotel (No. 13). The ammunition being stored in the Stanton Store while the horses were quartered in the hotel stable. With a feeling of security the inhabitants settled themselves for the night with the exception of three men (Guyon, Dart and Smith) who were doing guard duty.

Between two and three o'clock in the morning of September 4, 1862, about two hundred Sioux warriors were seen approaching. The sentinels sounded the alarm by firing their guns in the air. They were pursued by the savages with blood curdling war whoops and gun fire but reached the stockade in safety as did all the occupants of the hotel but in their hurry neglected to remove the horses and the bulk of the ammunition.

Much to the surprise of this horde of savages the walls of the stockade loomed before them. They did not attack this well armed barrier but contented themselves with burning five or more buildings and seizing and driving off about 65 horses. The N. E. Gornbom and Chas. Magnuson families and Mrs. Hodgson had sheltered themselves during the night in the school house but succeeded in the darkness preceding daylight in gaining entrance to the stockade.

With the coming of daylight a small band of Indians were discovered in the act of driving off cattle. Four men from the stockade attacked them and saved the cattle. In this skirmish two of the men (Aslog Olson and William Branham) were wounded. There were no fatalities among the whites. It has been estimated that three or more Indians lost their lives.

About 5 o'clock this same morning the Indians departed, dividing into three groups, one going toward Manannah, another in the direction of Greenleaf by the south road, and the third following the Rice City or Darwin road. On their way the Indians burned the houses of Dudley Taylor, William Richardson and Milton Gorton.

THE MANANNAH MASSACRE

The massacre at Manannah took place August 26, 1862, ten days following the Acton massacre. A group of eleven men who had found refuge in Forest City left there in the early morning to proceed to their homesteads in Manannah town and seek provisions and other needed supplies. Arriving at the home of Maybee they ate dinner and left hastily for the Carlos Caswell homestead where they left a yoke of oxen in the barn and proceeded to the Silas Caswell home, a distance of two miles. Here they loaded Wilmot Maybee's two horse wagon with provisions and bedding. Maybee in company with Joseph Page, Philip Deck and Linus Howe with Deck's one horse rig started on their return trip to Forest City. When they reached the home of Carlos Caswell, the rest of the party scattered to recover stock. The team driven by Maybee and Deck had entered the yard when they were ambushed by Indians who were hidden behind a pile of lumber. Page was killed and fell from the wagon and Deck and Howe had driven about 20 rods when they were killed. Maybee had driven about 40 rods when he left his team and ran toward the river but was soon overtaken and shot.

The killing was witnessed by Chauncey Wilson and Thomas Ryckman who were stationed some 60 rods distant. They were powerless in rendering assistance due to their guns having been left in the wagon. All of the group except the victims named reached Forest City in safety. Those not named above that were members of the party were Moody Caswell, N. C. Caswell, James Nelson and R. D. Cressy and David Hoar. The victims were buried in the Union Grove cemetery.

It is rather remarkable that there were only 12 victims of the Indian uprising among the settlers in Meeker County. This is largely due to the bravery of our sturdy pioneers and the assistance they rendered the settlers in reaching points of safety.

The names of the victims other than those mentioned are Caleb Sanborn killed September 17, 1863, on his claim in Section 35, Town of Ellsworth, and Daniel Cross a member of the party sent out to look for the missing Sanborn. He was shot September 18th only a short distance from the point where Sanborn was killed; Andrew Olson, a native of Norway, was killed and scalped by a band of Indians while engaged in salting his cattle on his homestead in Section 25, Acton town. The farm is now owned by Arthur Olson. James McGannon was killed July 1, 1863, while proceeding on horse back from Kingston to Anoka and following the boundary road between Meeker and Wright counties, presumably in the town of South Haven, Wright county.

KILLING OF LITTLE CROW

The writer has heard and read numerous conflicting stories regarding the killing of Little Crow and the disposal of his remains but is inclined to accept the story written by W. W. Pendergast, of Hutchinson, as a very correct statement of the killing and the same is confirmed by J. Birney Lamson (a son of Nathan and a brother of Chauncey) who for several years was a resident of Annandale and with whom the writer has exchanged visits.

This boulder marks the spot where Little Crow, the leader of the Sioux Massacre of 1862 met his death. Standing by the same is the compiler of this history, a sixth cousin of Chauncey Lamson, the slayer of the Indian chieftain. The boulder is located in section 36, Ellsworth town.

The little hamlet of Lamson, which in former years had a post-office, is six miles distant from this boulder. It was named by W. D. Joubert, who was serving as secretary to Congressman Heatwole when the post-office was established. It was thus named to perpetuate the memory of Nathan and Chauncey Lamson.

THE PENDERGAST VERSION

(Abbreviated)

On the morning of July 3, 1863, Nathan Lamson and his son Chauncey left Hutchinson for their home (five miles northward) to look after their stock which they found unmolested and toward evening started out to hunt deer. They were stealing carefully along a dim path or trail, leading northwestward. Lamson, Sr. (then 65 years of age) caught sight of a moving object in the bushes a few rods distant. Peering through the bushes he saw two Indians (afterward ascertained to be Little Crow and his son Wowinapa) picking raspberries.

Mr. Lamson thought this too good a chance to lose. He rested his gun against the trunk of a poplar tree and fired wounding Little Crow in the side who did not fall and catching sight of his assailant sent a bullet through the fleshy part of Lamson's left shoulder. The father dropped to the ground to reload. Little Crow seized his son's rifle and moved toward Chauncey. They saw each other and both fired at the same moment. Little Crow fell mortally wounded. Chauncey felt the wind of the ball on his check as it passed harmlessly by.

Chauncey, supposing his father to have been killed, hurried to Hutchinson to spread the alarm and reached there at 10 o'clock the same evening. The mother, nearly distracted, begged the men at the fort to go in search of her husband. William Gosnell was the first to volunteer. Birney Lamson and three or four other citizens and six mounted men of the Goodhue County Tigers set out immediately and reached Lamson's house shortly after midnight where they rested about three hours. In the early dawn they resumed their march. They soon reached the scene of the conflict and found Little Crow's body about six rods from the spot where Chauncey had fired the fatal shot.

Nathan Lamson s white shirt and his gun were found in the plum grove but no trace of the owner. On the return of the party to Hutchinson, however, he was among the first to welcome them. He had discarded his shirt fearing its color might attract the notice of the foe and his gun was left due to the lodging of a bullet in the barrel nine inches from the muzzle. He had concealed himself until nightfall and then, leaving his gun and shirt, made his way to Hutchinson, arriving about 2 o'clock in the morning.

Wowinapa escaped and rejoined the Sioux in Dakota. He was captured 26 days later by a party of soldiers near Devil's Lake. He admitted the slaying of his father.

DISPOSITION OF THE BODY

The following is an abbreviated report of the disposition of the body as written by Dr. John Benjamin of Hutchinson.

The body of Little Crow was brought into Hutchinson July 4. The boys of the town took advantage of the event by filling the ears and nostrils with firecrackers. These indignities I considered inhuman and with the assistance of Mr. Sharp we buried the body in an open grave and covered the body with gravel. A cavalry officer using his saber dug into the grave and severed the head from the body. I was informed by my children of his action and hastened to meet him and inquired his authority for this act. He replied that it was none of my —— business.

I took the head home with me and put it in a solution of lime with the intention of presenting it to the State Historical Society or leaving it in Hutchinson to carry out the wishes of the Lamsons.

The body, minus the head, was left one day too long for on my being superseded at the hospital by Dr. Twitchell he persuaded Mr. Dewing and Andrew Hopper to put the body in a box and sink it in the river but during the night some unknown person had removed the body and its whereabouts became a mystery.

In the latter part of 1863 an officer named Farmer in command of the commissary at Glencoe borrowed the skull to be used by Prof. Pond in a course of lectures. He agreed to return the same but this promise was never fulfilled.

There are many gruesome and conflicting stories regarding the treatment and disposition of the body after it arrived in Hutchinson but the reputable pioneer citizens of Hutchinson contend that these stories are without foundation. The scalp of Little Crow was delivered by Nathan Lamson to the Adjutant General of the state and he received the state bounty of $75.

THE JOHN McKENZIE EXPLOIT

One of the most colorful characters among Meeker County's pioneer settlers was J. H. McKenzie who resided for years in Dassel town and later in Dassel village. The citizens of this and adjacent counties will recall his attendance at county fairs where he made and sold white taffy. He regarded phrenology as a science and frequently lectured on that subject.

Big Job for Two

Late in the winter of 1864, Major Edwin A. C. Hatch of Fort Snelling decided he wanted Little Six and Medicine Bottle, who then were encamped on the Assinibone river between Pembina and Winnipeg, then known as Fort Garry. It was out of the question to lead an army troop into foreign territory to capture the pair, so he commissioned J. H. McKenzie and Onisime Geguire to the task on promises that they would be richly rewarded.

All the two white men had to do was to bring the Indian quarries over the border to Fort Ambercrombie, which was on American soil, and Fort Snelling troops would do the rest.

McKenzie and Geguire trailed the Indians to their camp and asked the chiefs to surrender peacefully. The chiefs scornfully rejected the proposal. The white men cajoled and promised them security, offering a chance at some "firewater" and a free ride to Pembina, a border village.

Aided by Canadian

The Indians would have nothing of Pembina, but they would go to Fort Garry, feeling that being still on Canadian soil they would be safe from their American hunters. Aided by a Canadian who agreed to handle the transportation, the party went to Fort Garry (Winnipeg).

Once there, McKenzie and Geguire saw to it that their "guests" received plenty of what historically is named as "toddies". The hosts drank water disguised as "toddies," hiring a half-breed to act as bartender. The party continued on through the night—the Indians demonstrating such a capacity that the white men added laudanum to the Indians' drinks. The half-breed is recorded as having watched with considerable delight the growing intoxication of the two Indians.

Medicine Bottle Resists

Towards morning, Little Six "passed out," and the captors decided to take the Indians away. Little Six submitted to being strapped to a board, but Medicine Bottle resisted, giving the captors considerable of a battle. They finally subdued him, however, and at daylight set out for Fort

OF MEEKER COUNTY 29

Ambercrombie with a dog team. A detachment of soldiers met them at Pembina and the Indians were as good as in the Fort Snelling guard house.

The trial dragged on for months. A court-martial finally decided the Indians should be executed. Newspapers carried editorial comment on both sides. There was small evidence that the two chiefs had actually murdered the men and women of whose deaths they were accused. None of the white witnesses could recognize them, the half-breeds on the stand recalling only the boasts Little Six and Medicine Bottle had made. That made small difference in the public mind, which was still concerned over the invasion of foreign soil. The Indians, however, were executed November 12, 1865.—Minneapolis Tribune.

"THE KINGSTON WATER POWER MILL"

The construction of this mill began in 1856 by A. P. Whitney & Co. and its erection was completed in 1858. It was the pioneer mill of the region lying west of the Big Woods. Previous to its operation the settlers were obliged to transport their flour from St. Paul, usually hauled by ox teams but history records that several settlers made the journey between these two points on foot and bore their flour on their backs.

The mill continued to operate until it was dismantled in 1896 and moved to Kimball. In 1859 the property passed into the hands of Hiram Hall and was run by Hall and Davis, Hall and Thompson, King and DeCoster, Hall and Thompson again and J. H. Thompson. It was sold to John Mattson and it was operated by the firm of Hottel and Andrews up to the time of its removal. The mill was used as a fortress during the Indian uprising of 1862.

THE WILD WOMAN OF MANANNAH
(Compiled from Early Records)

That truth is stranger than fiction is well exemplified in the life history of one of the pioneer residents of the town of Manannah. She is frequently spoken of as the "Wild Woman of Manannah." The historical background of this strange woman who successfully impersonated a man during the greater part of her adult life is extremely interesting.

Lucy Lobdell was born in the lumbering town of Long Eddy, Sullivan county, New York about 1831 or 1832. It is claimed that when she was only eight years of age she became efficient in the use of firearms and at the age of twelve surpassed all the men in that section as a marksman and handled an axe with the ease of an old chopper. She would be absent from home for days at a time. She had killed deer and on one occasion a full sized panther. She earned the title of "The Female Hunter of Long Eddy."

Lucy Lobdell had an unblemished reputation. The breath of slander had never touched her. She was popular with the male sex and could have had her choice of the most exemplary young men of the community.

A raftsman named Henry Slater came to the settlement at Long Eddy about 1850. He attracted the interest of Lucy and proposed marriage. She agreed to marry him if he proved himself a better marksman than herself. A trial of skill took place and much to the maiden's surprise and her future unhappiness Slater was victorious. Their married life was of short duration. One year after the marriage a baby girl was born; Slater had proven a worthless, dissolute and abusive husband and less than two weeks following the birth of his child deserted her, leaving them in destitute circumstances. He never returned, but occasional reports came to the settlement of his whereabouts and his conduct. He had become a drunken vagabond.

Mrs. Slater found a refuge with her parents and for two years supported herself and child by doing woman's work. At the end of this period, she donned man's attire and armed with her rifle roamed the forest and earned a living in hunting wild game. She spent two weeks of this early period in Meeker county. She built crude shelter cabins at various places and never entered any of the settlements except to dispose of her game and furs and secure needed supplies. She continued this manner of living for four years when she visited her child and finding her parents complaining of the care imposed on them, she placed the little girl in the poor house at Delhi.

She then started for Minnesota, paying her way in part by teaching singing schools. She lingered for a time in St. Paul, where she formed the acquaintance of Edwin Gribble, who had a claim on the upper shore of Lake Minnetonka. Her dress as this time consisted of calico pants, coat, vest and hat. They were partners but in all their relations Gribble had no suspicion that his companion was a woman. They slept under the same blanket when night overtook them in the forest. The partnership was term-

OF MEEKER COUNTY   31

inated and Lucy sold her interest in the joint ownership of the claim they held for a seventy-five dollar rifle and set out for Meeker county.

She spent the winter of 1856-57 with another male companion on the north shore of Kandiyohi lake where they were jointly employed to protect the townsite rights of Minneapolis speculators and again there was no suspicion on the part of Lucy's male companion that he was associating with a woman. On one occasion during this winter she was left alone with only a pet cat for company and compelled to live on squirrels and when she failed in her hunt, the cat, driven by hunger, would seek and kill them in their hidden retreats. This puss lived for years afterward in the home of Noah White, of Kandiyohi county.

In the summer of 1857, Lucy under the assumed name of LeRoy Lobdell took up her residence in Manannah and earned a comfortable living doing chores, chopping wood, hunting, washing dishes and general house work. She was skillful in all these tasks.

LeRoy Lobdell was well pleased with her disguise and enjoying true happiness, but fully realized the difficulty, without loss of character, of assuming woman's attire. She had little money but was an expert hunter, unoffensive and unobtrusive. She was a hale fellow well met with all the young people.

In the summer of 1858 her sex was exposed. The community, many of whom were of Puritan extraction were horrified by the exposure and the law was invoked to purge the community of the scandal.

William Richards filed information against Mrs. Slater (LeRoy Lobdell) in which he charged her with "falsely impersonating a man to the great scandal of the community and against the peace and dignity of the State of Minnesota," and asked that she be dealt with according to law; that "so pernicious an example might not be repeated in this land of steady habits."

The trial was an exciting event in those pioneer days. The hearing was before Justice Robson. W. S. Wylie, a young lawyer from Virginia and A. C. Smith, later president of the Meeker County Bar Association, were her counsel. There was no evidence introduced of any indiscretions on the part of the defendant and the court ruled that the right of females to wear male attire had been recognized from the time of Justinian and that this doctrine was too well settled to be upset in the case at bar and Mrs. Slater was discharged.

Mrs. Slater had become discredited in the community. She was ostracized and subjected to the rude insults of the vicious minded. It was too much for the proud, independent, self-centered huntress and she became deranged and in Meeker county annals became known as the "Wild Woman of Manannah."

The tragedy of her life had begun. She became a dependent on the county but through the kindly interest of Captain A. D. Pierce the Meeker county authorities appropriated the necessary funds to send her home to her parents, who gave her a prodigal's welcome. Captain Pierce received a letter from her parents extending their thanks to him and the county.

The tragedy of her life had been increased by her bitter experience. She was restless and discontented in the parental home and in 1859 again donned male attire and continued her roaming career for a few years when she became an inmate of the poor house at Delhi that gave shelter to her child whom she found had been sheltered in the family of David Fortman of Wayne county, Pennsylvania.

At times while an inmate of this charity home she would recount the experiences of her wandering life. She asserted that in eight years she had killed 150 deer, eleven bears, numerous wild cats and foxes and trapped hundreds of mink and other fur bearing animals. She told a story of a hand to hand contest with a wounded deer and ugly seams and scars on her body amply testified the truth of her story.

At the poor house she gained an intimate friend in Mrs. Wilson, one of the inmates, a deserted wife. They left the poor house and as man and wife they roamed the country together as Rev. Joseph Lobdell and wife. Mrs. Slater as Rev. Lobdell was bareheaded, her clothing was torn and dirty and she led a half grown bear cub by a rope. She delivered noisy and meaningless sermons and called herself a prophet of the new dispensation and claimed the bear had been sent to guide her thru the wilderness. The couple lived in caves and subsisted, in part, on roots, berries and wild game.

They were arrested at Stroudsberg, New York and returned to the Delhi poor house, where they remained as inmates for a brief period when they left the institution and made their home in a cave ten miles from Hovesdale but in 1876 they were arrested as vagrants and lodged in jail and her further life is shrouded in oblivion.

The daughter, Mary Ann Slater, was carefully reared in her adopted home and became an intelligent and attractive young woman. A mutual attraction sprang up between her and a man named Stone. A group of jealous young men of the neighborhood waylaid her and she was the victim of a cruel assault which nearly dethroned her reason but Stone's affection was undimmed. They were about to be married when Mrs. Stone revealed to them the fact that they were children of the same father.

A Patriotic Sacrifice

June 22, Rudolph Schultz, Charles Johnson and James W. Quick raised a liberty pole in Forest City with a small tin pan nailed to its top for a ball. The flag raised on this pole was home made. T. C. Jewett donated his Sunday-go-to-meeting shirt to furnish the white, Mat Standish his red flannel underwear and John Huy his blue denim overalls to emphasize their sacrificial patriotism. The celebration of the 4th of that year was the first celebration of the nation's birthday in Meeker county.

MY PIONEER GRANDMOTHER

(1810 - 1892)

By Frank B. Lamson

Note: I regard the experiences of my grandmother who was both father and mother to me during the years of her long and useful life as typical of the experiences of many of the early pioneer women in Meeker County.

When I speak of pioneers and pioneer life, there comes to my mind the memory of a beautiful woman, of slender build, her hair was snowy white, her face was wrinkled but her eyes were bright and in her movements she was quick and graceful.

The records tell me she was sixty years old when I came to know her but when some action of hers prompted a friend or neighbor to inquire her age, her reply would be, "I was sixteen my last birthday." She was past eighty when she was called to her final home but she was always 16 in spirit and action.

You might not have noted the beauty in her features that I observed, but if you could have known her as I knew her you would join with me in paying tribute to her memory. She took the place of both mother and father in rearing me from babyhood to manhood and was a wise counselor in her effort to shape my habits and mould my character.

Among the treasures of my youth is an autograph album on the flyleaf of which is the following advice:

"On this, the anniversary of your thirteenth birthday, let me leave this memento of my love and advice.

"Continue to do right. Set your standard high and then step by step reach the top. Never give up in the battle of life. Expect trials and meet them bravely, then you will best succeed in all you do. Love God and keep his commandments and then it will be well with you here and hereafter."

I speak of her today because I firmly believe she was a true type of many of the pioneer women of this state and county.

She was a native of Litchfield County, Connecticut, and from girlhood had been a member of the most cultured society. She was a member of Lyman Beecher's church and an associate of the members of his cultured family. She had studied medicine with Doctor Sartain, an eminent homeopathic physician of Philadelphia and was a trained nurse. Her New England home was one of refinement and lacked none of the comforts common to the better class of homes of that period.

When Grandmother was sixty years of age she lost her only daughter and she felt there were imperative reasons why she should establish a home in the west. She had friends in Wisconsin and, selling most of her personal effects, she became the directing spirit in piloting her family, consisting of a decrepit husband, an adopted daughter, age 12, and a grandson aged 2 to a sparsely settled section of Wisconsin about 12 miles from Menasha and Neenah, the nearest railroad stations. Here she established a new home in a typical log house.

In those days doctors were scarce and when it became known that she was skilled in the care of the sick she was called upon to minister to the suffering ones in that pioneer country. Many a time, at the risk of her own health, she traveled for miles, at night, with only a trail for a road and it may truly be said that no neighbor ever called for her services in vain. Many of those she aided were too poor to pay for her services, but it may be truly said that she was a ministering angel to many a poor mother and suffering child. She received some compensation which helped to meet the demands of her household.

I can recall that frail, slender little woman, with the weight of her years, wielding a brush scythe and helping to clear a small field that it might be put under cultivation. I have a very vivid remembrance of her and the old high spinning wheel as she walked back and forth driving the wheel with her hand and spinning the yarn for the socks and mittens her busy fingers knit during the winter nights. I can remember tears of gratitude coursing down her cheeks when a box of clothing came from New England friends and I recall her voice in song while she re-fashioned it to meet our needs.

I remember that her home was open to all who came in His Name and no matter how scant the rations or how cold the guest chamber she never apologized and her kindly welcome made up for anything lacking in food and shelter.

One of my earliest recollections dates back to the time of the Chicago fire. The same year fires raged throughout Northern and Central Wisconsin. Our home was threatened. I was placed in a tub and carried to a slough or pond in which there was about one foot of water. The tub was anchored in the water and I was told not to move until called for. I have seen many brave firemen peril life and limb at a fire, but to my mind I have never seen any person fight fire as she fought it, fighting, as she knew, to save her home and the lives she held dear.

I recall one winter, I think it was 1874, we experienced bitter poverty. My foster sister and I walked to school, a distance of two miles. Our dinner consisted of corn bread and scraps left from trying out leaf lard. That winter when Christmas came we were told that Santa Claus would not make his usual visit and I went to bed with a saddened heart. When Christmas morning came before any of the family had arisen there was a loud knocking at the kitchen door. When the door was opened a man was seen running from the house and on the steps were two sacks, one containing flour and groceries, while the other contained apples, cakes and nuts for us children. I learned in later years that this offering came from a good German Catholic neighbor whose children had noticed how scanty were our school lunches. This neighbor was carrying out the spirit of brotherly love that prevailed in so great a degree in those pioneer days.

We had very airy bedrooms in those days. I can recall looking through the roof boards at the stars, and in a windy blustering night finding my bed covered with small mounds of snow and water in various lavatory utensils frozen solid. Ten years brought great changes and we began to have most of the comforts and a few of the luxuries of life, but I would not have you forget that the luxuries of those days have become the necessities of today.

Those pioneer days had their pleasures and joys: There were the spelling bees and we could spell in those days. There were the kitchen dances, Virginia reel, Money Musk, and old Dan Tucker. We knew nothing of the Turkey Trot, Black Bottom, and Bunny Hug. Old and young were boys and girls together. There were no such distinctions as exist in our modern society. There were candy pulls and what a splendid gathering there was each spring in our neighbor's sugar bush, the coffee made with sap, the potatoes baked in the coals and ashes of the outdoor fire, the boiled chicken and chips for plates followed by the "sugaring off," the generous portion of hot sugar which we stirred with a stick in saucer or cup and no modern confectioner's candy tasted half as good as maple wax made by pouring our hot sugar on ice or snow.

I must not fail to mention the Fourth of July picnic, when the Declaration of Independence was read in its entirety by the rural schoolmaster and some stentorian voiced orator told us of Washington, Jefferson and Paul Revere, and to please the ladies did not fail to mention Betsy Ross and Molly Pitcher. The sports that followed included climbing a greased pole and the chasing and catching of a greased pig.

We greatly enjoyed the winter coasting parties and the different types of sleds used, all home made. I recall one pattern, and what fun it was to ride it. It is easily made—Get a hardwood barrel stave, nail a block of wood in the center and fasten a square board on top for a seat, straddle it and start down the hill but do not choose too steep a hill until you have learned to balance and steer it.

Time passed in its flight and when the lady of whom I speak reached the age of 74 she found herself through no fault of her own, without a home and again she sold her household effects and followed her adopted daughter to Minnesota, but age and failing strength prevented her from carrying on the same struggle she had undergone in those early years. It was no longer necessary. Nevertheless she was the directing spirit in her new home and presided over its household. Her new home was eight miles from a railroad station in a house on land owned by the husband of her adopted daughter. It was a crude frame house that had served as a granary. It was boarded on the interior with elm boards but not lathed or plastered. It was one story high with a floored loft that served as a sleeping room. The walls of the lower room were papered with newspapers and with rag carpets and rugs on the floor presented a homelike and comfortable appearance and not a murmur of complaint was voiced by her over her changed circumstances.

The country was new at that time. The homes were scattered. Our fuel was secured without expense. It did not take a skilled fisherman to supply us with fish, wild game was plentiful. We were amply and comfortably clothed and we were taught that cleanliness was next to Godliness.

Two years went by and we moved to a new and very comfortable home in an abandoned townsite three miles from a railroad.

In the summer of 1891 this dear pioneer grandmother was stricken with her last illness. She knew that the end was near and I wish you might observe as I did the heroic courage she showed in the face of severe suffering and approaching death. Death held for her no terror. It would have been a welcome release from pain and suffering could she have forgotten those dear to her who would be left behind.

She chose the clothing in which she would be laid at rest and asked to have alterations made under her directions, insisting that the sewing machine be brought to her bedside that she might supervise the work. How thankful she was for every ministering service during these days of pain and suffering. She named the pastor whom she wished to conduct the funeral service, selected the songs to be sung, and, mindful of the loved ones she would leave behind, selected among other songs "God be With You Till We Meet Again." She named the pall bearers, gave away her personal keepsakes and cheerfully, with no visible diminution of her mental powers, waited for the end which came as the rising January sun set its rays across the bed in which she reposed. She had lived a noble self-sacrificing life, one of service to others, typical of such characters as are only built by the experiences through which she passed. Her life brings to my mind the lines of her favorite New England poet which she frequently repeated:

> "So live that when thy summons comes
> To join that innumerable caravan
> That moves to that mysterious realm
> Where each shall take his place
> Within the silent halls of death
> Thou go not like the quarry slave at night,
> Scourged to his dungeon,
> But sustained and soothed by an unfaltering trust
> Approach thy grave like one
> Who wraps the drapery of his couch about him
> And lies down to pleasant dreams.

— CHRONOLOGY —

(Note: Detailed stories of the events named may be found in histories of the state available in all public libraries).

1849—June 1, 1849 to May 15, 1853, Alexander Ramsey's period of service as Minnesota's first territorial governor. He was succeeded by Willis A. Gorman who served until April 23, 1857 and was followed by Samuel Medary who was the last territorial governor.

1803—December 20. All of Minnesota west of the Mississippi River was ceded to the United States by Napoleon Bonaparte under what was known as the Louisiana purchase.

AGRICULTURAL DEVELOPMENT

(Contributed by Ralph W. Wayne)

"The husbandman that laboreth must be first partaker of the fruits."
—II Tim. 2:6.

The pioneer settlers of Meeker County 1855 found a region of great fertility that foretold its present development as one of the leading agricultural counties of Minnesota.

The first concern of these early settlers was to raise food crops for self sustenance. The distance to markets over blazed and well nigh impassable roads proved a severe handicap to the production of marketable crops. The growing of potatoes and cereals for home consumption was their only objective.

These pioneers soon learned that this virgin soil was well adapted to the raising of wheat (30 bushels to the acre was a common yield) and very little capital was required compared with the raising of livestock. There was a rapidly expanding market. Flour mills had been established at several points in the county and roads were undergoing improvement whereby it became possible to reach the marketing points, Carver and Minneapolis. The raising of wheat became the major agricultural enterprise.

Livestock production was of minor importance in the early years for various reasons; greater capital was required, buildings were inadequate, markets had not been developed, transportation facilities had not been provided and surplus stock was purchased by local livestock buyers at prices that often did not reflect the true value of the animal. No appreciable competition was afforded and the volume was small.

With the coming of the railroad in 1869 and the establishment of terminal markets wheat became the staple crop and the main source of income and paved the way to a greater development and a higher degree of prosperity. Every village reached by the present Great Northern railroad became a marketing center for cereal crops and eight water power and two steam power flour mills were in active operation.

With the passing years the once virgin soil was losing much of its fertility. The yields of wheat gradually decreased and in comparison with other farm products became less profitable. Until the early nineties when cooperative creameries were established all butter was made by the housewives and exchanged with eggs for household necessities at the local stores.

The prices were extremely low and most of the butter was of poor quality. With the introduction of cooperative creameries the outlet for dairy products was greatly enhanced. High quality butter commanding a reasonable price could now be produced. The herds of dairy cattle increased and with the development of the cooperative creameries Meeker County was destined to become one of the leading dairy counties of the state.

The Danielson Cooperative Creamery

The Danielson Cooperative Creamery at Rosendale is the oldest creamery in the county and enjoys the distinction of being one of the first three cooperative creameries in Minnesota.

The first meeting leading to its organization was held February 10, 1890, and it was placed in operation in February 1891. During the peak year of 1933 the production of butter was 303,104 pounds. The present butter maker Alfred E. Marohn is the operator and it is due to his personal effort that the grounds surrounding the creamery constitute the most beautiful creamery site in the state.

All of the cooperative creameries of the county were in operation within a period of ten years following the establishment of the Danielson Creamery. There were at this period twenty-one creameries in active operation. Of these creameries the following have ceased operation at the present time: Crow River, Greenleaf, Hope Lake, Lake Jennie, Lake Stella, Lamson. The fifteen remaining creameries in order of production is as follows: Watkins, Litchfield, Grove City, Eden Valley, Danielson, Cedar Mills, Star Lake, Kingston, Darwin, Corvuso, Dassel, Cosmos, Manannah, North Kingston, Forest City.

It will be observed that these creameries were established in community centers easily accessible to the farmers living in the territory adjacent thereto. The milk or cream was hauled to the creamery in horse-drawn vehicles prior to the advent of motor driven vehicles. With improved roads and auto transportation operating creameries were reduced until today there are including the Litchfield Produce Company and the Anderson Creamery at Litchfield 17 plants engaged in the manufacture of butter and the annual output of these plants is approximately five and one-half million pounds.

During the early period of the operation of these creameries whole milk was delivered by the farmers and after skimming the skim milk was returned to the farm and used for feeding purposes. Payments were made on the basis of a fixed price per hundred pounds of milk. Upon the introduction of the Babcock test it was soon determined that milk varied in butterfat content not only due to natural variation but "believe it or not" there were some farmers who watered their milk. Previous to the coming into use of the Babcock tester there was an instrument known as the lactometer which was used in the most progressive creameries of Meeker County whereby it was made possible to determine those patrons who watered their milk. These conditions led to payments being made for milk on the basis of butterfat content as revealed by the Babcock test. At a somewhat later period cream separators were installed on most farms which greatly reduced the labor of marketing as only the cream was transported to the creamery and by 1920 most creameries were only receiving cream.

In recent years certain farmers sought markets for whole milk which has resulted in certain Meeker County creameries installing separators to care for whole milk. The cream is churned into butter and the skim milk reduced to a powdered product.

Meeker County has become one of the leading dairy counties of the state. On January 1, 1934 according to census reports there were 54,560 cattle on Meeker County farms of which number 32,000 were dairy cows. Most of the dairy cattle are of the Holstein and Guernsey breeds and a few outstanding herds of Ayrshire, Jersey, Brown Swiss, and Milking Shorthorn.

At a somewhat early date in dairy development the Dassel community became one of the Guernsey centers of the state and the exhibit of this breed at the Meeker County Fair was equal if not superior to that of any county fair in Minnesota.

Many of the leading breeders of the county have adopted a constructive breeding program, and are enrolled in a cow testing association which enables them to select the higher producers for breeding purposes. In 1938 all cows in the Meeker County Association averaged 319.5 pounds of butterfat per cow which is about ten pounds above the state average for cows tested in such associations. The high herd in the Meeker County Association averaged 472 pounds of butterfat per cow. The blue ribbon cow produced 694 pounds of butterfat during the year. In addition to dairy breeds there are also outstanding herds of beef cattle, swine and sheep.

During the "Boom Period" following the World War there was marked activity in the production of pure bred livestock, consignment sales were held and rather fabulous prices were paid. In 1921 there was a deflation period and values met with a marked reduction.

In 1935 of the land area of the county 93.4 per cent was farm land. There were about 2500 farms averaging 145 acres in size. Of this acreage, 63.4 per cent was tillable of which 50 per cent was devoted to the production of grain, 27.7 per cent to cultivated crops, and the balance to tame hay, rotated pastures and minor crops. The acreage of alfalfa and sweet clover has been greatly expanded during the past two decades. Meeker County ranks seventh among the counties of the state in alfalfa acreage. Due to its high limed soil legumes grow exceptionally well.

Hogs and Poultry

Next to dairying, hogs and poultry contribute strongly to the farmers' income. Under normal conditions Meeker County produces between seventy and eighty thousand hogs annually.

Every farmer maintains a flock of poultry. In Kingston township chicken raising has become a specialty and although most of the farms are small as many as two or three thousand are maintained on a single farm. The following commercial hatcheries contribute to the success of those engaged in the raising of highly bred fowls: Mrs. J. H. Tummelson, Grove City; Mrs. George M. Baldwin, Litchfield; Litchfield Hatchery, Litchfield; Watkins Hatchery, Watkins; Riverside Hatchery, Kingston; Cosmos Hatchery, Cosmos; Snow's Hatchery, Litchfield.

Turkeys

The raising of turkeys has become an important industry with many farmers and as many as 75,000 birds have been raised and marketed in a single year.

INVENTION OF BINDER-TWINE KNOTTER
By A. A. Miller

John P. Johnson (John Moen) inventor of the twine-knotter used on self binders that came into use in the early eighties was a native of Norway, who settled at an early date in the town of Acton.

His first demonstration of his invention was in the Ecklund blacksmith shop in Grove City. My father brought home several samples of knots produced by his model and was very enthusiastic in speaking of its merits.

Johnson was cautioned by his friends not to exhibit the same publicly until he had been protected by patents. He did not follow this advice and exhibited the same publicly in Minneapolis. It is contended that representatives of the Appleby Company witnessed its demonstration and in 1881 the Appleby knotter was in use on the Minneapolis binder and is almost a perfect duplicate of the Johnson knotter. This knotter remains the same and ties in the same old way as that little device invented by the Acton farmer.

Hats off to the memory of John P. Johnson who received no lasting credit and no compensation for one of the greatest of all inventions to advance the progress of agriculture.

LIVESTOCK SHIPPING ASSOCIATION

(Note: Information secured from County Agent)

The Litchfield Livestock Shipping Association is the outgrowth of an organization in Harvey township known as the Harvey Debating and Literary Society established in the early nineties which later became known as the Harvey Farmers' Club and was formally organized at a meeting held in school district 29. This club was the first of its kind in Meeker County. The discussion of farm problems and mutual cooperation in their solution constituted the major portion of their frequent meetings.

The leaders in this movement were Anton O. Olson and N. E. Christenson. The value of this interchange of views and the possible solution of problems affecting the welfare of the farmer prompted N. E. Christenson to inaugurate a movement to establish similar clubs throughout the county. He was ably assisted in this endeavor by Charles Nelson of Litchfield township, H. T. Sondergaard (Litchfield butter maker), Messrs. Christgau, of Austin and N. E. Brown, of Elk River. The labor connected with the successful culmination of their purpose in the organization of a Farmers club in every township in the county was carried on during the winter months and resulted in the federation of these clubs into a county wide organization known as the Meeker County Farmers' Club and the election of the following officers: Chairman, Even Evenson; secretary, Anton O. Olson. Directors, Patrick Casey, J. H. Lawrence and N. E. Christenson. Annual membership dues were fixed at 25 cents per individual.

This county wide organization was active in promoting the interests of Meeker County farmers and established an exchange market among their members.

Halvor Christenson, of Harvey town, (father of N. E.) had a farm of 400 acres or more and with his sons produced sufficient livestock to ship by car load to the central market. This method of marketing secured for him a greater profit than was the case with neighboring farmers who were compelled to sell to local buyers at prices based in most cases on estimated weights.

The Farmers' Club of Harvey town urged N. E. Christenson to contact the County Farmers' Club that a cooperative shipping association on a county wide basis might be organized. When this proposition was presented to the club it created immense interest and the establishment of a packing plant to secure a home market for livestock was strongly advocated by those present. J. H. Lawrence, Patrick Casey and Charles Nelson were appointed to visit and investigate the packing plant at Fergus Falls, Minnesota. The result of this investigation prompted them to report that the financing of a similar plant was too great to be overcome and further action in this matter was abandoned.

The county club then centered their attention on the organization of a shipping association. Among farmers, other than the Christensons engaged at this time in the shipping of stock by car load were J. H. Lawrence and Patrick Casey and they joined in voicing the advantage of this method of marketing.

The Litchfield Livestock Shipping Association was duly organized with the following officials: President, N. E. Christenson; Secretary, Anton O. Olson; Directors, J. H. Lawrence and Patrick Casey.

This organization began operation in May 1908 in a shipment of their first carload of stock to the South St. Paul market. There was a very rapid expansion in business and during the first year of its operation it shipped 14 carloads of stock and its cash receipts amounted to $11,599.25. The peak year of 1919 resulted in the shipment of 217 carloads of stock and gross receipts of their shipments amounted to $625,930.61.

The volume of business met with a marked decline during the late twenties due to shipments by truck which compelled the association to adopt the same method of shipment and in 1938 two trucks were purchased since which time there has been a marked increase in their volume of business. During the active years of their operation (1908-1930) 3,932 carloads of stock were shipped and their gross receipts amounted to $6,700,147.25.

H. L. Halverson, of Litchfield town, the first manager, is deserving of supreme credit for the success of the Association. It was largely due to his leadership, marked business ability and integrity that the Association, during the years of his management (which terminated in 1935) association of the northwest.

Many prominent Meeker County farmers have served on the board of directors. N. E. Christenson was elected president to succeed Even Evenson and was followed by William H. Peters. Among those who have served as secretary are Anton O. Olson, George Taylor, Adolph Swanson and John Brandt.

The present officers are President, William H. Peters; Secretary, John Brandt; Directors, Carl J. Anderson, N. O. Evenson, Walter Constant, E. J. Boulion, Floyd Englund and Jens Williams. The present manager is A. G. Olson.

AGRICULTURAL EXTENSION SERVICE
(Contributed by Ralph W. Wayne)

The agricultural extension service in Meeker County owes the success it has attained to the mutual cooperation extended by the County Commissioners and Farm Bureau Association, University of Minnesota and the United States Department of Agriculture and a host of loyal supporters in carrying to a successful conclusion its various activities designed to improve living conditions in Meeker County.

The initial meeting to establish the Meeker County Farm Bureau was held in Litchfield, November 14, 1917 at which time the Board of County Commissioners authorized an appropriation of $1,000 contingent on an enrollment of three hundred members paying $2.50 each as an annual fee in the organization of the Farm Bureau Association.

An organization committee was named and the required membership was obtained and the Farm Bureau was established and the following officers elected: President, J. H. Lawrence; Vice Presidents, G. G. Robinson, F. F. Marshall, N. O. Evenson, and Simon Oster; Secretary-Treasurer, William H. Peters. The Committee was comprised of representatives of various public and official service organizations and was as follows; chairman, Matt Flynn, representing the county commissioners and other members were N. E. Christenson, Otto Tehven, Anna Onsdorff, Joseph Olson, Knute Johnson, N. D. March, Elmer Evenson, Henry A. Olson, A. W. Kron, H. I. Peterson, Mrs. G. W. Haskell, Mrs. Richard Welch, H. L. Halverson, A. W. Loewe.

To J. H. Lawrence and N. O. Evenson special credit is due for their outstanding and unselfish leadership during the establishment and development of the Farm Bureau. J. H. Lawrence served as president for the first 15 years of the organization's existence, and Mr. Evenson served as secretary for a period of 18 consecutive years.

They employed John Sheay as County Agent and outlined a program of activity. The office was officially opened May 23, 1918 and with the exception of holidays and Sundays has been open continuously to all who desire to obtain its form of service.

During the years following the organization of the Farm Bureau the farmers and general public have become increasingly sold to its usefulness as a service agency. The County Agents from 1918 to 1931 in order of succession were: John Sheay, T. G. Stitts, W. K. Dyer and R. H. Steidl.

Ralph W. Wayne, the present County Agent, has served since December 15, 1932.

The Home Demonstration Department came under the supervision of Clara O. Bly April 1, 1936. She was succeeded by Lois J. Miller, the present agent April 1, 1938.

Mr. Wayne was given an assistant January 1, 1937 in the person of J. R. Burkholder. In the conduct of 4-H Club work a part-time service during previous years, (1929 to 1935) the following agents have been employed in order of succession, Earl Hanson, Kenneth Hauks, Lola Runck and Elvira Weum.

The program of work is prepared annually by the executive committee.

Major Projects

Livestock — A large portion of the extension workers' time has been devoted to livestock which has included cow testing association work, swine and poultry improvement and general livestock problems. Due to the leadership of the Farm Bureau Association, Meeker County was the first county in the state to complete the T. B. Testing of all the cattle of the county.

Crop Improvement — Crop improvement has been an important phase of extension work and the development and use of legumes in Meeker County can be largely attributed to the educational activities of the extension service.

Home Projects — A full-time Home Demonstration Agent has been employed to direct this class of work. Groups have been formed in all sections of the county with a total annual enrollment of over 400 persons. These in turn reach a far larger number of homes with the subjects studied. The subjects covered are: meal preparation, home furnishing, millinery, clothing, poultry and nutrition. The group of ladies enrolled in the classes have been active in numerous community activities.

Employment Service — The extension service has served as an employment agency and has placed over 500 men annually on Meeker County farms.

Other Activities — Other activities have included cooperative marketing, disease control, weed and insect control, the R. E. A. as reported elsewhere, corn husking contests, community picnics, banquets, farm tours, etc.

The A.A.A. Programs — Under the government A.A.A. program, over 9,000 contracts and agreements have been made with individual farmers and the payments made total $1,250,000 which is more than twice the total annual property tax levy of the county for all purposes.

4-H Club Work

One of the most popular and publicly endorsed activities of the extension service and a corporation of loyal local leaders is the 4-H Club work. There are approximately 400 boys and girls enrolled annually in these clubs.

The value of this work is best measured by the effect it produces in the development of the rural boys and girls who engage in the work which is noted in the character of the individual and the leadership he assumes when he reaches adult life. With the growth in its membership one can not fail to note the increased activities. The fine cooperation extended by the County Fair Board during a five year period in which they have sponsored an all county 4-H fair has proven an excellent impetus to club work. Special credit for the success of these annual fairs is due D. E. Murphy, of Dassel.

The greatest value of club work is not found in winning of championships but the citizens of Meeker County are justly proud of the success of its boys and girls in state wide contests as follows: State champion pure bred beef heifer, four times state championships in dairy calf club, twice state corn champion, state clothing champion, state turkey champion for two successive years, state champion showman at Junior Livestock Show and state poultry champion.

RURAL ELECTRIFICATION

Reviewed and approved by Irving Clinton, Patrick Casey
and Ralph W. Wayne.

Meeker County was the pioneer in the establishment of rural electrification. It preceded all similar developments in the northwest.

The initial effort leading to the organization of the Meeker Cooperative Light and Power Company took place at a meeting of the directors of the Farm Bureau Association held June 28, 1935. Following a general discussion of the advantages of rural electrification under the R. E. A.; a committee was elected to investigate its possibilities. The members of the committee were Arvid Ruotsinoija, F. F. Marshall, Melvin Jebb, Irving J. Clinton, Henry A. Olson, F. E. Lawrence, H. B. Abrahamson, John Nordberg, C. H. Stenberg, Alfred Anderson, Chas. Ness, Adolph Waller, Wm. Leppa and County Agent Ralph Wayne as secretary.

This committee took prompt action whereby the secretary on July 1, 1935 made a preliminary application to the government authorities which was followed by an intensive educational campaign conducted through meetings in every township in the county followed by a questionaire prepared and mailed to every farmer in the county to determine the possible use of current and his attitude toward the development of the project.

The result of these combined efforts being favorable the committee conferred with the Litchfield village council whereby they sought to have the village secure the necessary government loans, build the lines and supply the current. Failing to reach an agreement with the village authorities after conferences extending over a period of six weeks the committee called a county wide meeting of farmers to perfect a county cooperative association. The meeting was held in Litchfield September 13, 1935 and was attended by 400 residents of the county and as a result the necessary procedure was taken to secure government approval. The Association was incorporated at $6,000 to consist of 1,200 shares of $5 each and a limited indebtedness of $500,000.

The solicitation was highly successful. John Nordberg of Collinwood Township led the field of local solicitors by selling shares of stock to 151 resident farmers of that town. The result of this county wide solicitation showed that the southeast section of the county had the largest number of stockholders which resulted (with the approval of the administrator at Washington) in the naming of Dassel, Collinwood, Ellsworth and parts of Greenleaf and Cedar mills as the first unit to be developed.

January 15, 1936 all the requirements of the R. E. A. at Washington had been met and $450,000 allocated to the Meeker Association to construct 420 miles of line to cover the southeast section of the county. With government approval H. McDonald was employed as engineer and P. J. Casey, attorney.

After several weeks of negotiation a ten year contract was entered into with the village of Litchfield for electric energy at the following monthly rates: First 50,000 K.W.H., 1.75 cents; excess to 100,000 K.W.H., 1.65 cents; all over 100,000 K.W.H., 1.50 cents.

At a later date the following retail rates were established as suggested by the R.E.A. authorities for farmer members of the Meeker Association. Minimum rate per month $3.50 to cover 40 K.W.H. of current; 4 cents per K.W.H. for the next 40 K.W.H. and 2½ cents per K.W.H. for all excess energy.

The construction loan contract was signed by the government and Association May 8, 1936 and the mortgage loan contract for $450,000 was also signed and recorded. The plans and specifications and other engineering details for the work of construction were prepared by Engineer McDonald and met government approval early in June and on June 12 the association advertised for bids to cover 125 miles of line. On June 27 bids were received and forwarded to Washington with the recommendations of the Association and on July 13, 1936 the contract was awarded to the Monroe Electric Company for $111,646.25. This contract was approved by the R.E.A. authorities at Washington July 22, 1936 and on July 30, thirteen months from the date of the first meeting to initiate the development the first pole was set one mile south of Lake Ripley on State Highway No. 22.

The formal dedication of the project took place at a Meeker County Farm Bureau picnic August 7, 1936 when several thousand Meeker County citizens were in attendance and addresses were made by R.E.A. Administrator Morris L. Cooke and E. A. O Neal, president of the American Farm Bureau Federation.

The first section was energized November 28, 1935 when approximately 300 customers were served. Since then two additional contracts for construction have been awarded and lines have been constructed reaching every section in the county and extending into several townships in adjoining counties. At the present time (June 1939) 1500 customers are being served, 676 miles of line have been built at an approximate cost of $850 per mile.

During the period of time the Association has been operating not a single customer has permanently dropped from receiving service and collections from customers have presented no problem.

The Association has met all interest obligations and in the fall of 1938 made a first payment on the principal.

Irving J. Clinton, secretary-manager, is deserving of great credit for his very capable management which has contributed to the marked success of the Association.

The service given the farmer customers shows an average monthly consumption of about 85 K.W.H. and the rural patrons are relieved of much of the drudgery of life on the farm and in the home.

— CHRONOLOGY —

1824—September 20. Laying of the corner stone of Fort Snelling, occupied by troops in 1824.

1849—March 3, 1849. Minnesota organized as a territory and September 3, the first territorial legislature convened.

1851—State capitol permanently located at St. Paul.

1854—In June the first line of railway reached St. Paul.

1857—First census gave Minnesota a population of 150,037. The same year the panic occurred that retarded the settlement of the state.

1858—May 11. Minnesota admitted to statehood.

1860—Heated political campaign. Lincoln wins election as President. Meeker County vote, Lincoln, 166; Douglas, 83; Breckenridge, 9.

1861—April 13. War declared between north and south. First Minnesota Regiment recruited. June 22, left Fort Snelling for seat of war.

1862—First railroad operated between Minneapolis and St. Paul.

1863—General Sibley conducted a military expedition to the Missouri River. Little Crow killed by Chauncey Lamson.

THE GRASS HOPPER PLAGUE

The grasshopper plague of 1876 and 1877 caused severe losses to the settlers of that period. Shortly before the grain had ripened they made their appearance in such numbers that the light of the sun was dimmed as they flew thru the sky and alighted on the ripening crops and began their work of devastation. They covered the railroad right of way and it took a train running from Dassel to Darwin three hours to make the run of five miles. The rails were so thick with the "hoppers" they looked like large steam pipes and the rails had to be scraped and sanded before the train could proceed. The experiences of the settlers inspired a local poet in a neighboring county to write the following lines.

> "I'll sing you a song of our Market Town
> Of the grasshopper times
>   In Market Town.
>
> Of noisy loons and long lean hounds,
> That in every street and lane abounds
>   In Market Town.
>
> Of how the people look forlorn,
> And wish that they were never born,
> For they can get no wheat or corn
>   In Market Town.
>
> Of how they sit from day to day,
> And growl and fret and never pray,
> And how they live no one can say
>   In Market Town.

— CHRONOLOGY —

1865—Close of Civil War. 25,052 troops furnished by Minnesota. Census gives state a population of 250,000.

1866-1872—Period of marked prosperity. Large immigration to Minnesota from Northern Europe. Great activity in railroad construction.

1873—Beginning of grasshopper raid which continued for five seasons.

1873—January 7, 8, 9 a blizzard swept the state and seventy persons lost their lives. Meeker County victims, Mike Condon and Mike Flynn of Forest City and Daniel Hoyt of Cosmos.

1873—The beginning of the financial panic of 1873.

1877—The state changed from annual to biennial sessions of the legislature.

1881—Minnesota's state capitol destroyed by fire.

1884—State prison at Stillwater partially destroyed by fire.

MEEKER COUNTY NEWSPAPERS

The history of any county would be incomplete without adequate mention of its newspapers and the men who patiently and nobly bore the privations of pioneering in a new country while chronicling the marriages, births and deaths, the coming and going of neighbors and friends, recounting the tragical events as they occurred, sympathizing with those borne down by sorrow, rejoicing with those whom fortune had favored, criticising unsound plans and theories for the upbuilding of the county and its various communities, freely advertising to all the world as far as the circulation would permit the advantages of their schools, churches, societies and clubs, boosting its industries without hope of reward and forever looking forward and never backward. To these men and women much of the county's prosperity is due. They deserve their meed of praise in this history.

The writer is indebted to H. I. Peterson, the veteran newspaper publisher of Litchfield, for much of the information embodied in the history relating to the varied publications in Meeker County. In 1867 when the Peterson family reached Meeker County by ox-team and prairie schooner to establish their home and grow up with the county there was a grave question whether Forest City (the county seat) or Greenleaf (location of the United States Land Office) would become the metropolis of the county. Both of these townsites had well founded claims to gaining this distinction but Forest City won as the location of the first newspaper.

THE MEEKER COUNTY NEWS

(1868 - 1872)

In the spring of 1868, Frank Belfoy, of French descent and a lawyer by profession came by boat to Carver, Minnesota and from there overland by ox express with a Washington hand press and printing outfit headed for Forest City. He made a night stop at Greenleaf where he met Olof Peterson (father of H. I. Peterson) with whom he discussed his newspaper venture. Then and there Olof Peterson enrolled as the first subscriber to a Meeker County newspaper. Mr. Belfoy reached Meeker County the next day and shortly afterwards issued the first copy of a weekly publication under the title: The Meeker County News.

The following year, 1869, marked the coming of the St. Paul and Pacific Railway (Great Northern) and the platting of the townsite of Litchfield. A county seat contest resulted and Litchfield was chosen as the future seat of county government.

OF MEEKER COUNTY 49

Mr. Belfoy moved his plant to Litchfield and resumed the publication of the News as a county seat newspaper. Very soon thereafter H. I. Peterson entered his employ as an apprentice or in newspaper slang a "printer's devil." The News retained its distinction as the only news dispenser in the county until the month of April 1872. The press was the first ever brought to Minnesota.

THE LITCHFIELD INDEPENDENT

In the spring of 1876 a third newspaper venture entered the Litchfield field of journalism named the Litchfield Independent, which was sponsored by N. C. Martin, Al Sanders and H. I. Peterson. The paper espoused and supported the principles of the Greenback party and in the purchase of the plant Martin was aided financially by W. M. and E. A. Campbell, Dr. V. P. Kennedy, A. Palm and Per Ekstrom. The first issue made its appearance May 30, 1876. Sanders retired from the firm one month later and Martin and Peterson remained at the helm. N. C. Martin was editor-in-chief. He was a brilliant and militant journalist, a lawyer by profession and espoused the cause of the Greenbackers until that party met its demise. About 1878 he sold his interest in the publication to E. P. Peterson, an attorney-at-law who later transferred his interest to his brother, H. I. Peterson, who holds the distinction of being the Dean of Minnesota journalism in his continuous publication of the same paper and at the age of 82 continues to write his editorials. The Independent became the recognized organ of the democratic party in Meeker County carrying for numerous years under its title head the words: Free and Unshackled. It survived all its previous competitors. The friends of the paper and its editor are not confined to party lines and in the later years of its publication the fairness, independence and impartiality of its editorial utterances have won the respect of its readers. Mr. Peterson was for years associated with his son, Roy, in the publication of the Independent but at present his grandson, John Harmon, is his associate. The circulation has shown a marked increase in later years and at present the paper has a circulation of 1900, well distributed throughout the entire county.

H. I. Peterson

BUILDERS OF CHARACTER

The home, the church, the school and the press should join influences in shaping the character of our youth. Woodrow Wilson once said: "The greatest force in the world today is individual character." If this were true in Wilson's day, it is doubly true today when 12,000,000 people are without employment. There will always be a place for the young man of good ability and unblemished character.

THE LITCHFIELD LEDGER

In April 1868 Frank Daggett, a veteran of the Civil War and a militant republican, came from Wabasha, Minnesota and established the Litchfield Ledger. W. D. Joubert was associated with him as a newspaper mechanic of good ability and the Ledger became a forceful competitor of the News which resulted in the sale of the News to Daggett in June 1874 when the merger resulted in a change of name to the Litchfield News Ledger. Frank Daggett was an able writer and the Litchfield Post of the G. A. R. was named in his honor. He died suddenly in 1876 at which time he was engaged in a newspaper warfare with the Litchfield Independent. It is of interest to note that the week of his death the Independent had put in type and printed an entire page of highly critical political articles directed against Daggett but on learning of his death suppressed its publication.

Frank Daggett

W. D. Joubert in partnership with Frank Belfoy succeeded Daggett as the editor and publisher and followed the policy of its former proprietor. He was an active republican and at one time served as private secretary to Congressman Joel P. Heatwole. The paper continued under their joint ownership until August 1881 when Belfoy died and Joubert became the sole owner. In 1920 Joubert died and the plant was purchased by C. W. Wagner and H. I. Peterson.

LITCHFIELD REPUBLICAN

January 24, 1871 H. G. Rising, a roving newspaper publisher, established the Litchfield Republican which continued publication until the autumn of 1871 when the editor abandoned the field and started a paper at Glenwood, Minnesota.

THE RAMBLER

The Rambler, a small humorous journal was established in 1876 by two compositors in the employ of the Litchfield News Ledger, Messrs. J. D. Hayford and N. P. Olson. It continued publication for a few months but during this period it afforded a fund of amusement.

SVENSKA FOLKETS ALLAHANDA

In 1882 a trio of young men published a newspaper in the Swedish language, The Svenska Folkets Allahanda, in the village of Litchfield for a period of eighteen months. Two of these men bore the names Gisslo and Peterson. The plant was moved to Minneapolis.

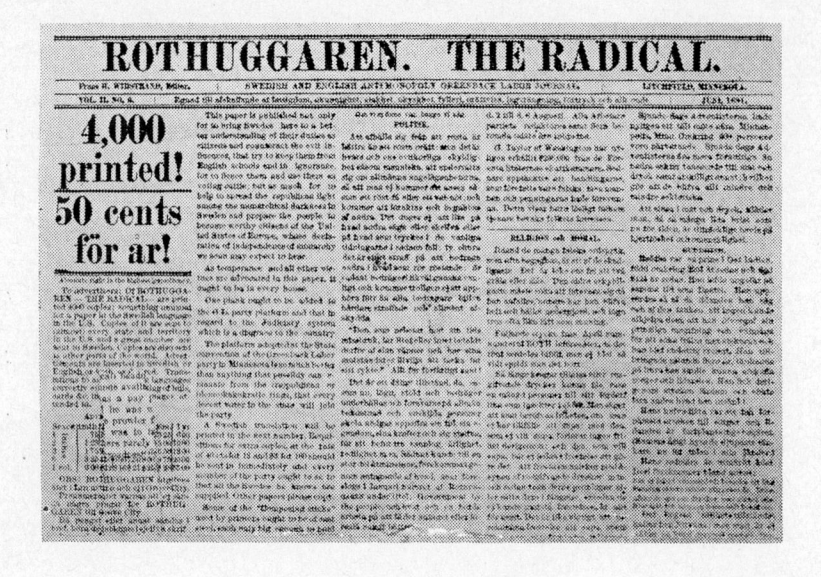

"THE ROTHUGGAREN"

Note—Root Chopper is the literal translation but Widstrand gave the translation as Root Lifter.

Franz Herman Widstrand, a native of Sweden, was born in Stockholm, Sweden, October 10, 1824. He received a university education, served in the Swedish government in various capacities and finally located in Minnesota. April 19, 1856 he homesteaded land in section 7 on the west shore of Lake Constance in Buffalo township, Wright County with the intention of establishing a socialist or communist settlement. He was not a successful farmer but in furtherance of his purposes he published in Buffalo the first issue of the Truth Teller in 1879 which was printed at varying intervals for about three years. It was also known at times as the "Agathocrat." His advanced views on morals, religion and politics did not appeal to the conservative people of Wright County and he removed to Meeker County where he had no definite place of residence but spent a large portion of his time with Dr. Erickson of Grove City. He again engaged in the publication of an intensely radical sheet which he named the Rothuggaren and the same was printed at intervals on the Litchfield Independent press.

Widstrand spent much of his leisure time in translating Paine's Age of Reason into the Swedish language. He was never married, the unfaithfulness of a sweetheart in his youthful years embittered him against all woman kind. In the later years of his life he was regarded as an insane fanatical radical and in the prolonged United States Senatorial election in the legislative session of 1875 in a voluminous letter read before the House nominated himself for that office. An extract from this letter reads as follows:

"I have been terribly disappointed here (Meeker County), have been shamefully abused by know-nothings, office holders and hypocrites. I was assaulted by H. L. Gordon, belied and robbed—All because I have tried to help the people against oppressors. Death at one stroke would have been far better than the mental tortures I have suffered."

Franz Widstrand lived like a hermit in rooms over what is now Tostenrud's Jewelry store at the time of his death. He died in poverty September 26, 1891 and was buried by sympathetic citizens in Lake Ripley cemetery.

The News Ledger in commenting on his death paid him the following tribute:

Notwithstanding his communistic, anarchistic and other radical teachings and practices, a more inoffensive man never lived. He never willingly harmed any living thing. Peace to his ashes.

THE LITCHFIELD REVIEW
By F. B. Lamson

The Litchfield Review, formerly known as the Litchfield Saturday Review was established in 1884 by Rev. Lewis A. and Fred Pier whose newspaper experience was acquired in the office and subsequent ownership of the Mantorville Express. This partnership was later dissolved and Rev. Pier became the sole owner. Rev. Pier supplemented his income by serving as pastor of the Christian church at Litchfield and greatly endeared himself to the citizenship of the entire county. He sold the paper to Frank Haven, an associate in the publication of the Review in 1888 and later became president of the Christian College at Excelsior, Minnesota. After a few years of service he removed to California and served as pastor of the Christian church at Whittier. He died about 12 years ago.

Rev. Pier

Frank Haven

Frank Haven was a son of J. N. Haven, a Wright county pioneer of Montrose, Minnesota. He was of the highest integrity and good ability. He continued the publication for several months. He died in 1890. He was succeeded by John T. Mullen, who had been employed as foreman of the paper where he had learned his trade. Mr. Mullen kept the paper up to its high standard and increased its prestige. He continued as editor and publisher until January 1898 when he sold to the present owner C. W. Wagner. Mr. Mullen is at present engaged in the real estate business at Litchfield.

It has been the privilege of the compiler of this history to enjoy personal and somewhat intimate relations with the editors of the Review previous to the present ownership and I take pleasure in recalling the years of my association and acquaintance. Rev. Pier was the officiating minister at my wedding and I was frequently entertained in his home. Frank Haven was a close friend and we enjoyed very confidential relations. John T. Mullen was and is a close friend and when I edited and published the Cokato Observer, now known as the Cokato Enterprise, he spent a day each week in my office due to my inexperience in newspaper mechanics.

My acquaintance with Mr. Wagner is somewhat limited but I have learned from responsible sources that in character and ability he is held in the highest esteem by the editors and publishers in Minnesota.

Mr. Wagner has played a large part in community activities. He served for four years on the village council and was a member of the library board for a considerable number of years. He was elected a member of the board of education in 1903 and served until 1922. Early in 1930 he was returned to the board and is still serving as a member. He has been its president for 20 years.

John T. Mullen

C. W. Wagner

THE CHRISTIAN GLEANER

During Rev. L. A. Pier's pastorate of the Christian Church in Litchfield he published and edited the Christian Gleaner, a monthly paper devoted to the interests of the Christian Church of Minnesota.

MEEKER COUNTY NEWS

The Meeker County News owes its birth to the prevailing political conditions existing in 1918 when it was the opinion of a large element of farming population that the agricultural interests of the county and state were not properly represented by a partisan press.

The cooperative movement has always been a strong factor in the business life of Meeker County and plans were formed for the establishment of a cooperative farmer owned newspaper. These plans were crystalized by the incorporation of the Meeker County Farmers' Publishing Company for a period of 20 years under the laws of 1913. The corporation bears date July 2, 1918 and is signed by Nels G. Dahlgren, Otto Tehven, H. C. Jensen, John Hahn, Herman Ramey, William Baden, John Morrow, and Neal Plaisted. At the expiration of this period there was a reincorporation, July 2, 1938 under the laws of 1933.

The first officers were: President, Nels G. Dahlgren; Vice President, William Baden; Secretary, Otto Tehven; Treasurer, John Hahn, which comprised with H. C. Jensen the board of directors.

The present officers are: President, Alfred R. Schultz; Vice President, Elmer W. Parsons; Secretary, Gus H. Carlson; Treasurer, Nels G. Dahlgren, who has been one of the directing officials of the corporation during the entire period of publication. Other members of the board are P. J. Settergren, H. N. Nelson, and Edmund Olson. There are about 270 stockholders.

One month following the original corporation (July 2, 1918) William T. Berg was employed to further the sale of stock and on August 31, 1918, the plant, subscription list and good will of the Dassel Anchor was purchased for a consideration of $6,000 from the owner and publisher, C. W. Henke. The name was changed to the Meeker County News and was published at Dassel during the remainder of the year when it was moved to Litchfield and established in its present location.

The paper has been managed until 1923 by the following parties in order of succession: O. E. Kelso, Elsie Weatherwax, and Guy J. Osbourne. April 16, 1923 Herman S. Johnson became the editor-manager and applied good business principles in the conduct of the paper and it grew in circulation and prestige and at the end of his ten years' service the paper had been placed on a sound financial basis.

On August 1, 1933, Roy T. Anderson, an employee of the News became manager and Phil J. Palm, a graduate of the Litchfield High School and Hamline University class of 1930, became editor. Mr. Palm from early boyhood had a strong leaning toward journalism as his chosen profession. He was connected with high school and college publications and in 1930 and 1931 was a member of the editorial staff of the Minneapolis Tribune.

H. S. Johnson

The Meeker County News has been a consistent supporter of the Farmer-Labor party and its candidates. Throughout its entire history it has never been subsidized by outside interests. All of its obligations have been made and met by its stockholders and it has maintained its independence in political matters.

The paper has increased its circulation and now has 2,970 subscribers and the plant has been improved with added equipment to a point that exceeds double the amount of the original investment.

GROVE CITY NEWSPAPERS

"UPPLYSNINGENS TIDEHVARF"
(Age of Enlightenment)

Grove City's first newspaper was printed in the Swedish language by Dr. Erickson under the title "Upplysningens Tidehvarf." The press on which the same was printed was one of the most unique in the history of journalism and was of his own invention. It was of letter press design and the impression was secured by stepping on the upper part of the press. The paper was published at intervals and soon passed into oblivion. Dr. Erickson was a druggist as well as the village doctor and was an extreme radical. He termed himself a "Free Thinker."

MEEKER COUNTY TRIBUNE

N. P. Olson who is at present the President and Treasurer of the Red-Wing (Minnesota) Daily Eagle established, 1878, the first English newspaper in Grove City under the title, Meeker County Tribune. It continued publication for four or five years, Mr. Olson's income being augmented by other business undertakings. When he became wholly dependent on the income of the paper it could not be continued and the plant was moved to East St. Cloud.

GROVE CITY TIMES

Grove City was without a newspaper for several years when N. P. Olson again entered the Grove City field and established the Grove City Times. The first issue made its appearance November 19, 1891. It was ably edited and published by Mr. Olson until 1894 when he sold the plant for a song to his employee, H. S. Rearick. The paper continued publication until 1923. From 1891 to 1923 the Times was for brief periods under the management of Al Sanders, Elgin Brown, Adolph Nelson and Anna Nelson-Hanson, M. J. Lynn and Oscar Ekbom. In 1923 the paper was owned by The Farmers and Merchants Bank of Grove City. The bank sold the subscription list to the Litchfield Independent and the mechanical equipment was scattered.

GROVE CITY GAZETTE

Grove City was without a newspaper from 1923 until September 1933 when T. W. Lewis established the Grove City Observer and conducted the same until 1937 when the same was sold to Robert Gordon (Son of S. Y. Gordon, ex Lieutenant Governor and ex state printer). Robert Gordon installed Modern equipment and enjoyed an excellent patronage. He changed the name to The Grove City Gazette. He sold the plant the same year to J. G. and Anna Carpenter of Sioux Falls and the paper had a somewhat checkered existence until May 31, 1938 when the same was purchased by C. E. Silverberg, an experienced printer and there is reason to believe that under his management the paper will merit and receive the liberal support of the Grove City territory.

DASSEL NEWSPAPERS

DASSEL NEWS

Dassel's first newspaper was established in 1878 by George Washington Barlow. It continued publication for a period of two years when it was discontinued and the plant was moved to Mandan, North Dakota.

DASSEL NEWS LETTER

John E. Bunker in 1882 established the Dassel News Letter which continued publication for about one year. It was printed on the Litchfield Independent press.

DASSEL TRIBUNE

In 1892 B. L. Goodkind, of New Jersey, established the Dassel Tribune. It lasted only a few months. He had secured a large number of paid in advance subscribers when he abandoned the field and left for parts unknown.

DASSEL ANCHOR

In 1893, Ed L. Peet and B. F. Sheffield of Minneapolis launched the Dassel Anchor and the Anchor held fast until September 1, 1917. During the 24 years of the Anchor's existence it underwent numerous changes in ownership. From 1896 to 1898 C. W. Henke was the editor and publisher. From 1898 to 1899 Vernon Brokaw and Reno Hayford, 1899 to 1900, A. L. Nelson, 1900 to 1902 S. J. Huntley. From 1902 to 1916 C. W. Henke was the pilot. He is an aggressive and able writer and is at present the editor and manager of the Winnebago Times. W. E. Struthoff was in control when the plant was sold and moved to Litchfield.

THE DASSEL DISPATCH

Early in the year 1918 C. W. Henke again made his bow to the Dassel community and established the Dassel Dispatch which has not missed an issue since that date. Mr. Henke severed his connection with the Dispatch March 1, 1925 when he sold the plant to J. Edwin Mallory of Chicago, Illinois, who continued as its editor and publisher until its sale in 1926 to L. R. Peel of Crosby, Minnesota. The Dassel Dispatch has a well equipped plant and is one of the most prosperous newspapers in the entire county. L. R. Peel is the proprietor but it is now operated under lease by Carold L. Johnson and serves well and faithfully the interests of the Dassel territory.

EDEN VALLEY JOURNAL

The Eden Valley Journal began publication September 27, 1892 with William O'Brien as editor and publisher. He continued until the early twenties when he sold the paper to Robert Kleschult who was succeeded by Al Martinson who sold his interests to Fay Child in January 1938 and Child sold to the present editor Edward J. Bahe, Jr., March 1, 1939. Mr. Bahe is a graduate of the School of Journalism of the University of Missouri.

— THE COUNTY LINE —

The County Line was established as a democratic newspaper during the McKinley-Bryan campaign of 1896. Two years following the close of the campaign in which McKinley was elected the "County Line" found itself out of line with public sentiment and it dropped off the line. The plant was traded by the stockholders, I. P. Shea, Joseph Friedman, M. E. Weilie and others for a house and lot in Wimbledon, North Dakota and the plant found its way to Swanville, Minnesota. At the time of sale J. L. Chapman was employed as editor.

WATKINS FORUM

Herbert H. Klitzke is the present editor and publisher of the Watkins Forum which is entering on its twenty-sixth annual visitations to the homes of the Watkins territory. He is ably assisted in his work by Mrs. Klitzke who operates the linotype.

CAUSTIC JOURNALISM

Meeker County newspapers in the early years were regarded as the personal organs of their owners. They engaged in wordy battles of an extremely caustic and personal nature but no personal encounters occurred and the editors continued to maintain friendly social and business relations. The same form of journalism, south of the "Mason Dixon's Line," would have produced a case of pistols and coffee at ten paces.

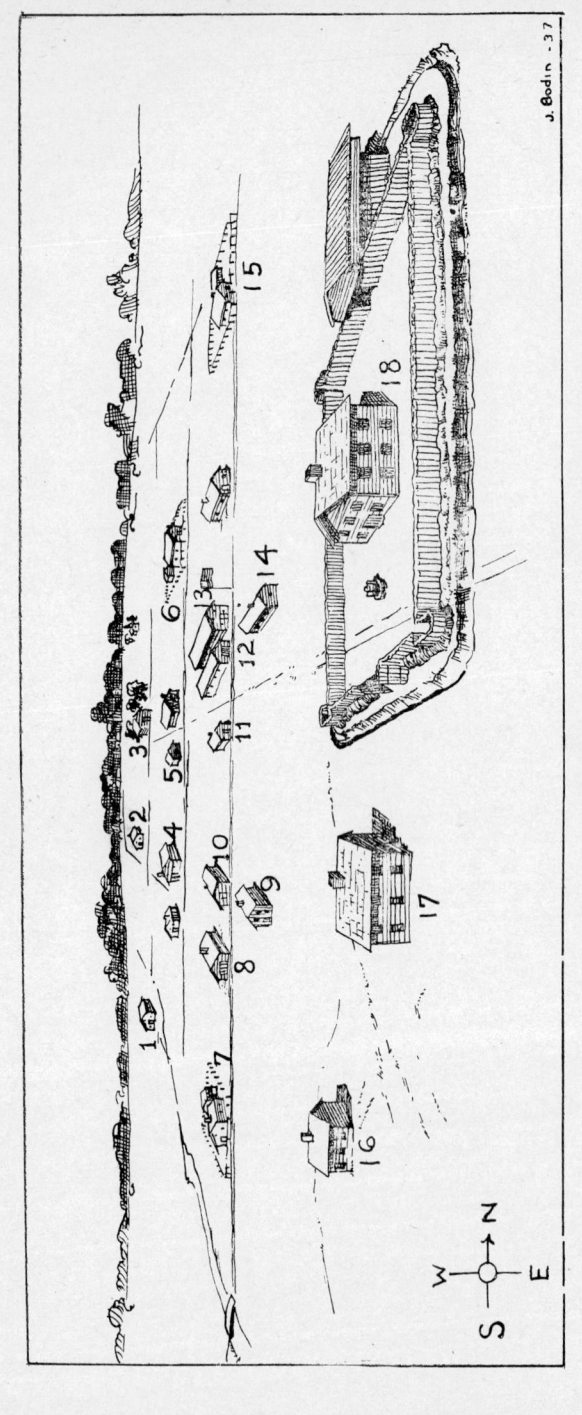

VILLAGE OF FOREST CITY AND STOCKADE — 1862

1, Robinson; 2, Hoyt; 3, Heath; 4, A. C. Smith's Shop; 6, Mallory; 7, Taylor; 8, Blacksmith Shop; 9, Welles; 10, U. S. Land Office; 11, Shoemaker Shop; 12, Hotel Barn; 13, Atkinson Hotel; 14, Atkinson's General Store; 15, Hamlet Stevens; 16, School House; 17, T. C. Jewett; 18, Stockade.

The buildings shown in the illustration represent the townsite (1862) in its entirety and is produced from a pen and ink copy of a penciled drawing by H. Koerner Strong, executed by John Bodin of Dassel, Minnesota.

This stockade was a haven of refuge for the settlers of Meeker County during the Indian uprising of August 1862.

Townships of Meeker County

In compiling this history of the towns of Meeker County we do not aim to fully list all the early settlers of these subdivisions due to the fact that they are quite completely listed in the Album History of Meeker County of 1888 and in the sectional histories of twelve of these towns published in 1938.

ACTON

Acton Township 119, Range 32 West.

In 1857 when the first settlements in the town were established the land area was 19,842 acres, water area, 3,130 acres. The lakes and streams teemed with fish and wild game was plentiful. At the present time, due in part to excessive drainage and drouth the lakes contain very little water.

The territorial pioneers were Peter J. Lund, Nels Waylander, Jesse Winquist, Howard Baker, Mrs. Ann Baker, John Blackwell, Robinson Jones, Abram Kelley, John and Peter Ritchie, Captain Robinson and John Winquist.

In the years that followed (1857 - 1870) there was a continued influx of settlers from the Scandinavian countries, Denmark, Norway and Sweden and their descendents constitute the major portion of the present population of the township. During the period from 1862, the year of the Indian outbreak ot 1865 very few if any settlers established homes in Acton.

The first white child born in the town was Sarah Lund, (Mrs. A. P. Nelson) daughter of Peter J. and Elna Nelson Lund, born, February 9, 1858.

The first school was taught in the home of Nels Waylander in Section 4 taught by a man named Algreen. It was in this same home that the first religious service was held in 1858, conducted by Rev. John Robson, a Methodist divine.

Acton, at the time of its organization embraced all of its present territory and in addition the town of Danielson and the south half of Swede Grove. Its name was given to commemorate the town of the same name in Canada, the home of the Ritchies prior to their coming to America.

The early settlers received their mail from the Lake Harold postoffice established in the home of Iver Jackson located in Litchfield town, close to the Acton boundary. The office was later moved to a point in Acton west of Lake Hope at which time August Hendrickson was postmaster. A later removal resulted in its location in the Acton townsite. It was discontinued with the establishment of rural delivery.

School district No. 4 was organized October 5, 1857. The present school building was erected in 1879 in section 17. Previous to its erection school was held in private homes. Among the homes thus utlized were those of Manda Olson, Lars Christianson and Nels A. Draxton. In the early years the enrollment was as high as 40 pupils and the average salary of teachers was $25 to $30 per month. In later years the maximum monthly salary was $90. At present there is an enrollment of seven entered in the Atwater school with bus transportation to and from their homes.

CEDAR MILLS

Township 117, Range 31 W. Acreage, 24,209.44;
677 acres were covered by water

The town derives its name in part from Red Cedar Lake, a translation of the Indian name Ranti-tia-wita. This lake formed a portion of the southern boundary of the neighboring town of Ellsworth.

The surface of the town is a slightly rolling prairie.

The first to make a settlement in the limits of the town was Daniel Cross, a native of Oneida County, New York, who established his home in section 13 in July 1856. At the time of the Indian outbreak of 1862 he took refuge with his family at Hutchinson. He was killed by the Indians in section 35 Ellsworth township, September 24, 1862. (A detailed sketch of Mr. Cross's life may be found on pages 200 and 201 of the Meeker County Album of History in the Litchfield Public Library).

Among the settlers of the township prior to the Indian outbreak of 1862 the following are deserving of mention: 1857; R. J. Brodwell, Philander Ball, Milton Coombs, Elmer Eighmey, David Hern, Doctor Hester, John and William Hunter, Charles H. Stinchfield, a German named Steinkopf and L. S. Weymouth. 1858; S. D. L. Baldwin, George R. Jewett and C. G. Topping. 1859; George Nichols and Jesse W. Topping. 1860; H. J. Lasher, J. M. Pitman and Seth Nichols.

Among the prominent settlers of later years who contributed in a large measure to the development of the township the following parties should be mentioned: James A. Elijah and E. R. Austin; A. C. Barrick, John Curry, R. D. Grindall, Edwin Gillett, C. B. Jordan, Edward Stafford, Arthur and Isaac Wheeler, and William Owens.

The first deaths were two children of Mr. and Mrs. Elmer Eighmey's in 1859.

The first school was taught by Sophia Pratt at the residence of Daniel Cross (now owned by the heirs of Mary Jordan in section 13) in 1860 and the first schoolhouse was erected in 1869 and E. B. Comstock was the first teacher.

The first religious services were held during the winter of 1859-60 at the home of H. J. Lasher by Rev. H. Adams, a Presbyterian minister, whose home was in St. Peter, Minnesota.

A post office was established in 1858 with C. G. Topping as postmaster. He was succeeded in 1861 by H. J. Lasher. At the time of the Indian outbreak Lasher buried the official records and supplies of the office in the ground and for several years following there was no post office within the limits of the town. In 1870 the office was reestablished with Thomas Vinacke as postmaster. Following him in order of succession were J. D. Baldwin, O. W. Stearns, E. B. Comstock, Elijah Austin, L. E. Austin, and Mrs. Julia Anderson.

A Presbyterian Church was organized in May 1879 with Rev. J. S. Sherrill of Litchfield as pastor and a membership of twenty-five. The first elder was John C. Curry but later he was joined by S. W. Barrick and J. W. Topping who occupied similar positions in the church organization. In

1882 a neat and substantial church was erected at a cost of $1800 on a four acre tract of land presented by Judge Vanderberg of Minneapolis. Services were held on alternate Sundays until 1887 when the church was able to support a resident pastor and services were held each Sunday. The church was dedicated July 16, 1883. Rev. D. E. Wells preaching the dedicatory sermon. Among the active church officials and workers were H. J. Lasher, J. W. Topping, S. W. Barrick, I. N. and R. A. Wheeler, and Franklin Curry.

A store was opened in 1870 by J. D. Baldwin who later took his brother into partnership. They sold the business to O. W. Stearns. They discontinued the mercantile business and opened a blacksmith shop and a few years later discontinued their business ventures.

In the fall of 1876 Ira Williams opened a general store and after a short business career he sold to E. Gillette who soon after disposed of the same to L. E. Austin who continued in business for ten years.

In 1887 a rival store was started by Elliott and Anderson but in March 1888 they sold to Standish brothers.

In 1888 there were two blacksmith shops in Cedar Mills village, owned and operated by Louis Kelm and Vigenske and Dumont. In 1858 a flour mill was erected by George Nichols in section 12 who continued to operate it until 1867 when it was purchased by C. B. Jordan and operated by Samuel Anderson. The mill later became the property of Dr. V. P. Kennedy and during the period of his ownership it was dismantled and passed out of the picture.

Cedar Mills town was organized as a township January 25, 1870 in a meeting held at the home of Isaac Wheeler, with thirty voters present. Wheeler acted as moderator and James A. Austin served as Clerk.

The following officers were chosen; Supervisors; J. M. Pitman; Chairman; E. H. Halsted and E. R. Austin. Clerk, J. A. Austin; Treasurer. John Dyer; Assessor, E. Gillett; Justices; V. P. Kennedy and A. C. Barrick.

COLLINWOOD TOWNSHIP
Township 118—Range 29

Collinwood was named after Collinwood, Canada, the former home of some of the early settlers.

The first claims filed in this township were by Dennis Felix in January 1858, and Levi Wilcox in the same year, but neither became settlers in the township.

The first settler was Charles C. Dewing in the fall of 1862. He was followed in 1864 by Thomas Fallon, and in the same year came Jacob and Thomas J. Hutchins, Jacob Blair, Elkanah McStotts, Alexander Ramey, Harrison Fuller, Philip Van Blaarecom, Hawkins Steel, Oliver Rasnick, E. K. Counts, George Fuller, Swan Johnson, John Forsberg, David, Noah and Lazarus Parks.

The major portion of the early settlers were from Virginia and the town was organized as New Virginia in the spring of 1866, and the following officers were chosen: Supervisors, E. K. McStotts, chairman, Canaan Counts and Hawkins Steel; Clerk, E. K. Counts; Treasurer, Jacob Hutchins; Assessor, Jacob Blair; Justice, Oliver Rasnick; Constable, Harrison Fuller.

The first marriage was that of John Taylor and Elizabeth Hutchins, in the fall of 1866.

In 1868 H. C. Bull located in Collinwood and established his home on lands bordering the north shore of Collinwood lake in what later became a part of the townsite of Collinwood. He was from New York. He was a young man of broad vision, ambitious and energetic. He had close relations with men of wealth in his native state. He firmly believed that Collinwood would become the metropolis and county seat of Meeker county and in 1870 he prevailed upon the board of county commissioners to change the name of the town from Little Virginia to Collinwood, and in company with L. G. Pendergast and D. E. Taylor layed out the townsite of Collinwood.

The plat was filed in the register's office September 26, 1870. Mr. Bull opened a store, became the first postmaster and erected an attractive residence facing the present school house which is occupied at present by a tenant of the owner.

Among the most prominent residents of the townsite at this time were Lloyd and Timothy H. Pendergast. They constructed and operated a water power grist mill and their home was one of the most pretentious in the entire county and became the social center of the community. At this period in the town's history Collinwood had a substantial hotel and two-story school building, and was the milling center of a large radius of territory. The mill dam kept the waters of the lake at a normal depth and it was one of the most beautiful and attractive lakes in the entire county. It would be difficult to conceive of a finer setting for a growing and thriving village that might expand in its development into one of Minnesota's most prosperous cities.

"Of all sad words of tongue or pen, the saddest are these, it might have been." This was undoubtedly the thought that entered the minds of Bull and the Pendergasts as they faced the development of that period in the townsite's history.

When the railroad, now known as the Great Northern, was surveyed through Meeker county the preferred survey passed through the townsite of Collinwood. The desired acreage for railroad purposes was owned by a man named Parks, who refused to make any concessions to the company and the railroad officials expressed their resentment by choosing the present location one mile north of the townsite. The villages of Cokato and Dassel were platted and the visions of Bull and the Pendergasts relating to the future of Collinwood failed to materialize. The struggle for the supremacy continued. A spur track was built one mile north of the village and for a time freight and passengers were received and discharged. In 1879 Bull and others gave up the struggle and succumbed to the inevitable and Collinwood became another "Sweet Auburn." Bull transferred his real estate and other interests to Cokato and became a prominent factor in the development of that village which has become an exceedingly close rival in wealth and population to Buffalo, the county seat. Mr. Bull was a member of the state legislature, session of 1891, and was the founder of the State Bank of Cokato.

L. G. Pendergast sold his milling and real estate interests to his brother, Harrison, and eventually established his residence at Bemidji, Beltrami county, Minnesota, and served that county in the state legislature, sessions of 1915 and 1917. It was largely due to his efforts that the necessary leglislation was secured to establish the Teachers Training College in that city. During his residence in Meeker county he was an unsuccessful candidate for the state legislature in 1874. The successful candidate was N. C. Hines, who had a plurality of 52 votes.

T. H. Pendergast, after the advent of his brother, Lloyd, and H. C. Bull, was for years the most eminent citizen of Collinwood town. He was a private soldier in the Civil War, had served as superintendent of the Hutchinson schools and was the leader in social activities in Collinwood and Dassel. In 1886 he was an unsuccessful candidate for county auditor of Meeker county, being defeated by Ambrose Walls. He became a state wheat inspector during the administration of Gov. A. R. McGill. In later years he established his home with his son, Mortimer, on a farm near Bemidji, Minnesota, but the last years of his life were spent at the Soldiers' Home in Minneapolis, where he died, and was buried in the Dassel cemetery.

The first school house constructed in Collinwood town was built in what is now known as District 17 in the fall of 1866. The school trustees were Jacob Blair, clerk; E. K. McStotts, treasurer, and Jacob Hutchins, director. The school was opened in the winter of 1866 and 1867 and was taught by E. K. Counts. The building was located in Section 18.

The first religious services were held in a grove in the Steelsville community. The first organized church was that of the Methodists who formed a class in 1868 with J. A. Quick as class leader. Mr. Quick served in the Civil War as a member of Co. I of the Thirteenth Indiana Cavalry. He located in Section 20 in 1868 and early in the eighties engaged in the manufacture of sorghum molasses. In 1885 he made 1600 gallons of this syrup which was reputed to be of the very best quality. He was elected county coroner in 1872 and defeated in the election of 1874 by Oliver Rasnick.

Collinwood is today largely populated by the descendants of Swedish emigrants. It is one of the substantial towns of the county but the picturesque beauty of its lakes and streams have been to a very large extent destroyed by excessive drainage.

In the early eighties a colony of Seventh Day Adventists was located in the vicinity of Lake Jennie, among those constituting this deeply religious group were the Wheelers, Maxons, Owens, Comers and Hawkins families. They held regular services at their several homes, were of excellent character and habits and extremely well versed in the scriptures. The most outstanding family of this group were the Hawkinses. The senior Hawkins was noted as the most successful gardener in Meeker county and his exhibits of vegetables and fruits invariably secured the first premium at

OF MEEKER COUNTY 65

the Meeker and McLeod county fairs. He was the first farmer in Meeker county to successfully raise a crop of sweet potatoes. One of the members of this family is Dr. E. P. Hawkins of Montrose, Minnesota, recognized as one of the most eminent physicians and surgeons in Wright county. This colony scattered in later years and there is doubtless no remnant left of the original group that, during their Meeker county residence, contributed greatly to the social, cultural and spiritual development of the Lake Jennie (Bonniwell's Mill) community.

COSMOS

Township 117 — Range 32 West

The town has an area of 23,030 acres and previous to its settlement 542 acres were covered with water but in the years which have followed excessive drainage has caused the lakes to well nigh disappear and very small ponds have taken the place of lakes that once teemed with fish.

The surface of the town is a low level prairie. The soil is a warm quick black loam of unusual richness.

The pioneer settler was Daniel Jackman, a native of Kennebec County, Maine, of colonial ancestry. He became a permanent resident and was closely connected with the development of the town.

Jackman's arrival was followed the same year by the arrival of the following settlers all of whom took up homesteads: Edward Chamberlain, Nelson Eddy, Hans H. Hanson, Daniel Hoyt, John Jameson, Isaac Layton, Ezra Matthews, J. M. McDonald, Ole K. Nelson, Ole Olson, Orrin A. Phelps, Iver H. Thompson and H. W. Young.

The following year (1869) the settlements were increased by the arrival of Albert Amerman, C. H. Duckering, Elisha L. Grindall, Christian and Lewis Halverson, John Rastue, J. T. and Thomas Royce, Ralph D. Waterman and A. B. Watson.

The first white child born in the town was a daughter of Samuel Hutchinson, January 18, 1871. The second birth was a son born March 27, 1871 to Albert, son of William C. Amerman. The first death was that of John T. Royce, April 16, 1871.

The first marriage was Ole K. Nelson and Mary Danielson in 1869. The first religious services were held by Rev. Kennedy, a Methodist minister in the school house named below in 1873.

The first school was held in the spring of 1870 at the home of J. T. Royce with Lilly Cathcart as the teacher. The first school house was built in 1871 and Miss Nellie Barrack was the pioneer teacher.

In 1871 a small school house was erected in the NE ¼ of section 27 the center of population at that time. It was later replaced by a larger structure that served as a community hall. This building remains intact in District 53.

The first wheat crop raised in the town was by Isaac Layton and H. W. Young in 1861.

The first house was built by D. Jackman in the summer of 1868. In 1874 a post office was established in the town named Cosmos and John A. Jameson was the first postmaster. Two years later he was succeeded by Isaac Layton who gave way in 1878 to Daniel Jackman. He resigned in 1880 and Mrs. Jackman became his successor.

Daniel Hoyt is credited with the naming of the township, Cosmos, the definition of the word represents the universality of created things and its synonym is harmony. Another name given to the town in the early days prior to its organization was Nelson in honor of O. K. Nelson. The very early settlers were English speaking people and came from New England and Canada. These pioneers, after a short period of residence sought homes elsewhere but Daniel Jackman and E. L. Grindall remained and have descendants residing in the township.

The town was organized January 25, 1870, at a meeting in the home of Daniel Jackman. Only nine voters participated in the election. The officers chosen were: Supervisors, D. Jackman, Chairman, John Jameson and Albert Amerman; Clerk, Daniel Hoyt; Treasurer, J. H. Thompson; Assessor, J. D. Jackman; Justices, Orrin Phelps and E. McMathews.

A preliminary meeting providing for the organization of the township of Cosmos was held at Beaver Falls, Renville County January 5, 1870 at which time the township was a part of Renville county. The organization was perfected at a town meeting held in the home of Daniel Jackman, January 25, 1870.

At a meeting held March 4, 1871 the town records show that Cosmos had been annexed to Meeker county. Daniel Hoyt, the first clerk of the township was one of its earliest settlers. He homesteaded a tract of land on the south shore of Thompson lake and prophesied that a railroad would pass thru that section which was fulfilled when the Luce line was built. Hoyt lost his life in a March blizzard while on his way to visit friends at Lake Lillian.

— CHRONOLOGY OF MINNESOTA —

1609—A portion east of the Mississippi river actively claimed by Virginia under second charter.

1679—May 2. Northern portion included in charter of English Hudson Bay Company.

1680—Father Hennepin's exploration of upper Mississippi river.

1762—November 8. French claim west of the Mississippi conveyed to Spain.

1763—February 10. French claim east of the Mississippi river ceded to Great Britian; also the northern portion of Minnesota, within present state limits, as a part of Canada.

1783—September 3. Portion east of the Mississippi river becomes part of the United States by treaty of Paris.

1784—March 1. Virginia claim relinquished.

OF MEEKER COUNTY 67

DANIELSON
Township 118 — Range 32 West

The town was named after Nels Danielson who homesteaded the N. E. ¼ of Section 2, November 28, 1863.

The town of Danielson in the years preceding its settlement embraced an area of 22,950 acres of which 974 were unavailable for cultivation consisting of low marsh ground, lakes and ponds. King and Belle lakes covered the larger portion of this area. The town was one of the last in the county to invite the settler. There were no permanent settlers until 1861 but Noah White in 1857 located a claim in the town but one year later moved into Kandiyohi County. In 1861 there was an influx of settlers who located claims in the township and became permanent residents. Among these were Berger Anderson, Andrew Dokken, Bethel Gunderson, William Hanson, C. L. Hanson, Nels Mattson, Soren Morton, O. K. Nelson, Peter Peterson, Oscar Phillips, Ole Solomonson and Nils Danielson Upsahl.

Nels Danielson

Among early settlers of subsequent years who have descendants now living the following are deserving of mention: Nels Fredrickson, P. C. Hanson, Christian Hanson, Peter Mortenson, Henry Solomonson.

The first white child born in the town was Arnt, son of C. L. Hanson, born November 13, 1866, and this child was the first death, the same date.

The first marriage was that of O. K. Nelson and Mary Danielson in 1868.

The first school was taught by Lizzie Martin in 1869. The first religious service was held in the school house located in Section 2 in 1869.

The first church in the town bore the name Arnt Dahl in memory of Arnt Hanson the first child born in the town and Rev. Dahl, the first minister.

Early Home of the Danielsons

Danielson was for several years part of a voting precinct including Swede Grove, Acton and Danielson but was organized as a separate town, March 12, 1872, and its name was chosen to honor an early settler, Nils Danielson Upsahl, of that name. The first officers were: Supervisors, Ole K. Nelson, Chairman, O. Solomonson and C. Fernelius; Clerk, Daniel Danielson; Treasurer, Berger Anderson; Justice, C. L. Hanson; Assessor, Daniel Danielson, Jr.; Constable, Lars Rasmuson.

DARWIN

Township 119 — Range 30

The name Darwin has no connection with the Darwinian Theory of the origin of man, but was named to perpetuate the memory of a prominent official of the St. Paul, Minneapolis and Manitoba Railroad.

The town embraces all of township 119 north of range 30 west. It is one of the most fertile sections of the entire county and contains lakes and streams that invite the summer tourists from the metropolitan centers during the vacation seasons of the year.

It was one of the first towns in the county to attract the early settlers of Meeker County. The first man to settle in Darwin was Patrick Casey, a native of Tipperary, Ireland. He came to America in 1849 and established a home in Allegheny County, Pennsylvania, where he was married July 8, 1851 to Hannorah McRaith. He left the Keystone State in the spring of 1856 and journeyed westward. When he reached St. Paul where he attached himself to a corps of surveyors (William and Michael O'Brien and Patrick Condon) headed by Captain Hayden and in May 1856 made a bee line for Meeker County, reaching Kingston June 16, 1856 and two days later he located a claim in section 33, Darwin town where he continued to make his home until his death.

The pioneers of 1856 were John Peiffer, Peter Stierens, Gotlieb Reef, Patrick Condon, John Doyle, John Dougherty and Timothy Dunn.

Timothy Dunn was an adventurous character who had joined the gold rush to California prior to locating his claim in Section 3, Darwin town. During the Indian outbreak he found safety for himself and family in Minneapolis. When he returned to his claim in October he found his farm buildings had been destroyed and he was compelled to begin life anew.

The pioneers of 1857 were William and Michael O'Brien, Bryan McNulty, William Cunningham, John McRaith, James Shelley, Jacob Reef, James Murphy, S. W. Ryan, William Keats, Richard Poole, Henry Bierman, John Curran, J. Powell, J. E. Bill, Capt. James Hayden, Edwin Fitch, Mark Warren and a man named Hitchcock.

The pioneers of 1859 were John S. Shields, Edwin and Lance Chapin and Sylvester Stevens. Of this number John S. Shields was a native of Canada. Upon coming to Meeker county he established his home on a farm in Section 34 Darwin town. He was in Forest City guarding the horses in a barn on the eventful morning of September 4, when the Indians made their attack on that settlement. In making his way to the stockade he barely escaped with his life. The horse he rode was the only one saved from theft by the Indians. He became prominent in town and county affairs and was elected to the State Senate on the Farmers Alliance ticket in 1886.

In 1860 the population of the town was increased by the arrival of James Deary, Michael Haggerty, Michael Nash, Michael Gallahue, Samuel Charlton and Colonel Andrews.

The names of these early settlers indicate that the major portion of these pioneers were of Irish descent. They were devout Catholics as are their descendants.

Darwin town was originally named Rice City, due to Capt. James Hayden having laid out a townsite of that name in Section 34 on the farm of John S. Shields.

Rice City town was organized April 5, 1857.

The first child born in the town was Mary Ann Pfeifer, daughter of Mr. and Mrs. John Pfeifer, born in 1857.

The first death was that of Edmund, the son of Timothy Dunn, who died in 1862.

The first school was taught by Mary Flynn in 1859 in a log school house near where Michael Harding's house stood.

The first religious services were held at the home of Bryan McNulty in 1861, Rev. Father Alexis (Catholic) of St. Cloud, celebrating mass.

The first marriage was that of John Doyle and Mary Lynch in 1861.

When the railroad passed thru Rice City town in 1869 and the village of Darwin was platted, the name of the town was changed to correspond with that of the village.

DASSEL TOWN

Dassel Township, 119—Range 29

The town was originally united with Kingston and when separated was named Swan Lake after the lake of that name within its borders. The township was organized as Swan Lake in the fall of 1866 with the following officers: Supervisors, John Smith, chairman, Frederick Spath and Wayne Russell; Clerk, G. D. Arrowood; Justices of the Peace, Andrew Davidson and William Maynard; Assessor, G. A. Arrowood. The name of the town was changed to Dassel in 1871.

The first settlers, C. L. Richardson and Edwin Ayres, surveyors, were originally from Mexico, New York. They built a cabin in Section 14 and lived there until the Indian outbreak of 1862 when they fled the country and their cabin was burned by the Indians. This section of the town was known as Ayres' Prairie.

The Indian massacre retarded the settlement of the town until November 1863, when Isaac and Anthony Russell, natives of Vermont, arrived with their families and took claims in Section 10.

Among the settlers of 1866 to 1868 who gained prominence in town and county affairs were Henry and Harlow F. Ames, Lewis and John Rudberg, William Maynard, John McKinney, Madison DeLong and Peter Johnson.

The first school house in the town was a log structure with a dirt roof. Light was admitted through two small half sash let into the sides. It was built in 1867 and located at the merger of the corners of Sections 10, 11, 14, and 15. Mrs. E. M. Winans was the first teacher.

George Cunningham was the first white child born in the town, 1865. The second birth was that of Ada Tuman, May 6, 1866.

The first death was that of the child of James and Margaret Littow.

The first marriage was that of Barney Cox and Janet Davidson.

ELLSWORTH

Township 118—Range 30

The pioneer settler in this township was Dr. V. P. Kennedy in June, 1856. He was followed by Thaddeus R. Webb, James Barret and Dr. Russel Whiteman. In 1858 there came a group of settlers, among whom were James Fallon, John M. Mousley, Alfred Mousley, John Hurley, W. H. Greenleaf, Dana E. King and a man named Hook.

The financial panic of 1857 checked all immigration and during the period between 1859 and 1860 there were few who sought homes within the town. Among the few who braved the existing conditions and established homes in this fertile wilderness during the period named were, George McGowan, Ira Pratt, Jr., Silas Pratt and a man named Matthews.

The first white child born in the town (1857) came to the home of Dr. and Mrs. Russel Whiteman. The second births and first deaths were in the townsite of Greenleaf (1860), twin babies born and died this same year. Mr. and Mrs. Greenleaf were the parents. The first adult death was in 1862, a Mr. Halstead.

The Indian outbreak of 1862 depopulated the town and very few settlers continued to reside within the limits of the town during this trying period.

"Hiram Sanborn, a settler whose family was at the fort in Hutchinson, was working alone on his claim in Section 35, Setpember 22, 1863 when he was brutally murdered by some roving Indians. As he had not been heard from for several days a detachment of which Daniel Cross was a member went from Cedar Mills to look for him. When they approached Sanborn's place they were fired on by Indians and Cross was killed. The next day the mutilated body of Sanborn and that of Cross, who had been scalped, were recovered and taken to the Hutchinson stockade."

FOREST CITY

Township 120 — Range 30

John Huy and Thomas Skinner who spent the winter of 1855 and 1856 in a crude cabin in the town of Harvey located in the early spring of 1856 in Forest City and established the townsite of that name.

Forest City has a background of history, unequalled by any other township in Meeker County.

Early in the year 1856 new settlers arrived among whom were Milton C. Moore and Elijah Bemis and the former became Meeker County's first register of deeds and the latter, the county's first sheriff.

During the same year (1856) the settlement at Forest City was further increased by the arrival of Walter Bacon, James Bramhall, Henry Clinton, Charles E. Cutts, Wait H. Dart, Isaac C. Delamater, Edward Fitzgerald, John Flynn, J. W. Griswold, Loring Huy, T. Carlos Jewett, John W. Johnson, John Kimball, Charles McAron, David Mitchell, John Patterson, John A. Quick, Rev. John Robson, Wyman Ryan, Charles N. Shed, Mathew Miles Standish, Judson A. Stanton, Samuel and Dudley Taylor, G. O. Thomas, Ogden T. Tuttle, W. H. Van Ness, Leander L. Wakefield, Jacob Weymer, Joseph Weymer, Sr., John Whalen, and John Wigle. Most of these first settlers took up claims, erected log cabin homes, and cleared small tracts of land for cultivation. Their nearest market was St. Paul and they were of necessity compelled to deprive themselves of all the comforts and conveniences of life, but wild game and fish were easy to obtain and they did not suffer the pangs of hunger.

The year of 1857 witnessed a new influx of settlers, many of whom left the country, a few remained and while none of these are now living there are several whose descendants are among the present residents of the county: H. M. Angier, James B. Atkinson, H. N. Baker, Jacob Ball, G. M. Blandin, B. F. Butler, W. S. Chapman, D. P. Delamater, Milton Gorton, Thomas Grayson, N. O. Griffin, L. F. Haines, A. F. Heath, John Heath, A. B. Hoyt, Jacob Knapp, Michael Lenhart, John and Michael Murray, Isaac Perrine, William Richards, Hamlet Stevens, John Sullivan, Allen Teachout, H. Walker, Charles and William Willis, James Willis and W. W. Woodman.

The hard times that followed the financial crisis of 1857 had a discouraging effect upon all emigration but nevertheless there were a few who were brave enough to face existing conditions and add their names to the honor roll of those that located themselves in the North Star State in the year of its admission to the dignity of statehood, May 11, 1858—J. A. Baird, N. W. Bannister, R. W. Brown, Dennis Cronin, John D. Evans, Patrick Finnegan, Charles and Samuel Getchel, Levi Getchel, L. W. Henry, Thomas E. Massey, Charles McPartheon, James Merrill, G. W. Parker, F. M. Scott, George S. Scholes, Jr., George S. Scholes, Sr., A. C. Smith, Sylvester Stevens, Rev. J. C. Whitney, U. S. Willie, a lawyer, and E. K. Wright.

The Indian massacre of 1862 resulted in the cessation of settlement in this section of the state and many left to acquire homes in more secure locations. Some never returned and others only after a long period of absence. The population had been greatly diminished by people leaving never to return and by those who had enlisted in the war to preserve the Union.

The first death was Frank Parsons, November 12, 1856.

The first religious services were conducted by Rev. John Robson (Methodist), November 1856. An organization of Methodists was formed in 1857 and services held in private homes, school houses and other available places until 1869. Rev. Thomas Harwood was the first pastor.

— CHRONOLOGY OF MINNESOTA —

1787—July 13. Territory northwest of the Ohio river organized over portion east of the Mississippi river. Slavery prohibited.

1800—Eastern portion included in Indiana territory. October 1. Retrocession of Western portion of state to France by Spain.

1804—March 26. Western portion included in District of Louisiana which becomes Louisiana territory (March 3, 1805) and Missouri territory (June 4, 1812). Territorial government ends with admission of Missouri (1821.)

1809—February 3. Eastern portion included in Illinois territory.

1814—December 24. Commission to delimitate Canadian boundary provided by Treaty of Ghent, Commission disagrees. Line finally prescribed by treaty of August 9, 1842 (Ashburton Treaty).

1817-1822—Commission of 1814 describes northern boundary of Minnesota.

1818—April 18. Eastern portion included in Michigan territory.

1820—Permanent American occupation begins at Fort Snelling. March 3. Slavery forbidden in western portion by Missouri Compromise.

1834—June 28. Western portion included in Michigan territory.

1836—April 20. Whole region included in Wisconsin territory.

1838—June 12. Western portion included in Iowa territory.

FOREST CITY VILLAGE

The first steam power saw mill was built and operated by John Robson near the village in 1858.

The first school house (District No. 2) was built in 1857 in Section 17. W. W. Woodman received the contract for its erection and was paid $250, the money being raised by subscription. The first teacher was T. Carlos Jewett.

Dudley Taylor and wife were the first hotel keepers in Meeker County, a large log building was erected for that purpose.

James B. Atkinson opened the first store about March 1, 1856, the first store in the county. In 1862 he admitted to partnership Mark W. Piper who operated the same during Atkinson's service in the Union Army. In 1866 he sold his interest to Atkinson and he conducted the same until 1879 when he retired from business.

Fitch and Stanton opened a store from 1858 to 1862. Thomas H. Skinner started in the mercantile business in 1862 which changed ownership several times between that date and 1888.

J. A. Baird operated a brick yard (the first in the county) for a brief period in 1858.

The first post office in Meeker County was established at Forest City in the fall of 1856 with Walter C. Bacon as postmaster. He was succeeded by James B. Atkinson. This position was filled, in succession, by the following persons: William Richards, J. A. Stanton, C. F. Woodman, O. C. McGray, Benjamin Manter, William Hardy, Nicholas Schreiner, Tess Atkinson and Hesse Peters.

The first Masonic lodge in Meeker County (Number 70) was instituted at Forest City May 18, 1867. The charter was dated November 14, 1869. The charter members were A. C. Smith, W. M.; J. B. Atkinson, S. W.; T. Carlos Jewett, J. W.; H. G. O. Thomas, Tyler; George W. Weisel, Sylvester Stevens, John S. Shields, Jesse S. Hipple and Perry D. Bentley. A. C. Smith continued to serve the lodge as worshipful master until the dissolution of the lodge December 23, 1871, caused by the removal of its members to the expanding village of Litchfield.

The Baptists erected a church in 1879 and continued to hold services.

FOREST PRAIRIE

Forest Prairie Township 121—Range 30

The town of Forest Prairie was a heavily wooded township and altho its soil is of unparalleled richness did not make a strong appeal to the pioneer who shrank from the necessary labor in opening fields for cultivation and it was ten years later than Forest City and Kingston in its settlement.

The first settlers in the town were Merrit B. Case, Charles T. Grote and James Hooser who came in 1866. Following them were Monroe Abbott, Hiram and Perry D. Bentley, R. K. Beecham, William Kielty, John Mayer, J. W. Polk, J. S. Reynolds, M. J. Roach, Sidney Scribner, George Smith, Benjamin F. and Charles F. Spaulding, Sylvester Waldron and his widowed mother, and Sidney Webb.

Among the settlers of 1867 were the following: Austin Brower, Stephen Cornwall, Daniel Duffy, Casper Hawkinberry, Peter Keilty, M. D. Stores, William Wortz and H. R. Williams.

While the hard, laborious work of clearing the land and the absence of available rivers affording a system of transportation had retarded the settlement of the country, the close of the Civil War brought a class of settlers who were impressed with the fertility of the soil and were inured to a woods life. These were the sturdy descendants of the Daniel Boone type of citizenship. They came from the forest sections of Ohio, Kentucky and Virginia. Eli Boring, Christian and Joseph Vossen settled in the town in 1868.

The first births (whites) within the limits of the town were the twin children born to Mr. and Mrs. George Smith in 1866. The first death of a white person was Mrs. George Smith in 1866.

The first school was taught by Mrs. James Hooser in section 26 (1868). The town was organized July 10, 1867 at which time the following citizens were prominent in the proceedings: B. K. Beecham, M. B. Case, C. T. Grote, James Hooser and C. F. Spaulding.

GREENLEAF

Township 118—Range 31. Acreage 24,736.07 of which 1,958.23 acres were covered with water.

The town was named in honor of W. H. Greenleaf an eminent pioneer citizen closely identified with the development of Greenleaf village. He located in Ellsworth township near the boundary line between the two townships and later became a distinguished citizen of Litchfield city and contributed to its early development.

The first settlers within the boundaries of the town were George Orcuth and a man named Pratt who located in Section 35 in the summer of 1856. They had turned the soil of three or four acres of land when one of their oxen was killed by the Indians. They became discouraged and abandoned their claims and went to Forest City and shortly thereafter left the county.

The first permanent settlers were the Kruger brothers, William, Herman and Charles, who located their homes in Sections 12 and 13 May 11, 1857. William remained a permanent resident but Charles and Herman established their homes elsewhere. The same year the following settlers arrived: J. V. Branham, Sr., Milton and Vincent Coombs, and George C. Whitcomb.

In 1858 and 1859 there was an influx of settlers among whom were: Charles Allen, Roland and Hendersen M. Angier, Jonathan Keech, Matthews, Maloy, George McGowan, Ira and Ira, Sr., and Silas Pratt, John A. Sampson, Michael Hanley, Louis Maher, Michael McGraw and Patrick Manning.

Following the Indian outbreak of 1862 and for several years thereafter all entries of settlers ceased but at the close of the Civil War in 1865 settlers arrived in large numbers. Among the prominent settlers of these years the following played an important part in the subsequent development of the township and are deserving of mention: Jacob Anderson, C. M. Beckstrand, Hiram DeLong, Olavas and Alexander Hanson, L. M., J. William, and Leonard Roman Johnson, John Knack, Martin Lawson, Daniel Nevins, J. A. Nystrom, John B. Pennoyer, John T. Putzier, and Martin Spelliscy.

Greenleaf was organized as a civil township August 27, 1859 and at that time its boundaries comprised the present township except the northern tier of sections which was attached to Litchfield and in addition included the present towns of Collinwood and Ellsworth. Those who took a leading part in the work of organization were W. H. Greenleaf, Dana E. King, George C. Whitcomb, George McGowan, Jonathan Keech, T. R. Webb and Dr. Russel Whiteman.

The first death is belived to have been the mother of the Kruger brothers in 1859.

The first school was opened in the Manning neighborhood. The first schoolhouse was erected in section 10 on the present site of the Beckville church. It was a log structure and the first teacher was Arvilla Dart.

The first religious services were held in 1860 at the home of John Sampson by Rev. Andrew Jackson. The Beckville Swedish Lutheran Church was organized and held services in private homes from 1859 until 1873 when the present church edifice was erected and Rev. P. Beckman, a settler of 1869, became the first pastor.

GREENLEAF VILLAGE

The townsite of Greenleaf was laid out and platted in 1859 by Dana E. King, W. H. Greenleaf and Bennett and Judson A. Brink.

Previous to the laying out of the townsite, William H. Greenleaf purchased the necessary machinery and having previously located a mill site in company with Bennett M. Brink erected a saw mill and improved the water power, which was located within limits of the townsite which embraced the southwest quarter of the southwest quarter of the southeast quarter and lots 5 and 6 of Section 30. Greenleaf and Brink operated the mill, 1858-1862 when Judson A. Brink purchased the interests of Greenleaf and Brink brothers operated the mill until 1864.

In 1862 Dana E. King and Judson A. Brink erected a flour mill at the mill site, but due to the Indian outbreak of that year, it was not operated until 1864. In 1865, Norman Pixley and Albert DeLong purchased the mill and operated it until 1876 when DeLong and J. R. McDonald purchased Pixley's interest and some years later they sold to a man named Leiser, who dismantled the same and moved the machinery to Traverse county. During the later years of its operation in Greenleaf village it was operated both by steam and water power. The saw mill equipment was moved in 1867 by Brink brothers from the townsite to a wooded section of country about one-quarter of a mile distant.

W. H. Greenleaf was a man of superior ability and during the early development of Meeker county was the most public spirited and enterprising of its citizens. He was a native of Allegheny, now Livingston county, New York, born December 7, 1834. The progenitor of the Greenleaf family was Edmond Greenleaf, who came to America in 1635 and settled in Newbury in the Massachusetts Bay colony. It is both fitting and proper that the townsite of Greenleaf, once a thriving village, and the township of Greenleaf should bear his name and perpetuate his memory.

The first grocery and hardware store combined was opened in 1862 by W. H. Greenleaf. In March, 1864 he added a stock of general merchandise and shortly thereafter formed a partnership with C. B. Jordan and two months later sold his interest to Jordan who continued the business for several years but subsequently sold to John Rank.

W. H. Greenleaf, after selling his interests to Jordan, erected, one year later, a second store building and opened another store of the same general character. This establishment he later sold to L. S. Weymouth who continued in business until 1884.

A third store was opened in 1868 and continued for one year. In 1888, Miss Sophia C. Pratt, the village postmistress, conducted the only store in the village. The first and only hotel in the village was opened by C. W. Butterfield in 1865 in the residence of Dana E. King which he purchased and enlarged as the necessities of the period required and was the landlord as late as the early nineties.

A seminary was started in the village in 1867 with Rev. W. C. Harding as principal and a Miss Todd as assistant. It existed for a period of two years. The first religious services were held in the upper story of the saw mill by Rev. J. C. Whitney, a Presbyterian clergyman.

A church edifice was erected in 1868 by the Presbyterian congregation of which Rev. W. C. Harding, deceased, was the first pastor. The Methodists had a religious organization and held services but did not erect a church edifice.

The first blacksmith shop was built and operated by Henry Keech in 1861 and was conducted by him as late as 1870 when he removed to Nebraska. He was succeeded in later years by James McCue and later by a man named Brown.

The United States Land Office, formerly located at Forest City, was removed to Greenleaf village in 1866 at which time Dr. Fletcher was the receiver and B. F. Baker the register. The office was moved to Litchfield in December 1869.

HARVEY
Township 120—Range 31 West.

Acreage 24,830.92. 464 acres are covered with water. The land is slightly rolling and is mostly prairie but a small portion was covered with heavy timber. The first settler was Rudolph Schultz who settled in the township in 1856. Others who arrived the same year were *Patrick Armstrong, Reuben Davis, Dennis, John, Thomas and Daniel Dougherty, Edward Fitzgerald, Mr. McCue, David Ralston, Dennis Shields, *Carl Shultz, John Tower and J. W. Walker.

During the years which followed and previous to the Indian outbreak of 1862 the following settlers established homes within the present boundaries of Harvey township (which prior to 1867 was a part of Forest City); E. O. Britt, Martin Branley, James Harvey, Samuel Hutchinson, Jorgen Lohse. *Fergus McCusker, L. F. McCusker, William Marks, Henry Parker, John C. Shultz, *John and *Robert B. Ralston and two men whose given names are not obtainable, Taylor and Thomas. Other settlers prior to the coming of the railroad.

(Names starred are listed in the biographical section of the Album of Meeker County History published in 1888 which may be found in the Litchfield, Minnesota public library.)

Harvey had very few additional settlers until the close of the Civil War when the town began to fill up rapidly.

The first marriage was that of Dennis Dougherty and Mary Finnegan in May 1869.

The first death was Eddie Dolan, eight years of age in 1870.

The first school was taught by Mary Flynn.

The first ground was broken for cultivation by Dennis Dougherty in 1856.

The township of Harvey was detached from Forest City and organized as a separate township in 1867. The first election was held in the spring of that year at the Dougherty Schoolhouse, now known as District No. 11. Philip Turck and Patrick Flynn were chosen supervisors and Andrew Smith, town clerk.

Harvey was named in honor of James M. Harvey, one of the heroes of the Indian outbreak. He was clerk of court of Meeker county 1863 to 1867. (See page 22).

KINGSTON TOWN AND VILLAGE

Township 120 and South half of 121—Range 29.

The town of Kingston covers the largest area of any of the similar subdivisions in Meeker County embracing all of township 120, Range 29 West and the south half of township 121 of the same range. In point of settlement and pioneer development it ranks second to Forest City among the towns of the county. It was named after Kingston, Ontario, Canada, the birthplace of J. B. Atkinson, one of the earliest and most highly honored settlers in the Kingston territory.

The Crow river, bisecting sections 18, 19, 20, 21, 22, 23, 26, and 25, forms a boundary line between the prairie to the south and the timbered portion to the northward. This condition prompted an earlier settlement of the southern portion of the township. The major portion of the pioneers of this town located their claims along the banks of this winding stream and the townsite of Kingston.

Mark Cates is awarded the distinction of being the first settler of the town in 1856, but he was speedily followed by the following influx of settlers: Henry, Cyrus and Warren Averill; Wellington Cates; Benjamin, Joseph and Nathaniel Dorman; Enoch and Rufus Eastman; John Fitzgerald; Patrick Flynn; Solomon Gray; Elmer Harper; William Higgins; Scott Hutchinson; John T. Kennison; John Lowell, Byley Lyford; John Martin; A. C. Maddox; Robert and Nelson Niles; Morris Power; Oliver Patch; John K. Perkins; Uriah Palmer; B. P. and A. P. Whitney and Joseph Weymer. These early settlers were of the very highest type of citizenship. Claude Brower, Ex-County Treasurer of Meeker County (son of a Meeker County pioneer) who had a personal acquaintance with these men, made the following statement in a newspaper article: "They were rugged pioneers, farmers, builders and lumbermen. Although the woods were full of wild game, the lakes and streams teeming with fish and the creeks and marshes affording an excellent opportunity for the trapping of fur bearing animals, they did very little hunting, fishing or trapping. They were men accustomed to manual and skilled labor. They made their own wagons, ox-carts, bob-sleds, boats, and built their houses, barns and other out buildings."

Histories and biographical sketches of these early pioneers inform us that the major portion of these settlers of the towns of Kingston and Forest City have a colonial ancestry that established their relationship to some of the most eminent men of our country's early history. The best blood of the New England Puritans, the Holland Dutch of the Empire State and the pure English and Scotch strain from the hill districts of the Southland flowed through their veins.

In 1857 Orrin Whitney, S. B. Hutchins, Benjamin Ruggles and E. H. Whitney joined the Kingston colony. The following year marked the arrival of F. V. DeCoster, George Scribner, A. H. and Jefferson Carville and John Doyle.

The territorial pioneers have passed from the scene of action but are survived by their descendants in this and other sections of our country. The trials, tribulations and hardships of these early settlers would fill a volume. Coming here without either money or the wherewithal to live through the struggling years, their endurance was severely tested. The land had to be prepared and seed purchased which in most cases was a serious problem. Their work remains and it is due to this hardy class of men and women that a foundation has been laid for the excellent development of all its resources.

The first death Morris Power in 1857.

The first marriage which was also the first in the county was that of Joseph Weymer and Mary Dorman in August 1857.

The pioneer religious services were held in the village over Whitney's store by Rev. J. C. Whitney in 1857.

A stock of goods was brought to the village in the spring of 1857 by A. P. Whitney and the first sales were made from his log cabin home. This same year a store building was built and operated by the firm of Whitney, Nourse and Upton. The following year, A. P. Whitney disposed of his interest and shortly after the business passed into the hands of Hines and Carmer. They were succeeded in turn during later years by the following: Hiram Hall; William Hall; Peck, Hutchinson and Durkee; Peck and Durkee and finally by the firm of Owen and Murphy who sold to Murphy Brothers. A second store was erected and operated in 1859 by N. C. Hines. He was succeeded by William Hall who sold to F. V. DeCoster who was succeeded by E. A. Briggs.

In 1888 the business interests of the village were represented by Murphy Brothers, dealers in general merchandise; E. A. Briggs, capitalist; Mr. Mahoney, the village smith and Samuel Dorman, wagon maker.

EARLY RECORDS

In reviewing the records of Kingston town it is interesting to note when one opens the covers of the sheepskin well bound volume in which these early records were kept that the book was purchased from Aaron R. Gray, No. 130 State Street Boston.

The record book's first four pages are devoted to the minutes relating to the organization of the town and we are told that this meeting was held at Woodman's Hotel. The polls were opened at 10 o'clock A. M. and closed at 4 P. M. A recess of one hour was taken from 12 M. to 1 P. M. Forty-one votes were cast. When the votes were counted, it was found that the following officers had been elected: A. P. Whitney, chairman; Supervisors, Charles Low, J. B. Salisbury, Benjamin F. Ruggles; Assessor, J. Simpson; Collector, W. W. Woodman; Overseer of the Poor, Byley Lyford; Constables, John M. Martin and Rufus M. Eastman; Justices of the Peace, W. W. Woodman and Charles Low; Supervisor of Roads, A. P. Whitney.

The period following the town's organization the transactions of the Board consisted very largely in the laying out of roads and the establishment of road districts. At the election of 1859 there were 35 votes polled and there was a marked change in the personnel of the officers chosen. It seems evident that these pioneers believed that "rotation of office is good for the country."

The annual town meetings of these early years were held in homes, stores and the grist mill.

The building of a new bridge across Crow river in the village of Kingston was brought to the forefront November 9, 1861, and continued to occupy the attention of the Board and citizens for a brief period and at a meeting held two days later definite action was taken and a contract was let to M. P. Littlefield for $295.

The first recorded general election is that of November 1866. Ignatius Donnelly, the republican candidate for congress, received a majority in the town of eight votes out of a total of 48 votes cast.

At the next general election held in November 1867, William R. Marshall, Republican candidate for Governor, had a majority of 4 votes out of a total of 66 votes polled. In the election of 1869 out of a total of 77 votes the Republican candidates had an average majority of 12.

At the election of November 2, 1869, the paramount issue was the removal of the county seat from Forest City to Litchfield. Kingston cast 42 votes for and 33 against removal.

CYCLONES VISIT KINGSTON

Kingston was visited by a cyclone June 10, 1929, which began its twisting course in Section 17, a few miles northwest of Kingston village and traveled in a southeasterly direction thru the adjoining townships of French Lake and Cokato in Wright County and spent its force near Cokato village. Serious damage resulted in the wreckage of farm homes and buildings in the track of the cyclone. Mrs. Gustave Wauttaja, aged 80, of North Dakota who was visiting her son, and Henry Wuornos, a farmer at a point near Kingston village, were killed. Several persons were injured but not fatally.

Three years later, July 27, 1932, another cyclone started its destructive course from nearly the same location. It was of greater force and did more serious damage in the destruction of property along its route which followed the same direction but bore to the southward. Eight farmsteads were completely wiped out and the Covenant Mission Church destroyed. August Nikka, age 73, was killed and his wife seriously injured. Several head of cattle were killed and buildings in the path of the storm were badly wrecked and damage was done to growing crops. The cyclone spent its force north of the Stockholm church hamlet.

A relief force of over 200 boys and men joined in the essential assistance needed in relieving the victims of the storm and the state contributed $6,000.00 to meet the needs of those left in destitute circumstances.

MARK CATES HOME 1856

The first frame house built in Meeker County is located in section 20, South Kingston.

The illustration is reproduced from a photograph taken by the Olson Studio, Litchfield, Minnesota.

ATTEMPTED BANK ROBBERY

September 20, 1919 was an exciting day in the annals of Kingston village. It was 1:30 p. m. when two well dressed young men of medium build entered the Kingston bank and engaged the cashier, Mr. J. E. Matsen, in conversation. Their appearance did not invite confidence and when Mr. Matsen observed the leader in the act of drawing a revolver he ducked behind the counter barely in time to escape instant death as the revolver was discharged. Mr. Matsen sounded the burglar alarm which so frightened the bandits that they proceeded to make their escape in their Buick car driven by a third party. Every effort was made to effect a capture and so persistent was this effort that they only made their escape by shooting an officer guarding a bridge at Elk River, Minnesota.

LITCHFIELD
Township 119 — Range 31 West.

The town contains about 23,040 acres and in the early years 2,805, were covered with water and a similar number of acres were covered with timber and the remaining portion is a rolling prairie. There were several beautiful lakes and among them Lake Ripley which teemed with fish and in the early nineties a resort was constructed on the south shore of the lake called Brightwood and numerous summer cottages were erected and a steamboat plied its waters. This resort was developed at a great expenditure of funds. It was not a financial success and was abandoned. During the severe winter of 1935 and 1936 the fish were smothered and tons of dead fish were removd from its shores.

The first settlement of this township was made in July 1856 by a party of Norwegian emigrants who came from Rock county, Wisconsin. These settlers were Ole Halverson-Ness, Henry Halverson, Ole Halverson-Thoen, Amos Nelson Fosen, Nels Hanson, Colberg and Gunder Olson, Ness, Halverson and Thoen had families. The others were single men. All of these parties took up claims in the southwest part of the town, one of the most picturesque locations in the county. Other settlers who arrived the same year were William Benson, Sven and Nels Swenson, Michael Lenhardt, Ferdinand, Christian, Frederick and William Cook.

In 1857 there was an influx of settlers among whom were Bengt Hanson, John Larson and his four sons, Nels, Andrew, Peter E. and Lewis; Hokan Peterson, Thorlson J. Cornelius, Ole Amundson, Nels Danielson, Kittel Haroldson, Henry J. Johnson, Ole, Andrew and Harold Kittelson; Jesse V. Branham, Sr. and his sons, Jesse V., Jr., William and Edward; Oscar Erickson, Nels Klemedson, Ola Johnson and Louis and Maximillan Cook.

In 1858 the following settlers arrived: Iver Jackson, Bengt Nelson, John and Thomas McGannon.

Among the settlers named, Ole Halverson Ness left the strongest impress of able leadership and the town bore his name from 1858 up to the time of the coming of the railroad in 1869 when its name was changed to correspond with the name given the county seat Village of Litchfield.

The first house built was the log cabin of Henry Halverson.

The first birth, Ole H., son of Henry Halverson (see page 3.)

The first death that of Dr. Frederick N. Ripley (see page 7.)

The first barn was built by Ole H. Ness, who occupied the same as a residence during the summer while his house was undergoing construction.

The first church services were held in the home of Ole H. Ness in the fall of 1858, conducted by Rev. William Frederickson, a minister of the Norwegian church, from Goodhue county, Minnesota.

The first school meeting was held at the home of Ole H. Ness, December 7, 1861, Amos Nelson Fosen served as Chairman and John Blackwell acted as clerk. The directors chosen were Thomas McGannon, Kittle Haroldson and Ole Ness. The construction of the first school house began in the summer of 1862 on the farm of Ole H. Ness but due to the Indian outbreak was not completed until after the war. The solid brick structure for the same purpose marks the site of the original structure.

Litchfield was originally a part of Round Lake township but was frequently designated by some of the settlers as Ripley.

The town was organized April 5, 1858 at which time it was named Ness.

MANANNAH

Township 121 — Range 31 W.

The town of Manannah was among the earliest in point of settlement of the towns of Meeker County. The portion of the town lying north of Crow River was heavily timbered while the south portion of the town is prairie. There is very little waste land in the township.

The first settlers of the town were Edward Brown, A. D. Pierce, and Nathan C., Ziba, Alonzo M., and Silas Caswell who settled (1856) on lands adjacent to Crow River where the townsite of Manannah was subsequently located. They were followed the same year by Moody Bailey, Carlos and Moody Caswell, Andrew Hamilton, John Tower and J. W. Walker.

The pioneers of 1857 were: John Adock, J. J. Baston, Mark Bridges, E. O. Britt, R. D. C. Cressy, David Dustin, Freeman T. Gould, Henry Fleming, Henry Faloon, Linus Howe, Henry Harrideen, J. Hubbard, J. C. Hollis, Jonathan Kimball, E. B. Kingsley, Robert Lang, Alexander Lee, G. W. Lamb, Porter Loveland, Robert Lyon, Charles and Wilmot Maybee, J. Marden, W. D. McGill, Ephraim Pierson, John Setter, James Shearer, S. Sterrett, C. O. Whitney, Henry Whitman, Chauncey Wilson.

The financial crisis of 1857 retarded further settlement but the following settlers located claims in 1858: Samuel Clyde, Robert Carroll and Michael O'Keefe. Among the settlers of 1860 were Joseph Page and Philip Deck, victims of the Sioux massacre.

The town's name was selected from an old Scottish history.

The town was organized, October 13, 1857 at the home of J. W. Walker, at which time the following officers were chosen: Assessor, N. C. Caswell; Justices, E. B. Kingsley and J. W. Walker; Constables, Mark Bridges, Nathan Caswell; Road Overseer, Ziba Caswell.

OLD PILE BRIDGE

N. Y. Taylor, Engineer

This bridge was located in section 32, one mile east of Manannah townsite crossing the middle fork of the Crow River.

MANANNAH VILLAGE

A townsite was surveyed and platted by a man named Halcott in lot 7 of section 30. This plat was filed for record. A post office was established in this townsite in 1857 with Jonathan Kimball as postmaster. The same year, Ziba, Nathan C., and Albert Caswell, erected a one and one-half story hewed log building in which the following May, Jonathan Kimball opened a hotel. This building was used by the settlers during the Indian outbreak of 1862 as a haven of refuge.

In May 1857 J. W. Walker opened a store and the same year he erected a dam across the Crow River which furnished power for a saw mill which continued to operate until after 1862 when it was destroyed by fire. Nothing remains to mark the definite location of the old and original townsite of Manannah, which the Caswell's and Walker expected would ultimately become the metropolis of Meeker County.

The present townsite of Manannah was surveyed and platted by Hines, Kimball, and Beedy and the plat was filed for record, September 6, 1871. Cressy s Addition was platted by R. D. C. Cressy and filed for record, November 16, 1874. It occupies a small part of sections 30 and 31.

The picturesque beauty of the present hamlet of Manannah indicates that in the hey-day of its glory it was supremely attractive, its high banks overlooking the mill pond, its well wooded streets and swift flowing river surrounded by its rich farms and clearings among the primeval forest have a charm that could not be found in any other of the original townsites of Meeker County.

In 1869 Ziba Caswell erected a dam which was partially washed out the following spring which was presumably rebuilt at the same location in 1872 by Hines, Kimball, and Beedy which furnished water power for the flour mill built by him in partnership with Otho H. Campbell and it was operated by N. C. Hines until 1874 who was succeeded in ownership and operation by Campbell and Caswell who in turn was succeeded by O. H. Campbell as the sole owner. He discarded the old millstones and installed the roller system of grinding and a sixty horse power engine giving the mill a daily capacity of 100 barrels. He sold the mill to A. D. Beal who in turn sold, in 1907, to Henry C. Parsons and Charles Hanson in 1907. They operated the mill for a period of three years and then disposed of their interests to William Schreiner who continued its operation until 1923. The mill was blown down in a heavy wind storm, and all of the lumber and machinery was sold on the ground. It was one of the last mills in the county to cease operation.

IMPORTANT DATES

1857—First birth, Hattie Estelle Kimball.
1857—First ground broken by the Caswells.
1857—Manannah post office established. Jonathan Kimball, postmaster.
1859—First death, Samuel Clyde.
1859—First religious service (Methodist) held by Rev. Kidder in the old townsite.
1865—First Roman Catholic Mass celebrated in home of Frank McIntyre by Father Anthony of St. Cloud.
1866—First school, District 12, Patrick McNulty, teacher.

SWEDE GROVE

Township 120 — Range 32 West

Swede Grove is one of the most fertile of the western tier of towns within the boundaries of Meeker County. In territorial days there were a number of lakes and streams that covered an acreage of nearly one section of land but at the present time due to excessive drainage there is only one lake (Peterson) that contains any water. In the early days most of these lakes were teeming with fish. There are citizens living in that township who recall taking fish in the spring from the small creeks with scoop shovels. Today there are no game fish in Peterson Lake, the only lake that contains any water and these fish are mostly carp, bullheads and a few small sun fish. The major portion of the township was a natural prairie with scattering tracts of timber land bordering the lakes and streams. With the drying up of these bodies of water the lake beds are used for pasturage. The services of a game warden are no longer necessary to prevent the unlawful taking of fish.

The first settlers established their homes in the town in 1857. Among them were: Nels Akerson, Bertha Elofson and sons (Nels, Andrew and Peter); Peter E. Hanson; N. E. Hanson; Helga, Amos and Nels Olson; Hans and Andrew Peterson; John Rosencranz and Nels Thorbjornson. In 1858 this group of settlers was increased by the arrival of Christian Erickson, John Larson, Hover Mickelson, Arslak Olson and H. Wilcox.

In 1859 Swen Nelson and a few others settled in the town but from that time until the close of the Civil War there were few if any who established homes in the town.

Swede Grove was a portion of the town of Acton until March 15, 1868, when it was organized as a separate unit and the following officers were elected: Nels Elofson, Chairman of Supervisors; Nels E. Hanson, Clerk and W. H. Wilcox, Treasurer.

The name given the town was Swede Grove due to the fact that it was settled almost exclusively by settlers of Swedish birth.

In 1864 a post office was established at the home of Nels Elofson and he became the town's first postmaster. He was succeeded by a Mr. Dahlquist who was in turn succeeded by Ole J. Levander. With the coming of the railway the office was removed to the townsite of Grove City (1870) and Mr. Dahlquist again became postmaster.

The first birth in the town was Peter Peterson, son of Andrew Peterson born January 3, 1859, and the second birth was A. P. Hanson born June 9 of the same year.

The first death was a child of Ole Nelson buried on the farm now owned by Ralph Busse.

The first marriage was John Larson and Hannah Elofson (1858.)

The first school (1859) was held in the home of Nels Elofson and was taught by Rev. William Baglund, a Baptist minister who also conducted the first religious services in the same home and year.

Hans Peterson was the pioneer settler who turned the first sod and sowed the first grain in 1859. Practically all the land in the town has been brought under cultivation. The farms vary in size from 40 to 200 acres with a few farms containing 400 acres or more. The raising of beef and dairy cattle has become the main source of income.

PETERSON LAKE

Peterson Lake has an historic background that is not surpassed by any other lake in Meeker County. It was around the shores of this lake in section 29 and bordering sections that the first colony of Swedish immigrants founded their first permanent settlement in Meeker County. It covered, in pioneer days, about 80 acres of water and had a very beautiful shore so well covered with growing timber that when the U. S. survey of the township of Swede Grove was made by U. S. Engineer Hardin Howlin he failed to locate this body of water teeming with fish and having a depth of 30 to 35 feet. It is not shown on the government plat book. Section 29 was a part of the government land grant to the St. Paul and Pacific Railroad Company. The main body of water covered the S. W. ¼ of the N. E. ¼ and the N. W. ¼ of S. E. ¼ with the exception of a few acres. This tract was purchased March 2, 1881 and March 2, 1883 was sold to Andrew Peterson for a consideration (named in the deed) of $800 and carried a mortgage on the same of $500. When Peterson discovered that he had bought a body of water instead of land he did not meet his tax obligations and the same was sold for taxes to Albert Johnson. When Johnson learned the conditions he did not keep up his tax payments and it was again sold for taxes to Lars Hillstrom. When Hillstrom died and his estate was settled his wife, Kersti Hillstrom, became the owner and June 17, 1924 it was sold to Charles A. Peterson. The mortgage was never foreclosed but was owned at different periods by ten different parties twice at a premium but the final sale of same was only one dollar. The tract is now owned by the Federal Land Bank of St. Paul, Minnesota.

UNION GROVE
Township 121 — Range 32 West.

Union Grove was named by a man named Allen. The why and the wherefore of the name selected is not capable of explanation.

Union Grove township prior to its settlement and subsequent development, was regarded as one of the most beautiful and attractive regions of country in the entire county. Its surface was diversified by alternate tracts of prairie and woodland. The town was well watered by the north and south forks of the Crow River, numerous ponds and Lake Koronis, one of the well known lakes of Minnesota, forms a portion of the northern boundary and its waters cover nearly one half of Section 3 and a small portion of Section 4. The soil is a rich sandy loam and in quickness of growth is not surpassed by that of any other township in the county.

The territorial pioneers followed the general course of the rivers and Union Grove attracted a group of settlers as early as 1856 when Lyman Allen, Lyman Baker, Andrew Hamilton and a Mr. Haywood made the first group settlement. They were followed the same year by a Mr. Brawn, S. H. Caswell, Alonzo Cook, S. Dickinson, John W. Goodspeed, James Hamilton, Cyrus Lewis, James Nelson, Judson Pierson and William Wheeler.

In 1857 there was an influx of settlers among whom were Albert Bridges, Florinda Bryant, Albert Alonzo Caswell, Jeremiah Leaming, James A. Lee, Charles and Wilmot Maybee, William Rodgers, Thomas Ryckman, and James Shears. These settlers were joined in the spring of 1858 by D. B. Hoar. From this date forward until after the Indian outbreak there were very few who settled in the township. In fact many of those mentioned in this list of pioneers abandoned their claims and homes at the time of the Indian troubles and never returned.

The first marriage was that of James Nelson and Elizabeth Caswell April 15, 1857.

The first birth is believed to have been a son of Lyman Allen born in 1857 and named Charles.

The first school was taught in a small log cabin owned by Nathan Caswell in 1859 by Miss Mary Caswell who later became Mrs. Gould. The first school house was erected in 1867 on the Southwest quarter of Section 24 and Miss Vina McNabb was the first teacher. The first religious services were held at the home of Thomas Ryckman in 1865 by Rev. George Hardy. During the year 1866, Rev. Griswold (Methodist) held regular services in the school house in Section 24.

Baker, Allen and Lewis were the first to raise a crop of wheat.

The first death was that of Samuel Clyde in 1858.

Union Grove was organized April, 30, 1866, at a meeting held in the home of Thomas Ryckman. C. D. Hill was chairman, Charles H. McCune, clerk with George W. Hardy and C. W. Puther and David Newcomb serving as members of the election board. The following officers were elected, Supervisors, Lucien J. Perry, chairman, David Newcomb and A. D. Pentler; Clerk, C. H. McCune; Assessor, A. T. Pentler; Treasurer, S. O. Campbell; Constables, James Nelson and William Stockdale; Justices, C. W. Puther and G. W. Hardy.

The Burr Oak Cemetery, comprising one acre of land, one half acre of which is in section 33 and the remaining acreage in section 34 was the gift to the Cemetery Association of David B. Hoar and Joseph Hubbard, and the first burial was Miranda, wife of Joheph Hubbard in June, 1870. It is well maintained and among the interments are the territorial pioneers, David B. Hoar, A. G. Petrie, Smith Flanders and Jeremiah Leaming. The last three named were veterans of the Civil War and other veterans of the same war whose graves are well marked are W. P. Hammond and James Stamps who has the distinction of having served during the war in both the Confederate and Union armies. The grave of Mrs. James Stamps has a monument that bears the following inscription:

"Kind friends beware as you pass by,
As you are now so once was I;
As I am now so you must be,
Prepare therefore to follow me."

THE JACOBSON STORE

The Jacobson Store at Crow River is one of the land marks of the Union Grove township and has been continuously operated by Ole Jacobson for 36 years. He has the respect and good will of all his acquaintances and customers. He is deeply interested and well versed in the history and struggles of the early pioneers. He served as postmaster of Crow River from 1905 to 1907 when the office was discontinued. Mr. Jacobson was born in Union Grove township, section 29, September 14, 1874 and married September 11, 1906, Lillian Anderson of New London, Minnesota. They are the parents of Clifford, born May 12, 1907 and Luella, born September 17, 1924.

CORVUSO AND CEDAR MILLS

The townsites of Corvuso and Cedar Mills are located on the Minnesota Western Railroad (formerly the Luce Line) in Cedar Mills township. Corvuso is in section 13 of Cedar Mills township and was originally owned and platted by the Penn Investment Company in 1923. It is midway between Cosmos and Cedar Mills and has a limited trade territory which has retarded its development. It has a well equipped creamery, postoffice and an R. F. D. postal route and a general store. Its taxable real estate value is $10,900.

Cedar Mills is located in sections 13 and 14 of Cedar Mills township and was originally owned and platted by the City Investment Company in December 1922. It has a postoffice, two general stores, lumber yard, hardware store, blacksmith shop, elevator, creamery, restaurant and barber shop. Its taxable realestate valuation is $12,045.

Incorporated Villages

COSMOS VILLAGE

Cosmos village was only a hamlet in 1907 when Henry Klawitter opened a blacksmith shop in the present village. The only other business places were a creamery and store. The mail was delivered from Brookfield, Renville county by R. F. D. carrier August Wehking who gave way to Warner Reinke and was succeeded November 16, 1905 by C. J. Larson who resigned in 1914 when Welch became carrier until 1921 when Henry Bergman was duly appointed as his successor and has continued in the service.

In 1922 the Luce Railroad now known as the Minnesota Western was in process of construction and the business district began to expand and in addition to the business places then existing, Otto Martinson opened a hardware store, Charles Ritter erected a dance hall, Ed Watson opened a soft drink parlor and Ed Mattson a grocery and Herbert and John Lietzau erected the present Lietzau barber shop. A post office was established April 26, 1924 with C. J. Larson as postmaster and the R. F. D. service was transferred from Brookfield to the Cosmos office serving a route of 28 and one-half miles.

During the passing years the village has had a slow but steady growth. It was not until September 24, 1926 that the present village plat was made and Cosmos became an incorporated village, from which date there has been some notable improvements. The village park embraces blocks 25 and 26 fronts the main street. It was developed and partially landscaped in 1935 by W. P. A. labor. A volunteer fire department was organized December 14, 1927 with 18 members and Ernest Grussendorf as fire chief. The equipment consists of a combination International truck with hooks, ladders, chemical and water tank and pump, purchased in 1930 in co-operation with the town and housed in a brick station constructed for that purpose.

In addition to railway transportation connecting Minneapolis with Clara City, Minnesota, there are two state highways. Number 4 extends north and south connecting the Iowa boundary with Paynesville and number 7 east and west from Minneapolis to Montevideo furnishing connections with trunk highways.

The population of the village according to the census of 1930 was 279 and the present estimated population is 375. In 1938 there were in process of erection four substantial residences by Floyd Jacobson, Ernest Lietzau, Carl Ulrich and Arthur A. Fleming and three additional homes will be built the present year. The village has contracted for the establishment of a water works system which is in process of construction.

It is a P. W. A. project in which the government furnishes $22,000 and the village an equal amount. The well with an 8 inch casing is 153 feet deep and a severe test insures an ample supply of "God's best gift to man."

The village corporation has an area of one square mile and embraces four quarter sections: the SW ¼ of 15; SE ¼ of 16; NW ¼ of 22 and NE ¼ of 21.

DARWIN VILLAGE

The village of Darwin was laid out and platted by John Curran and Martin McKinney and the St. Paul and Pacific Railroad Company. The plat was certified and filed October 11, 1869. The plat covers portions of sections 23 and 30.

The governing purpose of the early settlers of the town and village was to found an Irish Catholic settlement west of Minneapolis and St. Paul. The land adjacent to the present village had not been surveyed when Patrick Casey and others established their homes in the vicinity of Lake Stella in 1856.

On the bend of this lake which some historians refer to as Lake Casey, a townsite was platted and named Stella City, but later was named Rice City in honor of Edmund Rice, a railroad official.

The pioneer merchant was Alexander Cairncross. Other early merchants were J. F. Low, Moran and James Curran who were succeeded by Brown brothers.

The Minnesota and Dakota Elevator was built by C. D. Brown in 1870 and the Davidson elevator in 1869 which burned in 1880. The Cargill Bros. elevator was built in 1887 by Frank Chevre.

When the railroad passed thru the township the townsite of Rice City was abandoned and the settlers riveted their attention on the townsite of Darwin. The owners of the same had visions of great future development. It has been claimed by the early settlers that the excessive values placed on building lots prevented its growth and that the pioneer business men of the townsite were compelled to view the rapid development of Litchfield and Dassel and the subsequent decline of Darwin.

In 1888 the village had become little better than a whistling post. Mrs. M. A. Paquet conducted the only store and that with its elevators and the temperance pool room of Patrick McKinney constituted all of Darwin's business places. At this time the entire townsite could have been purchased for less than one thousand dollars. In the early seventies the post office was established in the depot with O. B. Knapp as the first postmaster who was succeeded in turn by John Feeney, W. E. Corkins, James McCabe, William Jensen, William Fortnum, James Maher and J. E. Nelson the present postmaster since 1910. One Rural Free Delivery Route has been established, Charles Victor Miller is the present carrier.

The Darwin of 1939 has a population of less than 200 but for its size is one of the live villages between Minneapolis and Litchfield, based on tonnage of freight handled. It is an unexcelled market for grain and with the establishment of its creamery in 1895 the foundation was laid for its development.

At the present time Darwin is well represented in all the common lines of business. When Darwin reached "rock bottom" in 1888 James McCabe established a general merchandise store and was succeeded by William Fortnum, James Maher and later by J. E. Nelson who sold to the present merchants, Edmunds and Krook. John McGowan opened a store about 1894 and later sold to Nordstrom and Carlson. The building was destroyed by fire in 1923. Alfred H. Oberg opened a general store in 1924 and sold the same to the present proprietor, Fred Colberg, in 1933.

Darwin established a publicly owned electric line connecting with the Litchfield plant in 1922. The village is free from all indebtedness and enjoys a low tax rate. The present officials of the village are: President, Earl Miller; Recorder, E. H. McGannon; Treasurer, John W. Freer; Trustees, J. A. McRaith, Albert Lukanen and Walter Walls.

The first officers of the village following its incorporation were: President, John Gallahue; Recorder, W. J. Caven; Trustees, J. A. McRaith, Hans Thompson and T. A. Doyle.

A Community Club was organized in 1937 and is quite active in every effort to safeguard the interests of the village thru trade promotion activities. It owns and operates a moving picture outfit and furnishes free entertainment each Thursday night during the summer months. The present officers of the club are President, Stanley Kelly; Secretary, Carl Martens; Treasurer, Arthur Hansen.

School District Number 42 was organized in 1880 and was a one room school until 1911 when the present two room school building was erected. The present school officers are J. W. Freer, W. H. Walls and Otto Johnson.

The Alliance Gospel Tabernacle was erected in 1924. It is undenominational but is allied with the Christian and Missionary Alliance with division headquarters located in St. Paul. Miss Grace Holbrook is the pastor. They have a membership of about 50 and their Sunday School has an average attendance of 40.

BRIAR CLIFF

The summer home of Mr. and Mrs. A. J. Horner, of Minneapolis, is located on the north shore of Lake Washington, one mile south of U. S. Highway No. 12, midway between Dassel and Darwin. In its natural and developed beauty it is regarded by the tourists as superior to any similar development within the boundaries of Minnesota.

Mr. and Mrs. Horner are extremely hospitable in welcoming visitors during the summer months.

BRIAR CLIFF

OF MEEKER COUNTY 93

DASSEL VILLAGE

Dassel Village, according to the census of 1930, has a population of 785 and its taxable valuation in 1937 is $200,638.

The foundation for Dassel's development as one of the most prosperous villages in Meeker County was established as early as 1865 and extended into the seventies. The territory embraced in the village and township in which it is located together with the towns which now constitute its trade territory was settled by a strong and sturdy class of citizens who, in the main, came from Virginia, West Virginia, Kentucky, Ohio, Indiana, and from Sweden. During the period between 1865 and 1870 they came by boat to St. Paul and thence by foot to their destination, but the major portion of these pioneers came by covered wagon. The names of many of these early settlers are recorded in the history of the towns of Collinwood, Dassel and Ellsworth. With the coming of the railroad in 1869 the influx of settlers increased very rapidly.

DASSEL IN THE MAKING

The original townsite of Dassel was platted by the St. Paul and Pacific Railway in 1869, now known as the Great Northern. There have been several additions to the original townsite known as Breed's, Rudberg's and Bell's additions. The east portion of the village was a part of the John McKinney homestead. The original townsite embraced a portion of the Madison DeLong homestead. DeLong's claim was jumped when he left it for a temporary period to move his family from Carver to their new home. When he returned he found Parker Simons, a civil engineer for the railroad company, in possession. Litigation followed, but there was an amicable settlement of differences and DeLong retained the tract south of the village where his sons, William and Frank, continue to reside.

Dassel was named in honor of Bernard Dassel, secretary for the railroad company. He was the traveling paymaster and continued as such until 1883 when this system of paying employees was discontinued. In later years Bernard Dassel engaged in the banking business at Browns Valley, Minnesota. He met with reverses and the bank failed.

During the year 1869 a number of buildings were constructed, but it was not until the summer of 1870 that a real boom occurred and store buildings, dwellings and a new school building were erected. This school building is now a part of the Kopplin Oil Station. A general merchandise store was established by Morris Brothers in 1869 and operated by them until 1872 when they sold it to Sam Bunting and in 1875 he sold the same to Rudberg Bros.

George Brower and William Bradford operated a saw mill in 1872 but in 1881 it took an aerial flight in a cyclone and was not rebuilt. J. Norgren and Co. established a general merchandise store in 1875 and were the leading merchants of the village for a long period of years. The building occupied by them is owned by C. J. Peterson who conducts a seed business. The first lumber yard was owned and operated by John Osborne in 1874. He sold the business a few years later and purchased a farm 2½ miles west of the village. The house built by him and the farm is occupied by his son, James.

George Brower built the Dassel house in 1872 and acted as landlord until 1875 when he sold it to Sam Bunting who managed the same until 1877 when J. H. Remick became mine host until February 3, 1883 when it was destroyed by fire. The present Park Hotel now occupies this site and is one of the oldest business houses in the village.

H. L. Babst opened the first hardware store in 1880 and sold the same to A. M. Bell in 1886. Bell sold to W. S. Bartholomew who sold to Gallagher and Co. In 1882 L. W. Leighton and J. M. Johnson opened the second hardware store and in 1887 Johnson became the sole owner under firm name, J. M. Johnson and Co. Some years later Peter Rudberg bought the business and in 1900 S. N. Gayner & Co. became the owners.

The pioneer drug store was established in 1872 by Lewis Rudberg and C. A. Morris. In 1875 Rudberg sold his interest to his partner who continued the business until 1880 when he sold to C. A. McCollom, M. D., and George P. Breed who sold to Rudberg Bros. in 1883. Jonas Rudberg, while enroute to Sweden, fell from a Philadelphia hotel window and was killed and the business was sold to R. F. Case, a registered pharmacist, who operated the store with marked success for several years but ultimately sold to McCoy and Co. Case moved to Starbuck, Minnesota, and died a few years ago in California.

OF MEEKER COUNTY   95

The Dassel Manufacturing Co. was established in 1883 and operated a well equipped foundry, giving employment to 15 men. It did not prove to be remunerative and the building was sold to E. Hagelin in 1887 who converted it into a flour mill and operated it until 1912.

In 1874 L. W. Leighton was the pioneer wagon maker. His shop was located on the present site of Gayner Bros.' store. The power used in turning his lathes and saws was furnished by horse tread power. He was quite diversified in his business relations, engaged with J. M. Johnson in the hardware business and became a member of the firm of Osterlund and Leighton in the general merchandise store and later severed his partnerships and engaged in the merchandise business, selling the same in 1898 to Murphy Bros. He then moved to Globe, Arizona, and died in Los Angeles seventeen years ago.

In 1886 Peter Johnson on his return from a trip to Sweden started a Swedish tile stove ("Kakelung") factory, the only one of its kind in the United States. It proved a poor competition with the American type of stoves and proved a losing venture. One of these stoves is on exhibition at the village hall.

Dassel Fire Department — 1883

From a pen and ink sketch by John Bodin, reproduced from a tintype in the possession of O. E. Linquist. The fire station was located on the Farmers' Corporation corner.

These gallant fire fighters from left to right, excepting the first in order, Frank G. Peterson (spectator), are L. G. Adkins, L. W. Leighton, Wm. Gallagher, Douglas Martin, W. L. Van Eman, C. A. Morris, A. M. Bell, J. J. Rudberg, George B. Breed, J. E. Bunker, J. W. Norgren, B. A. Records, C. H. Remick, S. O. Lindgren, P. F. Spath, P. M. Peterson and A. Linquist.

A woolen mill was established in 1876 with a well equipped plant by J. B. Lewis and Co. It was destroyed by fire in 1880. A stock company was formed and it was promptly rebuilt and continued operation for several years. They manufactured all types of woolen goods but specialized in the making of "Svenskt-Vadmal" which found a ready market throughout the northwest. They carried a pay roll of 22 hands, but in the course of time it went the way of all small town industries.

Frederick Spath started the first blacksmith shop in 1869. He was the father of Frank Spath, who continued the business when his father removed to his farm north of town.

Dassel's Boom Year

In 1886 the St. P. M. & M. Ry., now the Great Northern, relocated and straightened their right of way through Dassel for a distance of eight miles. Camps were established east and west of the village where hundreds of men were employed. Their pay rolls quickened trade and Dassel had the most prosperous year of its entire history.

EDEN VALLEY

Compiled and edited by Alban Ruhland

This vicinity's original settlement, a tiny hamlet known as Logering, had its beginning in the pioneer days of 1877, nearly a score of years before Eden Valley's earliest citizens platted their new townsite. Logering, bearing the name of the proprietor of its only general merchandise store, August Logering, was located about two and one-half miles east of Eden Valley's present site, on what is now the Nick Bischof farm. It consisted of the Logering store, a butcher shop, a feed store, a church and several homes. Its population was about twenty. A few of these inhabitants were Ed. Berns, Bartley McDonough, Charles Hamburger and Christ Kolman.

With the coming of the railroad, in the summer of 1886, came the developments which brought about the establishment of a new village within a few miles of Logering.

The officials of the railroad, known then as the Minneapolis and Pacific but later as the Soo Line, seeking a right-of-way through the territory, were finding it difficult, because of the excessive value placed on the land by the owners, to agree on terms for the property surrounding Logering. It appeared that they would fail, when Frank B. Smith, a landowner with property lying several miles west of the settlement, proposed to contribute a right-of-way and a considerable portion of the land necessary for a townsite, if a town were laid out on Eden Valley's present site. His proposal was accepted. And in the fall of '86 the original plat of the village was completed by Smith, Cossiart and the railway company. Three additions, of the land adjacent to Smith's included in the plat, were owned by Silas Cossiart, Luke Rails and Azariah Swisher.

Eden Valley Street Scene

The first building in this platted area, erected before it became the townsite, was a small blacksmith shop built in the spring of 1886 by Henry Hukriede on the present site of the Nick Stoffel store. The first dwelling, that which is now occupied by John Brula, was constructed by Bartley McDonough, and the second by C. J. O'Brien. The first child born in the village was Charles McDonough, son of Bartley McDonough, and grew to maturity and moved to Montana. He is the author of a song known as the "Montana Rose."

As the new village grew, its neighboring settlement, Logering, handicapped as it was by its inconvenient location with regard to the railroad, was gradually abandoned. Most of its residents moved to the new townsite which was soon developing rapidly.

By the spring of '87 two stores, two elevators and two hotels had been constructed.

Parker and Cossiart, who opened the first of the stores, had put up their building previous to the platting of the town, but they greatly enlarged this with the arrival of the railroad. It has since been razed, but was located on the west side of the main thoroughfare, one block from the railroad depot. The first depot agent stationed at the latter building was Lance Brown.

The second general merchandise store was Wm. Hardy's. This is now occupied by the Joseph Roedel store. Hardy's store, which he opened in December of '86, is believed to be the building in which the village was given its name, Eden Valley. There are several legends relating to the origin of the name, but in all probability, it is derived from the village's natural location near the western extremity of a valley extending several miles to the southeast.

In December of the year the town was founded, Anton Sattler came to Eden Valley and built the first hotel, the Pacific. This hotel, later known as the Arlington, was destroyed by the fire of 1913. The second hotel, called the Mansard House, was opened for business by Anthony Bell shortly after the Pacific was started.

In the spring of '87 the greater part of the present site of Eden Valley was still given over to wheat fields. The first grain elevator, which had been built by Hoskins and Reeves in December of 1886, was filled with grain before the first train steamed its way into the valley. The second elevator, that established by the railway company, was also raised during the winter of 1886-87.

J. M. Durkee, who arrived late in the eighties, and two others— Caspar Schmidt and John Sauer—who came to the village shortly before it was organized, were also among the first business men to erect general stores and open them for business in Eden Valley.

The store building now occupied by the O'Brien-Haines Drug Company is believed to be the oldest now standing in the village. It was brought here from Manannah when Eden Valley was only a few years old and has been in the O'Brien family for more than fifty years.

The records in the Register of Deeds office in Meeker County show that the village was organized and incorporated June 28, 1889, nearly three years after the Soo Line was built through this region and the townsite was platted.

Frank B. Smith, whose generosity had determined the site of the village, became its first mayor. Eden Valley's first board of trustees was composed of J. M. Durkee, John Carney and Nick Burggraf. C. J. O'Brien was elected as the first village recorder. James H. Doran was appointed by the council as its first attorney and James Jones as the town's first policeman.

One of the first public needs to be considered by the council was that of fire protection. And in the summer of 1890 a fire department was organized and the necessary equipment purchased. The membership of this original department included Nick Schommer, J. J. McGarrery, John Ross, Mike Schoen, O. P. Thurman, J. M. Durkee, S. N. Waldron, Mike Guelff, Dominick Gilley, John Scribner and P. H. Schommer. Periodic additions and improvements have made the department well equipped and prepared at the present time to supply the protection needed by the community.

The next major additions to the public service facilities of Eden Valley were the installation of a water-works system and the introduction of the telephone to the village.

The water-works system, including a well, tower, tank, pump and mains, was completed early in 1903. This original wooden tank was replaced by a steel gravity tank on an 80-foot steel tower in 1932.

The telephone service was installed by the Eden Valley Telephone Exchange upon the passage, in March of 1903, of a village ordinance granting them the right.

Until 1912- the streets of the village were lighted by common kerosene lamps, but in July of that year the council granted the Lethert Electric Company of St. Paul a franchise to establish and maintain an electric light plant here. During the years which followed, this plant became the possession of several successive owners until, in 1924, it was purchased by the Northern States Power Company which now furnishes the power and light for Eden Valley.

A history of the development of the business section, to be complete, must include some record of those business ventures, of various degrees of importance to the community, which were started when the town was young, but were short-lived.

Judged by its value to the town, one of the more important of these was the flour mill erected in 1893. The mill was brought to Eden Valley through the united efforts and financial assistance of the entire community. A cooper shop was started in connection with the mill. William Wolf and William Johnson were two of the many townsmen employed by the mill. Its first manager was L. L. Nehrlin. In 1908 the mill was destroyed by fire.

Three other business concerns which, for a variety of reasons, existed for only a year or two, were, a stave factory, a brick yard and a cheese factory.

The stave factory was sponsored by Dr. William Hambroer with Ed. Sulky as the foreman of the ten or more workers who were given employment there. At the end of the first season its operation was discontinued because of the unsuitable quality of the local timber.

M. E. Weiler and Joseph Friedman were the owners of the brickyard which was started in 1892. It was located about two miles west of the village on the Soo Line. Most of the brick used on the Assumption Church, the parochial school and the present Andrew Lahr store were manufactured there. Because of a lack of the necessary raw materials for brick formation, the yard's production was suspended after the second year.

The cheese factory, also started in '92, was an undertaking of the Schmidt and Sauer general merchandise firm. It, too, proved unsuccessful, lasting only a year or two.

Eden Valley's first creamery, a farmers' cooperative started in 1859, was located in a frame building down by the creek. This was purchased by George Ruhland in 1897. He directed its affairs until 1901 when R. T. O'Brien became its owner. In 1904 Henry Schoenecker purchased the plant and managed it until, in 1907, it became the property of its present owner, Elov Ericsson of Minneapolis. The present Eden Valley Creamery was then established and in 1910 its present building erected.

The Eden Valley Bank was the first institution of its kind in the village. This was later incorporated as the State Bank in Eden Valley.

The first post office in this vicinity is remembered to have been quartered in a little log building situated about a mile and a quarter northeast of Eden Valley. The first office established in the village proper was opened in the Parker and Cossiart store building in April of 1887. Samuel Cossiart was the first postmaster.

Eden Valley's first newspaper, The Eden Valley Journal, was founded in 1892 by William O'Brien. Its successive publishers have been R. J. Kleschult, Al Martinson, Fay Childs and the Journal's present editor, Edward J. Bahe, Jr.

Joseph Friedman, M. E. Weiler and J. B. O'Shay started a second newspaper, known as the County Line, in 1896. Its editor was a Mr. Chapman. This newspaper was not as successful as the Journal. It was discontinued after about two years.

The local educational system had its beginning in '87, when a two-room frame structure was erected and J. O. Winings was appointed as the first superintendent of schools. Among the earliest teachers were W. R. Salisbury, a present resident of Eden Valley, and Miss Elizabeth McGowan, now the owner of a millinery shop at Litchfield.

This original school building was enlarged to four rooms in 1897 and later to six rooms. In 1927 it was razed and replaced by the present modern public high school. (See frontis piece.)

The parochial school was established in 1901.

Eden Valley's first religious services were held in the old Christian Church. The second church was a little German church and the third, which was established in 1894 by Rev. J. Bastian of St. Nicholas, was the Assumption. The Elders of the Church of God organized their congregation in 1899 and erected their present church building in 1900. The Evangelical church was built in 1888. St. Peter's church was built in 1904 and the St. Paul Lutheran church in 1911.

The greatest catastrophe which Eden Valley has experienced in the fifty odd years of its existence, was the fire of 1913. this was discovered at the depot during the noon hour of a hot, dusty day in June. It is believed that sparks from a locomotive ignited the wooden platform and the flames, aided by a strong wind and a very dry season, spread rapidly. The depot and several nearby structures were soon ablaze. Despite the combined efforts of the local townsmen and hundreds of citizens brought by train from neighboring communities, the flames remained beyond control until six o'clock that evening. Before the blaze was extinguished a large section of the town lay in smouldering ruins. In addition to the depot, at which L. L. Boilen was then agent, Steve McCarthy's lumberyard, The Arlington Hotel, then managed by R. T. O'Brien, and John Becker's livery stable were destroyed. The Cossiart building, then occupied by the Wm. Kersten general store, was also damaged, but its metal siding prevented the blaze spreading further. The value of the property destroyed was estimated at nearly $50,000. Two of the buildings which were burned, the depot and the lumberyard, have been rebuilt.

Today, Eden Valley, with a population of nearly six hundred fifty, is a thriving business community with excellent parochial and public schools, five churches, a creamery, grain elevator, bank, theater and weekly newspaper.

Eden Valley's most active organization is its Chamber of Commerce which was organized in 1936. Among its numerous accomplishments are the installation of a "Whiteway" street-lighting system, the purchase of an athletic field and ball park, and its campaign to advertise Eden Valley's ideal location for tourists; in the heart of one of Minnesota's fairest resort regions.

GROVE CITY

Grove City's growth and development dates from 1869 when the first dwelling house in the present village was erected by Olof Levander on the site of the residence now owned and occupied by Mrs. Peter Redin.

During the summer of 1870 the St. Paul and Pacific Railway laid their tracks through Acton township and established the station of that name two miles east of Grove City. The post office of Swede Grove was one mile to the north. The distance between the station and the post office and the confusion of names prompted the settlers to petition the railroad company to move the station to its present location which request was granted. There was a fine spirit of cooperation existing between the farmers and the railroad officials and the settlers furnished the teams and labor to prepare the ground for the depot and the side track. The present section house was built in 1870. The post office was moved about the same time into the house of Olof Levander.

The question of a uniform name for the station and post office excited general interest. The railroad company desired to honor one of the high officials of the road by naming the village Farley and this name was in process of adoption by the post office department but did not meet the approval of the citizens and A. P. Nelson suggested the present name which met with general approval. The name Grove was intended to convey its connection with the previous name of the office while City suggested the faith of the settlers in its future growth. The name was officially adopted. If Jim Farley or any of his ancestors had been postmaster general at this time it is highly probable the name of Farley would have been adopted and the patrons of the post office (Americans of Scandinavian birth and descent) would have their mail directed to an office named in honor of a distinguished Irish American of Catholic faith.

Grove City was surveyed and platted by the railroad company on the northeast quarter of section three, Acton township in the summer of 1870 and the plat recorded in the Register's office August 26, 1870. Lawson's subdivision to the townsite was made and filed September 11, 1877 but is not included in the corporation. Bengtson's addition was platted and filed September 16, 1920. Among the first settlers were Olof Levander, A. P. Nelson, Swan Hokanson, George Okeson, Mark W. Piper, A. S. Wilcox, Andrew Okeson, and E. P. Eklund.

102 CONDENSED HISTORY

The main street in 1878 extended north from the Fairway Store corner.

The upper illustration is the west and the lower the east side of the street.

OF MEEKER COUNTY 103

The first white girl born in the village was Lilly Levander (Mrs. John Tait) daughter of Olof and Sigrid (Lundgren) Levander who was born in January, 1871.

The first Christmas service was held in the section house in 1871 and conducted by Reverand Beckman. The soul hungry settlers gathered in such numbers that improvised plank seats were used to accommodate the crowd. A. P. Nelson used to relate that on Christmas morning he was awakened by the pastor's singing of the old Swedish hymn, "Var Halsad Sjona Morgonstund." "All Hail to Thee O Blessed Morn."

The first business building in the village of Grove City is the rear portion of the present Reuben Anderson Crocery now occupied as a shoe shop. It was erected by a man named Stevens and is now known as the Grimsgard Store building.

The first grain elevator was located on the railroad right-of-way opposite the Merchants and Farmers State Bank Building. It was built by a man named Davidson from St. Paul.

The first flour mill was situated where the present Nelson Lund Company garden lots are located. It was owned by farmers and was a losing investment. Charles Lindberg purchased the same. It was destroyed by fire in 1884.

The first hotel was erected in 1874 by Louis Olson, father of Mrs. Charles King. It was known as the Swede Grove House and was located on the site now occupied by the Kopplin Gas Station.

The first church was the Baptist, organized in 1866. The Swedish Lutheran was organized in 1868 and the Norwegian Lutheran in 1876.

School district No. 23 was organized in July 1867 and school was taught in an alternation of the homes of the settlers. In 1875 the district was reorganized and the first three months' term of school was taught in a private home and about the same time a four room school house was built. The enrollment continued to increase and in 1904 the present building was constructed and in 1936 the combined gymnasium with class rooms was erected.

Among the physicians and surgeons in the Grove City community who have engaged in practice Dr. A. C. Cutts is deserving of special mention. He met the needs of the public for a period of 19 years (1900 - 1919) and continues to be held in fond remembrance.

Other physicians and surgeons deserving of special mention are Dr. Robb and later Dr. H. E. Cassel, of Litchfield served the Grove City community. He was educated in Sweden and was considered one of the best qualified surgeons in central Minnesota. The resident physician at the present time is Dr. S. Peterson.

Grove City was incorporated February 14, 1878. The first officers were: President, A. S. Wilcox; Trustees, N. Loberg, C. C. Reitan, and P. J. Malmquist; Recorder, Nels Paulson; Treasurer, (C. J. Erickson, Dr.)

Among the early business men and firms whose name are recalled by many of our citizens are: C. C. Reitan, M. A. Brown, John Hartstad, E. P. Eklund, N. W. Waylander, Peter Redin, N. E. Hanson, O. N. Lindell, Swan

Hawkinson, Nels Paulson, C. E. Fenstad, A. J. Floren, Otto Dersch, O. B. Anderson, Barney Bresden, Nels. Lagergren, C. M. Carlson A. O. Lawson, Hans Norgard, P. J. Malmquist, Swan Hokanson, Ole Pehrson, Nels Elofson, Axel Nelson, John Christenson, O. W. Hawkinson, O. L. Dudley.

All of these pioneers in the business life of the village have "crossed the bar." It is fitting that we should pay our tribute to four men who contributed in a marked degree by their public spirit in promoting the growth and development of Grove City, namely B. Bresden, O. N. Lindel, A. P. Nelson, and Jens Grimsgard. The last two named have the distinction of having continued in the same lines of business for a period of more than fifty years.

The pioneer blacksmith shop was opened by E. P. Ecklund in 1869. He continued its operation for many years. The needs of the community in this line of service were met in subsequent years by O. B. Anderson, Louis Hawkinson, P. J. Malmquist and Lars Lagergren, the last survivor of the trade dignified in the minds of the public by Longfellow's poem, "The Village Blacksmith." Anderberg, Nels W. was the pioneer painter and paper hanger. He continued in this line of labor until 1937 when he retired from active work. He receives and merits the respect of the community.

Grove City had no banking facilities until 1890 when the Merchants and Farmers Bank was organized with E. S. Griffith of Minneapolis as cashier. He was succeeded in 1895 by Aaron Liedholm who gave way in 1926 to N. A. Christianson. The bank discontinued business at the height of the depression in 1929.

The present First State Bank was organized in 1907 with Frank Carlson as cashier. He was succeeded in 1912 by A. A. Miller who holds that post at the present time. This bank weathered the storms of the depression and celebrated its thirtieth anniversary of continuous service in December, 1937.

Telephone service was established with a local exchange in 1898. Adolph Anderson is the present manager.

The water works system was installed in 1898 and the mains have been extended to meet the needs of the village. A sewage system was constructed in 1922 which serves the major portion of the village.

Electric light and power service was made available in 1913 when the village erected an electric line to connect with the Litchfield plant. A contract was entered into with that city whereby Grove City secures the current at the switch board at a price that ensures a profit to the city in its distribution to consumers. With proper economy in the management of village affairs the revenue thus derived should, in time, reduce the tax levy.

The only surviving fraternal organizations in the village is the A. O. U. W. which was chartered November 4, 1880. The V. F. W. Post No. 934 was organized January 18, 1932 and its Ladies Auxiliary on March 17, 1932.

Three grain elevators, a modern creamery, a bulk oil company three produce companies and a trucking company contribute toward making the village a desirable marketing center while the commercial, mercantile and professional needs of the community are well represented by energetic, public spirited and capable business men.

The Grove City Community Club was organized 1934. The membership with few exceptions embraces all of the business and professional men of the village. The present officers are: President, M. L. Martinson; Secretary and Treasurer, L. M. Nelson. The club owns a moving picture projector and furnishes free outdoor moving pictures each Saturday night during the summer and autumn months. The main objective of the club is to engage in such activities as will advance the social, financial, agricultural and commercial interests of the Grove City Community.

Grove City owns a park of several acres of natural beauty. In the early years a small lake formed its western boundary and sail and row boats plied its waters in summer and it formed a skating rink in the winter months. The dried bed of the lake is now used as a ball ground and the park serves as a tourist camping ground. The park with its adjacent tract of land embraces 92 acres.

WATKINS

Contributed by E. J. McCarthy.

The village of Watkins is located near the northern boundary of Meeker county and has a population, according to the census of 1930, of five hundred and twelve people.

The village is primarily a trading center and supplies the needs of its residents and those of its trade territory. Its stability and growth is due to the character of its citizenship which is largely of German extraction with the exception of a scattering of Americans of Swedish and Irish descent. These citizens are thrifty, strongly attached to the soil and progressive in thought and action.

The village developed rapidly following the coming of the Soo railway in 1886. The actual site of the town is the farm then owned by Danville D. Spaulding. The original plat of the village included only two blocks immediately south of the railroad right of way which has been materially enlarged to meet the needs of its growing population.

Immediately following the construction of the railroad bed, the company erected a depot and grain shed and J. R. Martin was the first depot agent. In the fall of 1886 Michael Becker, anticipating the coming of the railway, built a small store building on the site of the present village hall. This building, at present, is a part of the Math Turner residence. Mr. Becker hauled his stock of goods and equipment from Litchfield and was prepared for business when the whistle of the engine announced the coming of the first railroad train into Watkins. The customers of this early period came from construction camps and the rural population adjacent to the townsite.

There was a division of sentiment regarding the name to be given the embryo village. It was suggested that it be called Danville, in honor of Daniel Spaulding who owned the land on which the townsite was located, while another suggestion was Watkins, the name of a Soo railroad official. The town was duly incorporated, bearing the name of the latter gentleman. The first officers of the village were, President, C. F. Spaulding; Recorder, P. H. Schomer; Councilmen, Chas. Kupper, Val Hoffman, Nicholas Schillo.

The establishment of the railroad stimulated the influx of settlers into the heavily wooded sections of land tributary to the railroad which furnished a ready market for cordwood and railroad ties. The lands were cleared and cultivated and a fine market established for the products of the farm. In later years there has been a marked development in dairying and this has contributed in a very great degree to the prosperity of the village and Forest Prairie township.

THE WATKINS CREAMERY

The Watkins Creamery was promoted by Henry and Charles Ehlers and was financed as a stock company by the business men of the village. It began operation in the early nineties and in 1909 was sold to the Farmers Co-operative Creamery Association.

It was moved to its present location in 1914, when the present building was erected and modern equipment installed. There have been added improvemnts in the succeeding years until at the present time it is recognized as one of the most modern and best equipped plants in central Minnesota, and has the largest production among Meeker county creameries. It has 300 farmer patrons and in 1937 it produced 760,000 pounds of butter. The quality of its butter is unsurpassed by the creameries of Minnesota, evidenced by the fact that at the Internationald Dairy Congress held at Berlin, Germany in 1937 the Watkins exhibit in the fresh butter class was awarded the gold medal. It had a score of 19 out of a possible score of 20 points, which score was not exceeded by the exhibits of the competing creameries of the United States. The herds in the Watkins territory consist of highly graded Holsteins and Guernseys.

The success of the Farmers Co-operative Creamery Association, of Watkins, is largely due to the efficient management of its officers and Board of Directors, the loyalty of its patrons and the excellent service of its operator, John B. Ellering, who has been in the employ of the company the past nine years.

The English translation of the illustrated certificate awarded John L. Ellering is as follows:

INFORMATION—Concerning participation at the International Exhibit Show of Butter and Cheese, given by the International Creamery Fair, sponsored by the Eleventh Creamery World Congress at Berlin, August 1937, John L. Ellering, Watkins, Minnesota, participated in the International Quality Examination for butter with highest class samples.

The business managing president.

Chairman of the Labor Committee   General Secretary

URKUNDE

ÜBER DIE TEILNAHME AN DER

Internationalen Leistungsschau für Butter und Käse,

VERANSTALTET BEI DER

Internationalen Milchwirtschaftlichen Ausstellung

ANLÄSSLICH DES

XI. MILCHWIRTSCHAFTLICHEN WELTKONGRESSES BERLIN AUGUST 1937

John L. Ellering — Watkins, Minn.

WAR AN DER INTERNATIONALEN QUALITÄTSPRÜFUNG

FÜR BUTTER MIT 1 PROBEN BETEILIGT.

DER GESCHÄFTSFÜHRENDE PRÄSIDENT

DER VORSITZENDE DES ARBEITSAUSSCHUSSES   DER GENERALSEKRETÄR

THE CHURCH OF ST. ANTHONY

The first church was built on the site of the present church in 1890 and the parish was incorporated September 25, 1891. The rapid growth of the parish necessitated the construction in 1912 under the pastorate of Rev. Anton Vilman of the present structure. It is regarded as the finest piece of architecture in Meeker county. It has been served by the following pastors: Rev. Alois Kastigan, Rev. Anton Vilman, Rev. Francis Roemer, and the present pastor, Rev. Bozja from November 1931.

COLLINWOOD TOWNSITE 69 YEARS AGO

These ox-teams were returning from unloading ties for the railroad. Andrew Swanberg (deceased), a veteran of the Civil War, is driving one team. This picture is reproduced from a tintype taken by J. N. Kunions. (Illustration contributed by Cokato Enterprise.)

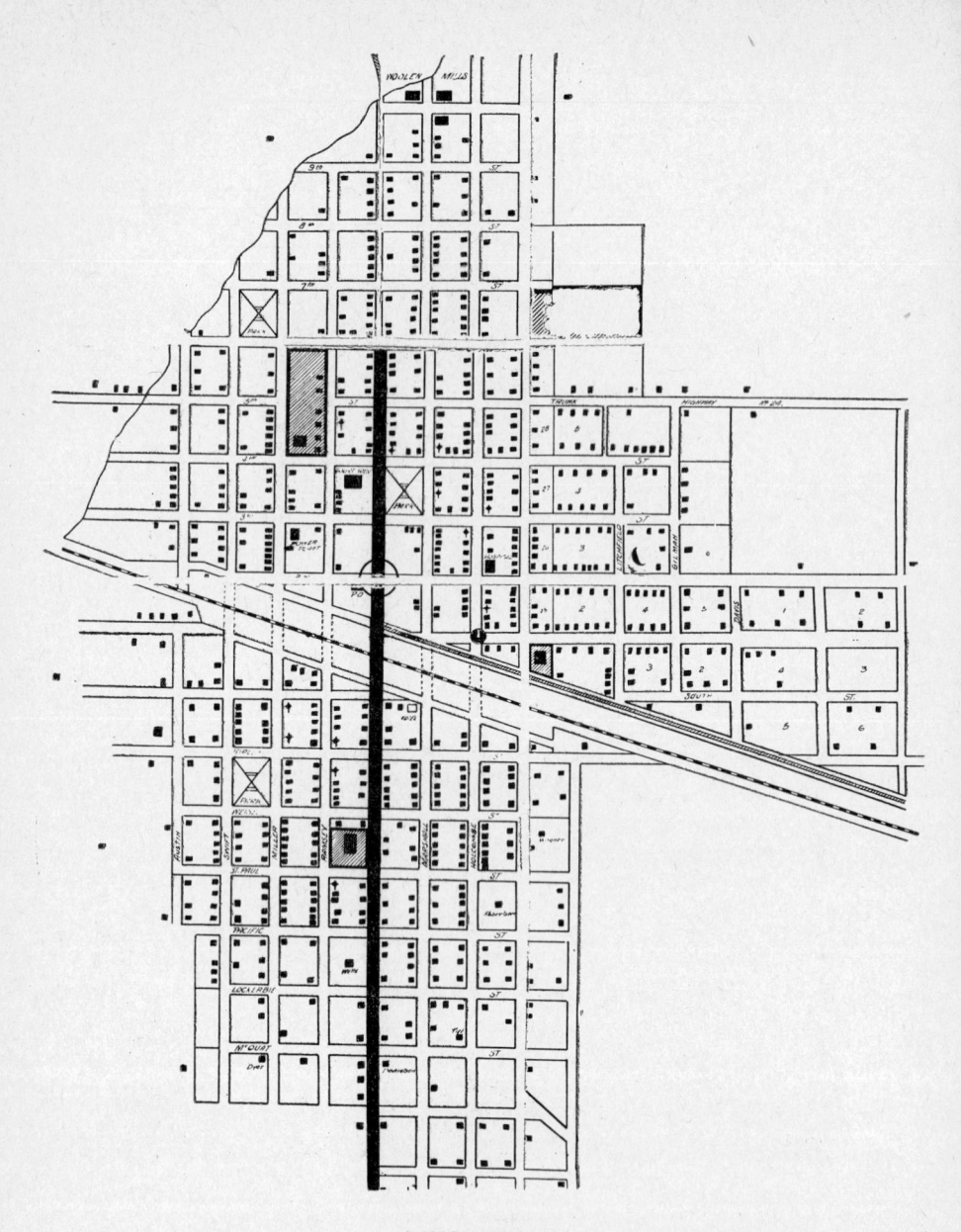

LITCHFIELD

Courtesy of C. W. Wagner

This map does not portray all of the incorporated portion of
Litchfield Village but shows the business district and
the greater portion of the residential section.

LITCHFIELD VILLAGE

The Village of Litchfield, County seat of Meeker County, was not even a dot on the map until 1869, when the St. Paul and Pacific Railway (Great Northern) established its right-of-way thru Meeker County and the railroad station was erected and named in honor of E. D. Litchfield, a London capitalist and heavy stockholder in the railway company.

George B. Waller was the owner of what became the original townsite of the Village. He deeded a one-half interest of the selected tract to the railway company and joined the company in platting this portion as the first unit of the County's present metropolis. The plat was filed July 16, 1869, and lots were placed on the market at a reasonable price. Lots on Sibley Avenue in the business section sold as low as $100.00 for a 25-foot frontage. The present price in the preferred business district is $150 to $200.00 per front foot.

A county seat contest between Forest City and the embryo villages of Litchfield and Darwin was inaugurated and at the general election of November 2, 1869, Litchfield won over Forest City by a plurality of 82 votes. Very few homes had been erected prior to this time. George B. Waller had erected a residence and a house was in the process of construction by J. M. Miller.

The establishment of the county seat at Litchfield caused a rapid influx of a substantial class of business and professional men. The business buildings and homes located in Forest City were placed on skids and hauled to Litchfield. A few of these buildings remain to serve as historical landmarks of this eventful period.

Main Street Litchfield 1874
Courtesy of J. H. Happ

EXISTING LANDMARKS

The present residence of Mr. and Mrs. George Hatch (which housed the Adam Claus saloon at Forest City) located at 114 Marshall Avenue North, was moved to Litchfield in 1869, where it first served as a unit of the Exchange Hotel. The Ole Langren residence located at 815 Sibley Avenue North, was the Stanton store at Forest City prior to 1869. A portion of the Charles Holt blacksmith shop was originally the James B. Atkinson saloon in Forest City. The barn of A. O. Askeroth near Holt's blacksmith shop is constructed in part of the lumber used in the building of the Stockade at Forest City. Among the outstanding landmarks of Meeker County is the residence owned by the Wandok Sisters, located at 508 Armstrong Avenue North. This building was moved in 1870 from Greenleaf Village, where it served as the United States Land Office when the owner, W. H. Greenleaf, was the Receiver. It was located on the west side of Armstrong Avenue where it served as Litchfield's first school house. It was owned for a time by William Roehl and moved across the street to the rear of the Shelp residence where it was used as a furniture and repair shop and later was sold to Thomas Wandok and occupied by him as a cigar factory. It was again moved to its present location and serves as a residence. It is occupied at present by Clarence Nordine and family.

Illustration by Courtesy of Henry Becklund

Among the enterprising business and professional men who established their residence in Litchfield and contributed to the growth and development of the Village during the year of 1869, we mention the following as among the first business and professional men: General merchandise, C. D. Ward and S. A. Heard; hardware, W. S. Brill; lumber yard, Joseph James; photo studlo, C. L. Angell; livery Chase and Dunn; hotel (Litchfield House) Charles Elmquist. Railway Land office, Hans Mattson; physician, Dr. George H. Weisel; lawyers, Charles Strobeck, Newton H. Chittenden and Frank Belfoy.

During the seventies these pioneers in the settlement of the Village were joined by men of marked ability in their chosen fields of labor, a detailed record of their varied careers of activity may be found in the Meeker County Album of History (1888) on file in the Litchfield Public Library.

The first banking house, having any degree of permanency was the Meeker County Bank of which W. R. Merriam and Walter Mann were the promoters and leading stockholders.

The growth in population of the Village is fully shown in the census reports of the following years: 1870, 353; 1880, 1,250; 1890, 1,899; 1895, 2,044; 1900, 2,280; 1910, 2,333; 1920, 2,790; 1930, 2,880. The estimated population of Litchfield (1939) is 3,300.

The commercial life of the Village represents all lines of business. The professions are represented by men of ability and character. The Village is not seriously restricted in its trade territory by competing cities of equal or superior commecial importance. The competing cities are as follows: East, Minneapolis, 64 miles; West, Willmar, 28 miles; North, St. Cloud, 42 miles, and South, Hutchinson, 22 miles. Litchfield is connected

OF MEEKER COUNTY   113

with the outside world by the Great Northern Railway and its public highways; U. S. Number 12 and State Highways Numbers 12, 22 and 24.

Litchfield has had from its earliest years a live and active business men's organization that continues its program of activity in furtherance of the civic, commercial, industrial and social life of the village. The present president is H. A. Plate, V. A. Sederstrom serves as secretary and A. H. Youngstrom as treasurer. In conjunction with the board of directors they comprise the governing body. They meet on call of the president to consider questions of special import and are prompt in attendance and there are few absentees at their meetings and a unanimity of action invariably results. Their Christmas decorations and programs possess especial merit.

WHEN WOOD WAS KING 1870 - 1890
Courtesy of the Olson Studio

Litchfield may properly be termed an agricultural city, dependent very largely on the products of the soil, dairying, stock raising and poultry. These sources of income are supplemented by motor traffic and its nearness to lake resorts. The only industry not directly connected with the agricultural resources is the Litchfield Woolen Mill which in years past has maintained 100 or more men and women on their pay roll. The fact that Litchfield is the seat of county government contributes much to the commercial life of the Village.

Litchfield is recognized as an excellent marketing center for dairy products, the Land O'Lakes creamery, the Litchfield Produce Company and the Anderson Creamery Company furnish the farmer a competing market and the buttermilk drying plant gives the farmer a market for his surplus product. There is also an excellent market for poultry by the firms named. There are two outstanding hatcheries (State accredited) the Litchfield Hatchery and Snow's Hatchery that contribute materially to the expansion of the poultry industry.

THE LENHARDT HOTEL

The Lenhardt Hotel, formerly the Howard House, is among Litchfield's most substantial business buildings. It is a solid native brick structure and was erected in 1880 by Colonel Jacob M. Howard, a veteran of the Civil War who came to Meeker County in 1867 and purchased a farm in Greenleaf town. In 1872 he came to Litchfield and erected the first independent grain elevator dividing his efforts in the operation of the farm and buying and shipping of grain. In 1887 he retired from active business and devoted his attention to the management of his varied interests and the upbuilding of Litchfield. He was one of the leaders in the organization of the Woolen Mill Company and became its first president. He served as mayor of Litchfield in 1885.

In October 1901, Erhardt Lenhardt purchased the hotel from which time it became known as the Hotel Lenhardt. In 1900 a three story solid brick addition was constructed which with the original structure provides accommodations for twenty-three employees and a guest capacity of 40 rooms, a roomy lobby, ladies' parlor, dining room, coffee shop, with barber shop and rest rooms in the basement. The hotel is heated throughout with steam. The guest rooms are comfortably furnished and have running water and there are a few rooms with direct bath connections.

The present proprietor and manager is E. M. Lenhardt. The hotel enjoys a fine patronage and is the only strictly modern European hotel between Minneapolis and Willmar.

Their spacious dining room furnishes ample facilities for banquet gatherings and their excellent menus of home cooked viands is hard to excel. Their Sunday dinners attract visitors from a large radius of territory. The Lenhardt Hotel is a distinct asset to the village.

A RESIDENTIAL CITY

Litchfield excells as a residential city. Its attractive homes, well kept lawns, graded tarvia treated streets and three public and railroad owned parks lend beauty to the Village. Its High School building is one of the finest and most commodious structures of its kind west of the Twin Cities. All the leading church denominations are represented and its public library adds to the cultural life of its citizens.

Its recreational facilities are of an appealing nature to the youthful and adult population and the transient visitor. The Village has two excellent theatres, an illuminated atheletic field under construction, golf grounds and tennis courts, there is hunting and fishing in accessible territory with good hotel and tourist camp accommodations.

The Village has social clubs, ladies' civic organizations, scout troops, and during the winter months public skating rinks. The following fraternities are represented: K. C.; A. F. & A. M.; I. O. O. F.; A. O. U. W.; M. W. A.; American Legion; Veterans of Foreign Wars and ladies' auxiliaries; D. A. R. and an uncharterd organization of the Sons of Veterans of the Civil War.

The Village has a privately owned hospital, well equipped with all modern appliances and an excellent corps of graduate nurses. The medical fraternity is composed of eminent physicians and surgeons.

The public buildings are of a substantial character and consist of the G. A. R. Hall, Public Library, Fire Hall and Community Building (formerly the city owned opera house) which has been remodeled and serves as a civic and social center for the entire county. It contains office rooms for the city officials.

The U. S. Post Office building was erected in 1936 and is a substantial structure. The office has four rural routes covering a mileage of 194 miles and serving 695 families. The present postmaster is Roy Peterson and the office staff consists of B. W. Grono, assistant and the following clerks, George Rethlake, Ralph S. Hawkinson and Roy Mortenson. There are three city carriers; Kenneth Peters, Arvid Rudberg and Frank Theisen. The R. F. D. carriers are Hugh I. Angier, Walter R. Hills, Clifford W. Risdon and Baldis Koenig. Harold Oslund is the fireman and laborer.

Litchfield has a number of excellent musical organizations. It has a band of 25 pieces under the able leadership of Professor Ernest C. Meyer. The city council makes a liberal appropriation toward its support whereby free concerts are given in the park each Wednesday evening during the summer months. The Litchfield Band is a continuation of the pioneer musical organization of fifty years ago which was under the leadership of Professor O. A. Olson, deceased.

SANITARY SEWAGE SYSTEM

Litchfield has a well equipped sewage and disposal plant that meets all the requirements of its residential, industrial and business district.

The facts connected with its establishment and development constitute an interesting and constructive episode in the municipal progress of the village.

In 1912 Erhardt Lenhardt, one of the largest holders of real property and owner of the present Lenhardt hotel became the leader in advocating the construction of a sewage and disposal system. The conservative council took the matter under advisement but delayed action due to what they regarded as a prohibitive expense but finally consented to engage the services of an able engineer (L. P. Wolf) to present plans and specifications for its construction. The main sewer was to extend from the Lenhardt Hotel to Jewett's Creek, a distance of one and one-half miles. The engineer's estimate of expense was $15,500.

Emil Aveldson, superintendent of the Electric Light Plant and other municipal utilities was called into conference and as a result of his investigation and a careful analysis of the engineer's plans and specifications expressed the opinion that the sewage system and disposal plant could be constructed for $10,500.

On the basis thus afforded the council advertised for bids. Mr. Lenhardt's confidence in the Aveldson estimate prompted him to submit a competitive bid with the expressed understanding on the part of the council and Lenhardt that in the event he should secure the contract, Mr. Aveldson would superintend the construction.

The Lenhardt bid was the lowest bid by $5,000 and he was awarded the contract and the work completed without any increase in the fixed salary paid Mr. Aveldson as superintendent of the village utilities. Mr. Lenhardt had a slight element of profit.

The further development of the sewage system up to the time of Mr. Aveldson's retirement in 1920 was under his supervision at an approximate saving to the taxpayers of $35,000.

WATER WORKS

The water works system was established in connection with the installation of the electric plant in 1890. The system consists of wells, town, an 80,000 gallon tank and about four miles of main. There have been further extensions and additional wells provided during subsequent years covering the years that have elapsed since the date of installation and at present the entire village has been covered.

Aveldson, Emil (son of Ole and Hannah Olson-Enevoldson) was born in Harvey township, May 29, 1874.

The parents were natives of Malma, Sweden, and upon coming to America, established their home (1870) in section 18, town of Harvey. On this farm they reared a family of six children, all of whom are living at the present time. Here the subject of our sketch grew to manhood, attended the district school and acquired a good common school education and assisted his father in the development of the farm. Early in life he exhibited a marked talent in mechanical work.

In 1898, following his father's death, in 1893, Emil Aveldson moved to Litchfield and soon thereafter secured employment in the village electric light plant as an assistant to the engineer. He became schooled in electric engineering work by this practical experience and a correspondence course, conducted by the International School at Scranton, Pennsylvania.

In 1920, Mr. Aveldson severed his connection with the village and with his background of practical experience he engaged in general contracting. He was successful from the start and received four contracts the first year. These contracts covered the installation of water and sewage plants in villages located on the Great Northern Railway. In the years following the completion of these contracts he has engaged in general construction work and drainage systems in addition to water works and sewage systems. These operations have been confined to Minnesota, with the exception of four years of contracting service in Florida. At present Mr. Aveldson's work has been confined to R. E. A. projects. He served as county surveyor (1923-1924). Emil Aveldson married, Nov. 23, 1899, Mary A. Olson (daughter of Andrew G. and Sigrid Pehrson-Olson) born January 13, 1877. Four living children were born of this union. Elvira Marie (Mrs. R. G. Reiter) born May 12, 1904. Child, Richard, born December 16, 1929. Margaret Ruth (Mrs. A. O. Payette) born January 27, 1907. Child, Robert, born Nov. 9, 1925. Ernest, born May 19, 1911. Conrad Emil, born Oct. 8, 1914. Mrs. Aveldson died November 17, 1917.

CENTRAL HEATING PLANT

In 1909 (under the supervision of Emil Aveldson) a central heating plant using exhaust steam from the utility plant was developed. The mains, at this time, covered a distance of two blocks of the business district and replaced eight privately owned heating plants. These were extended during his and J. C. Bang's superintendency until, at the present time this plant heats the entire business district, numerous residences, court house, public school building, community building and the Episcopal and Catholic churches.

GRAIN MARKETS

Previous to the development of the dairy and poultry industries of the county the marketing of grain was the main source of income to the farmers and contributed in a major degree to the commercial and financial growth of the villages of the county. In those early years Grove City and Litchfield villages were the leading markets for these products of the farm, A. J. Whitaker, formerly railroad agent at Litchfield, is authority for the statement: "There was more grain marketed at either Grove City or Litchfield than is now raised in the entire county." From sworn statements on file at the court house we learn that during the year 1938 the elevators and seed houses of the county marketed 1,708,302 bushels.

The Darwin Elevator

Darwin with only one grain elevator, under the efficient management of A. J. Kelly, received 499,932 bushels which was within 3,269 bushels of grain marketed at Litchfield's five elevators and the seed company. The grain received at the Darwin elevator is not produced in its entirety in Meeker county but it has developed such a well established market that barley is received from the two Dakotas and other points equally distant.

Other marketing centers in Meeker county handled (in bushels) the following amounts of grain; - Grove City 220,234; Dassel, 210,605; Watkins 141,400; Cosmos, 50,353; Cedar Mills, 46,577; Eden Valley, 36,000.

Meeker County Industries

LITCHFIELD MUNICIPAL LIGHT AND POWER PLANT

LITCHFIELD INDUSTRIES

ELECTRIC LIGHT PLANT

The combined municipal Light, Power and Water Works plant was established in 1890 at an expenditure of $25,000. The equipment of the light plant consisted of one alternator, one arc machine and a 60 horse power steam engine with the necessary boiler equipment. The current was turned on July 4, 1890.

During the ten-year period, 1890-1900, the plant was under the management of the following parties in succession: Isaac Miller, his son, W. H. Miller and Fred Hanke.

Emil Aveldson Takes Charge
1900-1920

In 1900 Emil Aveldson took charge and under his able supervision there was an ever increasing improvement in the extension of lines, better equipment and increased patronage. In 1913 the first extension of electric service beyond the village limits took place. A contract was entered into with Grove City (8 miles distant) whereby that village constructed a line to connect with the Litchfield plant at the switchboard and current was furnished that village at 3½ cents per K. W. H. Several farm homes adjacent to the line were served.

At the expiration of Mr. Aveldson's term of service in 1920 he turned the management over to his successor, J. C. Bang, in good serviceable condition, and free from all indebtedness.

J. C. Bang's Management
1920-1039

Mr. Bang has proven an able and efficient successor to Mr. Aveldson.

In 1922 extensions were made at the expense of the plant to serve the villages of Atwater and Darwin and it became apparent that the serving of these villages and the rapidly increasing local consumption created a condition that demanded a remodeling of the plant. This requirement resulted in the installation of much new equipment and a new power house. The improvements were made under the direction of Superintendent Bang and were followed in subsequent years by additional improvements. The local distribution covers 70 miles of rural lines which serve three villages and includes a white way system covering the business section of the city. These additions and improvements covering the period from 1920 to 1933 which include the central heating plant and water works system (See Litchfield village) amounted to $400,000 of which the entire expense has been met by the revenue from these utilities with the exception of $6,000 of unmatured bonds. In addition to the service extended the patrons of the plant the village has been given free service in light, heat and water which if paid for at commercial rates would amount to $9,000 annually. Litchfield claims the distinction of being the only municipal plant in the United States to finance the construction of rural lines.

J. C. Bang

Since 1934 the local and rural distribution has been extended and connection was made in 1936 with the Meeker Co-operative Light and Power Association whereby they are served at a transforming station three blocks west of the plant at the present price of 1¾ cents per K. W. H. for the first 50,000 K. W. H.; next 25,000 1½ cents and additional current at 1¼ cents. (See article relating to Rural Electrification).

The local domestic rate starts with 6 cents for the first 30 K. W. H.; next 170, 2 cents and additional current, 1 cent.

The Litchfield commercial light rate begins at 6 cents for the first 50 K. W. H. and graduates to a rate for current in excess of 400 K. W. H. to 3 cents with a special rate of 2 cents for all current used for heating and refrigeration. The Litchfield Power rate is slightly lower in the upper brackets and graduates downward to 1½ cents for current used in excess of 3,000 K. W. H.

Mr. Bang's period of service as an electrical engineer covers a period of 54 years of continuous generating electric service and he is the oldest man engaged, at the present time, in this line of work. The Litchfield plant in its economical and business-like management serves as a monument to his efficiency.

OF MEEKER COUNTY 123

At the annual meeting of the Minnesota Electric Association held at Rochester, Minnesota, February 23, 1937, Mr. Bang was awarded a certificate which reads as follows:

Know All Men by These Presents
J. C. Bang
Having Completed Fifty Years
of Faithful Service
Within the Electrical Industry
is Qualified for the Honor of
GOLDEN JUBILEE PIONEER

Signed by the president and secretary of the Asoociation

THE LITCHFIELD CREAMERY

The Litchfield Creamery was organized January 20, 1894 under the title Farmers' Cooperative Dairy Association. At this meeting by-laws were adopted and the following officers were elected: President, John W. Johnson; Treasurer, E. B. Benson and Secretary-Manager, Henry Ames. Others chosen to complete the board of directors were H. I. and Nels H. Peterson.

A site was purchased at the present location for $300 which was increased in later years by the purchase of additional ground. The construction of a creamery building was begun and May 5, 1894 H. T. Sondergaard was employed as buttermaker and the creamery was placed in operation.

The creamery continued operation and increased its patronage and at a meeting held June 11, 1903 it was deemed necessary to construct a new creamery building. Other meetings followed and as a result the main building was erected in 1903. Due to a greater patronage, in 1926, the creamery was enlarged by the construction of an extension to the building increasing the floor space used for operating purposes by about 750 square feet. During all the years of the creamery's operation there has been a continuous addition of modern machinery and equipment and the present plant represents an investment of $25,000.

The product of the Litchfield Creamery is of excellent quality. Its supply of milk and cream comes from a varying radius of territory. There are over 200 patrons. During the year 1938, 550,000 pounds of butter were produced. During the most prosperous years of the creamery's operation, prior to the period of the depression, monthly checks were issued to a single patron in the amount of $500.

The present officers of the Litchfield Creamery Company are: President, John Brandt; Secretary, Charles Ness; Treasurer, N. W. Nelson and other members of the governing board are Will Mitchell and Otto Marquardt. The operator and manager since 1935 is Emil G. Oman.

LAND O'LAKES CREAMERIES, INC.

The Land O'Lakes Creameries, Inc., is a nationally known organization and is admittedly the largest farmer owned and controlled corporation engaged in the purchasing and marketing of butter in the world.

This famed corporation is the direct result of an organization of the dairymen of Meeker and adjoining counties who held a conference in the county agent's office in Litchfield, November 23, 1920. The purpose of this gathering was the discussion of problems affecting the marketing of creamery products. As a result of the meeting an organization was effected which embraced creameries in Meeker, Wright and Kandipohi counties under the corporate name Meeker County Creamery Association which proved so successful that similar organizations were established in the counties of the state. These county organizations were combined in a state association and incorporated as "The Minnesota Cooperative Creameries Association.

John Brandt, the owner of a dairy farm in Forest City township became its first secretary and later was elected president. There was a marked expansion in business and its field of activity was extended into the states of Wisconsin and the two Dakotas and the name of the association was changed to Land O'Lakes Creameries, Inc. The territory is divided into twenty districts. The creameries of Kandiyohi, Meeker and Wright counties constitute District Number One, a recognition of the fact that they were the initiators of the Land O'Lakes Creameries, Inc. Unit number one is composed of twenty-one creameries in the counties named.

MILK DRYING PLANT

The Milk Drying Plant at Litchfield was established as a cooperative association in 1926 at an expenditure of $74,000. The corporate title is The First District Association which embraces 17 creameries located in Kandiyohi, Wright and Meeker counties. This plant was the first of its kind engaged in the drying of sweet buttermilk and in 1936 added the drying of skim milk. It is claimed there are only 70 similar plants in the United States. A large portion of the product is marketed through the Land O'Lakes Creameries, Inc., and eventually reaches the metropolitan centers of the country where the major portion of these shipments are used by bakers, confectioners, ice cream manufacturers, packing houses and meat markets.

The gross income from the plant during the past year amounted to approximately 35 to 40 thousand dollars and in several of the years past has more than trebled this amount. In the process of manufacture eight pounds of powder is produced from one hundred pounds of milk. Twenty-seven employees are carried on the payroll. The present officers of the plant are: President, John Brandt; Vice President, G. W. Carlson, Grove City; Secretary, D. J. Doyle, Darwin; Directors, Albert Rick, Ed. J. Boullion, B. T. Hovey, N. O. Evenson, John Werness and Alfred Carlsted. The office force consists of C. H. Leaf, manager; cashier and bookkeeper, F. F. Phillips; assistant bookkeeper; Hazel Phillips; stenographer, Effie Cole.

ANDERSON CREAMERY COMPANY

The Anderson Creamery Company was organized, building erected, equipped with modern machinery and opened its doors for business April 25, 1936. There are four employees engaged in the operation of the plant. Their annual production amounts to about 500,000 pounds and the bulk of their product is sold thru jobbers in the Philadelphia market.

THE ANDERSON CHEMICAL COMPANY

The Anderson Chemical Company had its start in 1911 when Alfred Anderson using his residence garage as a base of operations produced a butter culture that he placed on the market which almost immediately found favor with creamery operators throughout the northwestern states. Their use improved the flavor of butter and it was found that dairymen who used his product secured higher scores than was obtained by non-using competitors. The butter that received the highest scores at the international butter and cheese exhibit in Berlin, Germany contained the Anderson butter culture. In the early years his shipments were made by parcel post.

Mr. Anderson continued his experimentations in the garage and developed other products that came into public use: whey sterilizer, neutralizers and washing powders, all of these products were developed from recipes based on Mr. Anderson's previous experience. The business increased to such an extent that in 1926 he purchased the buildings located on the present site which he later enlarged to provide for the manufacture and storage of thirty products of his plant that find a ready market in Minnesota, Iowa, Wisconsin, Nebraska, Montana and the two Dakotas.

The Anderson Chemical Company is recognized as among the leading industries of Meeker County. The volume of business is steadily increasing. The Anderson products are guaranteed by Mr. Anderson and carry the following label: "Use according to directions and if dissatisfied your purchase money will be cheerfully refunded."

Alfred Anderson was born in the province of Varmland, Sweden. At the age of fourteen he came to America and found employment on a farm for three years during which time he learned the use of the English language and became an assistant in the Litchfield Creamery and later became its operator for a period of fourteen years during which time he developed his best selling product (butter culture) and has been its dispenser for twenty nine years. Mr. Anderson is the sole proprietor of the business that bears his name.

LITCHFIELD PRODUCE CO.

On March, 1912 a partnership was formed by John C. Peifer, Frank A. Peifer and Arthur F. Peifer, known as the Litchfield Produce Co. They commenced business in the old Union House, Litchfield, buying and selling eggs, poultry, cream, hides, fur and wool. During these early days the partners did all the work, hiring one or two others to help out during the busy season.

The business proved successful and it was not long until it became necessary to enlarge their quarters. This was done by building additions from time to time and the acquiring of more ground on Block 63, until today most of this block is covered by the plant while other buildings about town, both owned and rented, are now occupied by the company.

Early in the company's history John C. Peifer moved with his family to Benson, Minn., where he founded the Benson Produce Co., while his brother Frank remained at Litchfield as manager of the Litchfield Produce Co. soon to be followed by his son Arthur F. as Manager who has guided the destinies of the company ever since. In 1918 the partnership was joined by Richard Peifer, a brother of Frank and John, and in 1919 D. B. Payne was taken into the company.

On February 27, 1931, the company was incorporated, the first officers being Arthur F. Peifer, President; John Peifer, Vice President and D. B. Payne, Secretary. Special attention was given at this time to production of a very fancy pack of dressed poultry which was marketed under their ELPECO brand and soon this brand was recognized throughout the east and south tops for fine Minnesota dressed poultry, turkeys, ducks and geese as well as for frozen mixed whole eggs, frozen egg whites, and sugared egg yolks.

In 1934 the company purchased a local ice cream plant which they operate under the name of tthe Litchfield Ice Cream Co. This business has been greatly enlarged with truck routes established thruout the territory for the daily delivery of "Litchfield" ice cream and frozen novelties.

The history of the company has been one of constant expansion. Some 70 buying stations are now established in the territory serviced by a fleet of trucks, which bring to Litchfield and to a branch plant established at Melrose, Minn., the produce purchased at these points which is processed and made ready for eastern markets. The pay roll varies with the season, the low point being in February when 75 people are employed and from this gradually increasing to adout 210 persons in December. The annual pay roll exceeds $100,000.00 which helps business in all the towns serviced by the company.

Most all the products of the company are shipped to eastern and southern markets. It requires more than 400 refrigerator cars annually to move the produce processed at the Litchfield and Melrose plants, which is valued in excess of two million dollars.

THE LITCHFIELD WOOLEN MILLS

The Litchfield Woolen Mills were established in 1885 by a stock company. The officers chosen who constituted in part the holders of the capital stock of $25,000 were J. M. Howard, Hamlet Stevens, B. P. Nelson, N. W. Hawkinson, D. Flynn and D. Methven, manager, and John Rodange, secretary and treasurer. The capital stock was increased in 1887 to $50,000. It has been in the past Litchfield's greatest industrial asset carrying on its pay rolls as high as 150 to 200 employees. The mills were incorporated in 1913. Their capacity was expanded during the World War period when government contracts for their products were obtained. The production was again increased in 1929 and in 1936. The mills reached the peak of employment in 1937 when three shifts of employees were used and 150 people were employed. The plant is in operation and has fifty employees on their pay roll. The present manager is E. E. Strout and J. M. Sweet is the superintendent.

LITCHFIELD WOOLEN COMPANY

The Litchfield Woolen Company is the outgrowth of a section of the Woolen Mill plant established in 1889, which was reorganized and became a separate and distinct unit in 1934 under the ownership of F. R. Lasley. The company has enjoyed a substantial business from that date forward. Their field of operation extends throughout Minnesota and twenty additional states. They specialize in making a batting of old wool material furnished by their customers. They produce a bat 27 x 90 inches and feature the statement that they can save you money by using the contents of the home rag bag. Their stock is washed and sterilized before carding.

LITCHFIELD HATCHERY

The Litchfield Hatchery was established in 1925 by Leo Baumgartner and W. K. Dyer who through all the intervening years have been and are the sole proprietors.

The hatchery has an egg capacity of 175,000. They hatch six different breeds of chickens but make a specialty of white leghorns. They also hatch each season an average of 100,000 turkey poults. They were the pioneers in promoting poultry raising in Meeker County as a profitable source of income. The Litchfield Hatchery was the first in the county to start the hatching and raising of turkeys on a commercial basis.

TURKEY FARMS

The Litchfield Turkey Farm which has a state wide reputation had its initiative in a turkey farm located in the southwestern section of the city by Leo Baumgartner and W. K. Dyer. Their success prompted the establishment of the present farm of eighty acres, one mile east of the city. They joined with Ray McGraw, Richard and Art Peifer and engaged in raising turkeys for the commercial market. They raise an average of 10,000 turkeys each season.

There are numerous turkey farms established throughout the county that maintain flocks in excess of one thousand. Next in rank to the Litchfield farm is the Plainview Turkey Farm operated by Orville B. Dalk in section 35, Cosmos town which markets in excess of 5,000 turkeys annually. Other turkey breeders that raise flocks in excess of 1,000 birds are W. J. Nelson, Litchfield township; Albert P. Anderson, Collinwood; Albert Colberg, Dassel; Walter A. Tintes, Manannah; Harry Marks, Kingston; N. F. Johnson and George Philippi, Dassel, Carl J. Anderson, Greenleaf; Henry Olson and R. E. Baumgartner, Harvey and numerous others who raise flocks between 500 and 1,000.

SNOW'S HATCHERY

Snow's Hatchery at Litchfield is one of 25 hatcheries operated and controlled by E. H. Snow of Sleepy Eye, Minnesota. The plant at Litchfield has an egg capacity of 120,000 chicks. They specialize in eleven breeds. The plant is operated by B. H. McDonald who has the supervision of four additional plants. During the hatching season three employees are carried on the payroll.

The Electrik Maid Bake Shop

The Electrik Maid Bake Shop was established in 1923 by Mr. and Mrs. F. J. Koktavy. They do a wholesale and retail business. Their wholesale trade territory covers villages and hamlets for a radius of forty miles. Their eastern trade extends eastward as far as Minnetonka Lake. The bakery has a daily capacity of 2,000 loaves and additional products are all types of cake and pastries. The firm carries nine employees on its pay roll supplemented by three members of the family.

The New Bakery

The New Bakery was organized and opened for business in 1933 by Wayne H. Rappy. It supplies the villages in the territory between Litchfield and Willmar. The bakery has a daily capacity of 5,000 loaves of bread and other products consist of all varieties of cakes and pastries. They carry 22 employees on their pay roll which amounted to $17,000 in 1938. They cater largely to retail trade.

LITCHFIELD BOTTLING WORKS

The Litchfield Bottling Works were established in 1878 by John Rodange who associated with him, as a partner, Jacob Reese. The name of this firm was Rodange and Reese and later the Reese interests were purchased by Mr. Rodange. He was succeeded in ownership by Johnson and Roos and later it was owned and operated by Clyde Crosby. The plant was purchased from Leslie Burns in 1924 by Oscar and August Anderson, the present proprietors. This firm does a flourishing business. The plant bottles sodas of 12 or more flavors and specializes in Howell's Root-Beer which product they market in Wright, Meeker and Stearns counties.

LOVEN SEED COMPANY

The Loven Seed Company was established in 1923 and has expanded into the largest distributing agency of varied farm and garden seeds between Minneapolis and Fargo, North Dakota. Their seeds are purchased from farmers and wholesale seed houses. During the planting season they carry seven employees on their pay roll.

BROWN PRINTING COMPANY

The Brown Printing Company was organized in 1922 by E. B. Brown and James H. Phelps and was operated by these gentlemen until 1924 when Mr. Brown became the sole owner. The plant has been expanded and at present four employees are carried on the pay roll. The plant specializes in commercial printing and receives orders from a large area of territory. The Lamson History of Meeker County was printed by this company and he has had very pleasant business relations with Mr. Brown and his loyal employees.

DASSEL INDUSTRIES

Dassel has gained the distinction of being the seed corn center of the great northwest. T. H. Pendergast, deceased, of Collinwood town, was the pioneer promoter of this industry. The Dassel News Letter of March 8, 1884 carried an advertisment in which he offered seed corn of guaranteed quality to the farmers of the Dassel territory. The following year he entered into a contract with Northrop, King & Co., of Minneapolis whereby he sold them his entire crop. The corn was dried in racks provided for that purpose, located in the Collinwood flour and feed mill which he owned and operated at that time. Pendergast did not continue in this industry but disposed of his holdings and moved to Minneapolis.

It remained for Andrew Larson, the owner of a farm in Section 12, Collinwood town, to promote the movement that has resulted in the supremacy of Dassel as a seed corn center. He was young, ambitious, and progressive when he entered into a (longhand) written contract with Northrop, King and Company to market the corn of a 20 acre tract of the then popular corn, Pride of the North. The venture was successful and spread rapidly and this initial seed producer remains active in this field of endeavor.

In 1908, Carlsted Brothers and other farmers followed his lead and started curing the seed raised on their farms and retailed their product. In 1911, the Carlsteds shipped ten barrels of seed corn to Pretoria, Africa, picked from their field in Section 15, Collinwood town, which won first prize in the state wide contest, producing 106.8 bushels to the acre.

THE C. J. PETERSON SEED HOUSE

C. J. Peterson engaged in a limited way in the seed corn business as early as 1916 by the establishment of a small drying plant in which one of the early units of his present well equipped plant is the Steelsville pioneer school building in which the writer taught Mr. Peterson's brothers and sisters the rudiments of their early education. The Peterson plant has a capacity of 15,000 bushels.

MEEKER COUNTY SEED COMPANY

The Meeker County Seed Company, successors of the Dassel Seed Company was organized by Arne Arneson and Knute Johnson in 1916. They established a commercial business, erecting a drying house with a capacity of 15,000 bushels. They purchased the property of the Dassel Milling Company and continued to manufacture flour and feed but found it necessary after a brief period to discontinue the manufacture of flour to expand the seed corn and other field seed business.

October 1, 1928, a corporation was formed that took over the business under the name of the Dassel Seed Company. During the peak year of 1935 they contracted with the farmers for the product of 1,600 acres and marketed 40,000 bushels of seed corn. In October 1936 the plant was sold to the Interstate Seed and Grain Company of Fargo, North Dakota and is now operated under the name of the Meeker County Seed Company with Mrs. Edith M. Bodin as their local manager. Their plant is the largest seed corn drying plant in the northwest.

THE HAAPALA SEED HOUSE

In 1906, Andrew Haapala engaged in the production of seed corn for his own use and disposed of his surplus product to neighboring farmers and was among the first in promoting the growing of the famed variety, Minnesota 13.

In 1913, his son Levi began operating along similar lines and his 1917 crop of 600 bushles found a ready market in the spring of 1918 at $11 per bushel. This led to the establishment of his present well equipped modern plant.

He places on the spring market all the popular varieties of field corn including hybrids and one special type of sweet corn. Mr. Haapala was the first producer in Meeker County to introduce the use of hybrid corn. Mr. Haapala is of Finnish descent and is a splendid representive of this element in the citizenship of Meeker County.

RICE LABORATORIES

The Rice Laboratories, Inc. of Dassel was organized in 1935 with O. H. Rice, president; Knute Johnson, vice president; and L. R. Peel as secretary-treasurer and business manager. The Dassel plant is the only one in the state engaged in the manufacture of dried yeast or yeast culture. The product is used extensively in the feeding of poultry and swine and there is an increasing market for their product from New York to San Francisco and as far south as Texas. The death of Knute Johnson, December 13, 1936, resulted in a reorganization of the company with L. R. Peel as president-manager; C. G. Porter, vice president; and F. V. Johnson, secretary-treasurer. In 1936 they constructed a factory especially equipped for the manufacture of their product.

SORGHUM MILL

O. M. Mattson established a custom sorghum mill in Dassel village in 1935. It is a modern up to date plant and no better quality of sorghum can be found in the markets than is produced by Mr. Mattson.

FOX FARMS

There are three fox breeders in Meeker County. Among those engaged in this line of business are: J. W. Miller, Section 17, Collinwood town; Fred Nordstrom, Jr., section 25, Darwin town and W. L. Albrecht, section 13, Cedar Mills town.

SQUARE DEAL EGG ASSOCIATION

The township of Kingston leads all other units of the county in the production of poultry and eggs.

The Square Deal Egg Association is a non- incorporated cooperative association of poultry raisers that truck eggs and poultry bi-weekly to Minneapolis and sell their products direct to the retailer. The receipts of these shipments are pro-rated weekly to the poultry raiser. The Christianson State Accredited Hatchery in the Kingston townsite is an excellent feeder of the industry. It has a 52,000 egg capacity.

MINK KENNELS

R. J. Broderius, the present mayor of Cosmos village and the proprietor, in partnership with his wife, of the Rainbow Hatchery in that village has, in process of development, a mink farm. They started this unique sideline to their hatchery in the fall of 1936 with six females and one male. The 1937 litter increased the number to thirty and the 1938 litters numbered seventy and in 1940 they expect to be able to market breeding stock and pelts. The interesting feature of connecting their poultry plant with the breeding of mink is that unfertile eggs form a most desirable ration for the mink. The average litter of a mink is about five and at birth they resemble very closely a mouse in size and color. The mother weans its young when they are two months old and they are then fully developed.

Financial

It is the judgement of the compiler of this history that there are few, if any, counties in the United States that have not met with serious reverses, resulting in loss to stockholders and depositors, due to banking difficulties caused in part by the depreciation in the value of loan securities.

It is the opinion of the writer that there is nothing to be gained by recounting the somewhat sordid stories that might be related regarding the banking institutions of past years.

Let us rather regale ourselves with the thought that under our changed banking laws there will be no repetition of these experiences in the future. "Let the dead past bury its dead." We are not living in the past but in the present and for the future. There are seven banking institutions in Meeker county under conservative management. The depositors are protected against loss to the amount of five thousand dollars by reason of their holding membership in the Federal Deposit Insurance Corporation.

NORTHWESTERN NATIONAL BANK

The Meeker County Bank was organized in January 1878 by Walter Mann and W. R. Merriam, who later became Governor of Minnesota. These gentlemen were, at that time, Vice President and Cashier of the Merchants National Bank of St. Paul.

In perfecting the organization of the Meeker County Bank, Mann became President; W. R. Merriam, Vice President; H. B. Gates, Cashier. At a later date the control of the bank was taken over by a stock company and transferred to the Northwestern National Bank. During the entire period of the banking service of the Northwestern the depositors have met with no financial losses.

The resources of the Northwestern National Bank exceed $1,000,000. The present officers are President, William S. McGee; Cashier H. A. Becklund, who has been connected with the institution for thirty-three years; Assistant Cashier, A. L. Tostenrud. Other employees, Tellers, Mildred Oslund and Miles Johnson; Bookkeepers, Ethel Tuman and Fay Carlson, Stenographer, Myrtle Oslund.

STATE BANK OF LITCHFIELD

The State Bank of Litchfield was organized by the First Bank Stock Corporation, embracing the First National Bank of Minneapolis and the First National Bank of St. Paul, together with about one hundred additional banks in the leading cities of the Northwest, including Litchfield.

This newly organized bank acquired all the assets and assumed all the deposit liabilities of the Bank of Litchfield, which bank was facing dificulty due to the banking crisis then existing not only in Meeker County, but throughout the United States. This protected all depositors against any possible loss in the Bank of Litchfield, and was done with the co-operation of heavily interested stockholders of said bank, who assumed liabilities very much in excess of legal requirements.

The State Bank of Litchfield opened its doors to the public, December 18, 1929, and has enjoyed the confidence of its customers and the public since its organization.

At the close of business December 31, 1938, its capital stock and surplus was $128,818, and its aggregate deposits were $892,000. Its resources exceed $1,000,000.

The present officers are: President, C. W. Wagner; Vice President and Cashier, A. E. Pfiffner; Assistant Cashiers, R. W. Swanson, D. N. Tharalson and A. H. Youngstrom. Other employees are: Maryon Taylor, Assistant Auditor; Ethel Burington, Stenographer; Book-keepers, Howard Nelson and Mary-Alice Pemberton.

FARMERS STATE BANK

The Farmers State Bank of Darwin with a capitalization of $10,000, was organized and incorporated July 15, 1914 with the following officers: President, E. E. McGrew; Cashier, J. E. Nelson, and the following stockholders of that period have continued as such since its organization: E. H. McGannon, John McGowan and W. F. Kline.

Soon after the incorporation of the Bank, E. E. McGrew severed his connection with the bank and John E. Nelson succeeded him as president.

The bank has had the unwavering confidence of its depositors from the date of its organization and with the exception of the brief period of the national bank moratorium, its doors have never been closed to business. No losses have ever accrued to the depositors. Its banking territory met with a marked expansion during the period following the moratorium, due to a curtailment of banking facilities in adjoining territory and the business relations established at this time has enabled them to hold many of the customers secured during this trying period in banking conditions.

The present capital remains at $10,000. The bank's surplus is $3,000.

The present officers and directors are J. E. Nelson, President; J. A. McRaith, Vice President and W. F. Kline. J. W. Freer, the present cashier, has served since 1935. He is ably assisted by R. E. Simns as assistant cashier and Vilas Nyre as bookkeeper.

The bank celebrated its twenty-fifth anniversary June 14 of the present year.

DASSEL STATE BANK

The Dassel State Bank is the successor of the Wright State Bank located at Wright, Carlton county, Minnesota, organized November 15, 1916 as State Bank 1304. The bank passed under the control, July 20, 1918, of the following stockholders: S. O., E. C. and C. Ilstrup and A. E. Anderson of Cokato, B. J. Ilstrup of Minneapolis and John P. Applequist of Wright, and later Henry E. Groth and H. B. Peterson purchased stock.

The bank at Wright was moved to Dassel and opened the doors of the institution to Dassel patrons February 4, 1934. In closing their banking relations at Wright they declared a stock dividend of fifty per cent. At the time of the bank's reorganization and location at Dassel, all requirements of the State Securities Commission had been met. It was one of the few banking institutions in the state to open its doors after the bank holiday and had a one hundred per cent bill of health.

The present bank officers are S. O. Ilstrup, president; Eva C. Ilstrup, vice president; A. R. Anderson, cashier, and directors Nels Wreisner and Ade Wreisner. Their capitol stock is $20,000 and their surplus $5,000.

THE FIRST STATE BANK OF GROVE CITY

The First State Bank of Grove City is the only banking institution in the village and was the first bank to operate under a state charter. Its organization was perfected and it began business in December, 1907.

The bank was originally capitalized at $15,000 which was expanded in 1920 to $25,000. It has been a correspondent of the First National Bank (formerly the Security National) of Minneapolis during its entire existence.

The affairs of the bank have been so well and ably managed that it was able to meet the adverse conditions of the depression period without loss to the depositors and has a surplus of $5,000, and has built up its reserve. It was one of the few banking institutions of the state to resume operations after the bank holiday. The present officers and board of directors are: president, Louis Johnson; vice presidents, O. P. Wilner and William Carlson; cashier, A. A. Miller; directors, L. F. Holm and L. M. Nelson. The working force in addition to the cashier consists of F. A. Schmidt, L. Liedholm and W. L. Miller.

STATE BANK IN EDEN VALLEY

The State Bank in Eden Valley is the successor of the Security State Bank and the State Bank of Eden Valley both of which were located in that village. The State Bank in Eden Valley was organized January 2, 1932. Their capital stock is $20,000 and their surplus and undivided profits amount to $12,000 with resources of $250,000. The bank is a locally owned and managed institution and its officers and directors are as follows: President, E. A. Arnold; Vice President, Jacob Bischof; Cashier, R. S. Schmid; Assistant Cashier, M. E. Finken. All of these officers serve as directors together with C. L. Arnold, Henry Schoenecker and Mary and Peter Stoffel.

FARMERS STATE BANK OF WATKINS

The Farmers State Bank of Watkins, Minnesota was organized in the year 1914, receiving its charter on October 12th of that year, with a capital of $15,000.00 and a surplus of $3,000.00, the first officers being; John J. Ahmann, President, F. H. Welcome, Vice President, and M. W. Vogel, Cashier.

The bank has always enjoyed the confidence of the community and has grown and prospered with the surrounding territory. It is celebrating in this year of 1939 its silver anniversary, twenty-five years which has seen a World War, inflationary periods, depressions and periods of prosperity, and has always been able to meet the tests of all times, without loss to a single depositor. From its beginning in small rented quarters in the old Central Hotel building, it moved in 1920 to its present location which it owns and which affords spacious and modern banking quarters. At present its resources are over $300,000.00, with capital, surplus and undivided profits of well over $31,000.00. It is also a member of the Federal Deposit Insurance Corporation.

The present officers are N. H. Ley, President; P. H. Weber, Vice President; R. H. Ley, Cashier; Gerald Ley, Assistant Cashier, all of which together with M. Brixius constitute its present Board of Directors.

FIRST STATE BANK OF COSMOS

The First State Bank of Cosmos was incorporated and opened its doors for business, April 9, 1914. It is capitalized at $10,000 and has a surplus of $2,000.

At the time of the depression the bank was not closed except during the moratorium. The depositors united in a voluntary 30 per cent reduction of their deposits and there were no further losses. Nine per cent of the entire amount has been returned and there is every assurance that the entire 30 per cent will ultimately be paid.

All the bank stock is held by local people. There has been no increase in the capital stock and surplus. The present officers and directors are: President, C. Theodore Johnson; Vice President, E. H. Maag; Cashiers, H. L. Swanson, and E. A. Hackbarth, Mrs. Eleanor G. Swanson serves as assistant cashier. The bank, during the past five years, has had a steady increase in its deposits.

Political Trend

Meeker county has been predominantly republican in every presidential election since its admission to statehood with the exception of the elections of 1912, 1924, 1932 and 1936.

The growth and development of public sentiment in opposition to the existing leadership in the republican party in their control of state affairs began in 1910 when the Progressive Republican League was organized with George S. Loftus as president and Frank B. Lamson, secretary. Among the active members of this militant organization, which embraced the followers of Theodore Roosevelt and Robert M. LaFollette, were Hugh Halbert, of St. Paul; James Peterson, of Minneapolis; J. A. A. Burnquist, Theodore Christianson, Ernest Lundeen, W. I. Nolan, Lynn Haines and Peter Youngdahl, the forceful leader of the Anti-Saloon League. The organization made its influence felt and was largely responsible for legislation being enacted that conformed to the progressive platform of principles advocated by Theodore Roosevelt and Robert M. LaFollette.

It is freely admitted that the membership in this state-wide organization represented different shades of progressiveness but they were united in their opposition to the ultra-conservative forces in control of the state and national government.

The organization was disrupted and ceased to function in the early summer of 1911 due to a division of sentiment among its members regarding the presidential aspirations of Theodore Roosevelt and Robert M. LaFollette. During its brief existence it had sowed the seed of progressiveness throughout the state. This seed fell on fertile ground in Meeker County as was evidenced in the presidential election of 1912 when Theodore Roosevelt carried the county over Wilson by 359 majority and Taft, who was regarded as an ultra-conservative received only 560 votes in the county and failed to carry a single precinct.

The followers of LaFollette were regarded by the supporters of Roosevelt as ultra-progressive.

George S. Loftus was a sincere follower of LaFollette. He had named one of his sons after this militant progressive. Loftus carried on the fight to wrest the control of the state from the reactionary control of the existing republican leadership and may properly be regarded as the political godfather of Magnus Johnson and Ernest Lundeen.

The Non-Partisan League under the leadership of A. C. Townley extended its organization into Minnesota and was strongly supported in Meeker county. The League is acknowledged to have been the beginning of the Farmer-Labor movement in Meeker county and the state at large.

The League's attempt to bore from within and ultimately control the republican party was a dismal failure. Townley became a discredited leader of the progressive forces and the Farmer-Labor party came into existence.

Magnus Johnson became the acknowledged state-wide leader of the newly formed organization and became known throughout the state as a sincere advocate of the principles he espoused.

The republican party retained its strength and prestige in Meeker county in the campaigns of 1914, 1916, 1918 and 1920, but in the election of 1922 Henrik Shipstead, the Farmer-Labor candidate for United States Senator carried every precinct in Meeker county except Dassel village, Grove City and the first and third precincts in Litchfield village. His majority in the county was 1785 over the internationally known Frank B. Kellogg. Magnus Johnson, candidate for governor carried every rural precinct in the county but lost out in all the village precincts. In the presidential election of 1924, Robert M. LaFollette was an independent candidate for president and received a majority of 153 over Calvin Coolidge in Meeker County. Magnus Johnson, candidate for United States Senator, and the state candidates of the F. L. party had substantial majorities in the county. A new leader of the Farmer-Labor party appeared in the person of Floyd B. Olson, a man of strong personality and marked oratorical ability. He was the Farmer-Labor candidate for governor and carried the county by a majority of 1,032 over Theodore Christianson. The Farmer-Labor Party had become a real power in Meeker county and throughout the state. Henrik Shipstead had retained his position as United States Senator, Floyd B. Olson had been twice elected governor and Magnus Johnson had won a seat in the United States senate and served one term as representative in congress.

The death of United States Senator, Thomas D. Schall in 1931 resulted in the appointment of Elmer A. Benson to fill the vacancy with the understanding that at the expiration of his appointed term of office he would become the Farmer-Labor candidate for governor while Olson would file as a candidate for United States Senator. "The best laid plans of mice and men gang aft aglee." Floyd Olson died in office and Lieutenant Governor Hjalmer Peterson became his successor.

Magnus Johnson did not approve of the political deals formulated and entered the lists as a candidate for the gubernatorial nomination against Elmer A. Benson but was defeated in the primaries, and Benson became governor. Ernest Lundeen won the United States senatorship. With the exception of Stafford King for State Auditor and Mike Holm for Secretary of State, all the state officials of the Farmer-Labor party were elected and the party controlled the lower house in the state legislature. During Benson's administration it became apparent that the more radical element of the Farmer-Labor party exercised marked control of the party.

In the campaign of 1938 there was a revolt from the machine controlled organization, headed by Hjalmer Peterson, who entered the primaries in opposition to Governor Benson, who won the nomination. The followers of Peterson joined an independent movement and supported the republican nominee, Harold Stassen who won the election by 291,000 majority over Benson. The republican state ticket was elected together with a majority in both houses of the legislature favorable to the principles advocated by the newly elected Governor. The republicans also elected seven out of nine congressmen. Meeker county gave Stassen a majority over Benson of 3,593 and he carried every precinct in the county except Cosmos village.

The banner Farmer-Labor precinct of Kingston, the home of Magnus Johnson, gave Stassen 156 majority over Benson.

The republican party is seemingly in the saddle again under the leadership of Harold E. Stassen.

THE COUNTY OPTION CONTEST

Meeker county became a dry county at a special election held June 14, 1915. There was a total of 2,247 votes cast of which 1,633 were recorded against license and 1614 in favor of license, a majority of 19 votes for the drys. The following precincts gave majorities against license in order of rank: Kingston, Collinwood, Dassel, Dassel village, Acton, Greenleaf, Union Grove, Grove City and Litchfield village. The precincts returning majorities in favor of license in order of rank were, Forest Prairie, Manannah, Cedar Mills, Ellsworth, Cosmos, Forest City, Harvey, Darwin and Danielson. Forest Prairie was the banner town for the wets with a majority of 185 and Kingston was the peak precinct for the drys with a majority of 122. Danielson trailed for the wets with a majority of 8 and Litchfield village for the drys with a majority of 10.

HONORS BESTOWED

Meeker county has had a rather unusual recognition in the election and appointment of its citizens to official positions in state and national government. It can be truthfully said that there has been no abuse of trust in the administration of the duties of these offices during the period of their service.

Hans Mattson and Peter E. Hanson have served as Secretary of State.

T. C. Jewett, the territorial pioneer, served as Court Commissioner of the Alaska Territory.

A. T. Koerner was honored by election to the office of State Treasurer.

S. W. Leavitt served as chairman of the State Board of Control.

Magnus Johnson achieved a national reputation as U. S. Senator from Minnesota and represented his district in congress.

William Campbell and Bernard Anderson have served as United States Marshal for Minnesota.

Mrs. Anna Determan has served as a Regent of the Minnesota State University and member of the State Board of Control.

Charles H. March is serving at present as a member of the Federal Trade Commission.

WILLIAM CROOKS ENGINE NO. 1

The William Crooks Engine No. 1, famous locomotive which opened up transportation for Meeker county pioneers, is attracting nationwide interest these days as an exhibit at the "World of Tomorrow" exposition in New York City.

It's a far cry back to 70 years ago when Litchfield was platted and the William Crooks was greeted with acclaim. For at that time it had been the fastest engine in these parts since June 28, 1862, when it was put on the rails at St. Anthony after being barged up the Mississippi river from LaCrosse where the rails ended east of the "Father of Waters."

Built in Patterson, New Jersey in 1861, it was placed in service on the St. Paul and Pacific railway, now the Great Northern, as Minnesota's first railway locomotive. Few old timers can remember when it made monthly stops at Dassel, Darwin, Litchfield and Grove City. From its pay car cash was dispensed to railroad builders and other early workers by Bernard Dassel, for whom this Meeker county village was named.

Patriotic

MEEKER COUNTY WAR SERVICE

Since the organization of Meeker County there have been three wars to test the patriotism of Meeker County citizens: Civil, 1861-1865; Spanish American, 1898 and World War, 1914-1918.

There were two of our pioneer settlers who were veterans of the Mexican War, whose graves may be found in the Ripley cemetery, W. H. Branham and J. B. Salisbury.

The county was sparsely settled in 1869, the census of that year gives a population of 928 and only 300 adult males but the official records show that there were 126 men on the war service rolls from Meeker County. There is grave doubt in the mind of the writer whether any county in Minnesota can show a higher percentage record.

THE GRAND ARMY OF THE REPUBLIC

The G. A. R. (Grand Army of the Republic) and its allied organizations, Women's Relief Corps and Sons of Veterans, were among the active organizations throughout the northern states following the close of the Civil War and extending through the nineties. These organizations were a live force in Dassel and Litchfield and influenced the civil and social life of these communities. No fraternal organization in the entire country can or will ever compare with the G. A. R. in its loyalty of interest in the welfare of its individual members.

The Frank Daggett Post No. 35, G. A. R. was organized July 8, 1883. The Daggett Post erected a memorial hall in 1885 at an expenditure of $5,000. It is a solid brick structure and contains numerous pictures of Civil War Veterans and relics of the rebellion and Indian Massacre. The building is now the property of the city. It is said to have been the only meeting place owned by the G. A. R. in Minnesota.

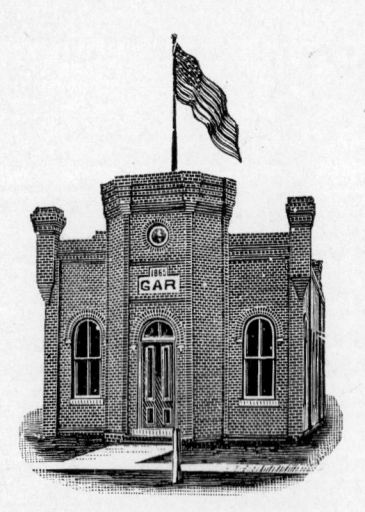

An allied organization, Women's Relief Corps No. 16, was organized January 2, 1886 with sixteen charter members.

A second allied organization, the Sons of Veterans, organized as the Yorrick Camp was instituted in Dassel village December 5, 1885 and was moved to Litchfield in August 1887 and renamed the J. C. Braden camp No. 10. The Sons of Veterans organizations were quite numerous throughout the entire state and assisted very materially in all patriotic demonstrations.

OF MEEKER COUNTY 143

This camp after a short period of existence surrendered its charter but later was reorganized as the J. B. Atkinson camp but failed to retain its chartered standing but continues to meet as the Atkinson Camp with Hugh I. Angier as the commander. A complete roster of Meeker County citizens who enlisted in the Civil War is published in the Meeker County Album of History on file in the Litchfield library.

FOREST CITY HOME GUARDS

To protect the village of Forest City from raids by the Indians and to impede their progress eastward thirteen men and three women determined to make a stand in defense of the town. The names of this heroic group are recorded on page 22 of this history.

Jesse V. Branham, Sr., a man 59 years of age, made a forced ride of 100 miles to convey this information to Governor Ramsey whereupon the Governor commissioned G. C. Whitcomb (county treasurer of Meeker County) captain to organize a company of Home Guards. He arrived at Forest City the morning of April 23 and immediately using the thirteen men as a nucleus perfected a company of Home Guards.

Roster

Officers: Captain, G. C. Whitcomb; Lieutenants, J. B. Atkinson and Hamlet Stevens; Sergeants, William Branham, H. S. Howe, Daniel McGraw, F. G. Gould,; Corporals, A. F. Heath, H. J. Hill, T. C. Jewett, Samuel Hutchins, J. M. Harvey, R. B. Ralston, N. H. White, A. B. Hoyt.

Privates

Branham, J. V. Jr.; Bradshaw, J. H.; Behrman, H.

Caswell, William; Condon, Patrick; Cobb, Jesse F.; Chapin, E. A.; Chapin, D.

Grayson, Thomas; Gorton, M.; Gibbins, Oliver; Garrison, J. B.; Gibbins, Eli.

Heath, J.; Hamilton, A.; Holbrook, D. M.

Johnson, Henry; Johnson, W.

Kruger, Charles; Kruger, Herman.

Lang, James; Lutons, H.

McGraw, Michael; Mousley, Alfred; Mickelson, H.; Maybee, C. D.

Nelson, Andrew; Nelson, James.

Olson, Aslog; Olson, Halga; O'Doughertay, Thomas.

Payson, C. E.; Page, G. R.

Rogers, Jerome; Ragan, Thomas.

Stevens, Sylvester; Smith, Lory; Smith, A. C.; Sperry, Albert; Smith, Henry L.; Sholes, G. S., Sr.

Todd, O. B.; Thomas, Joseph; Tornborn, Nels.

Wilcox, William; Waggoner, G. W.; White, S. W.

SPANISH AMERICAN WAR

TWELFTH REGIMENT U. S. VOLUNTEERS

The regiment was commanded by Colonel Joseph Bobleter. All of the Meeker county members of this regiment were enrolled in Company L. under the command of Captain Paul E. Henninger. The list is as follows:

Corporal, George P. Dunn; Privates, Lawrence E. Baum, John J. Caswell; Leonard B. Caswell, Andrew Hawkinson, George W. Lindgren, James H. Phelps, Edward Rodange, Waldo Taylor, William H. Young.

Two Meeker county boys served in the 13th Regiment: F. O. Holm and J. J. O'Loughlin. Harvey E. Bigelow served in the 14th Regiment.

15TH REGIMENT U. S. VOLUNTEERS

The regiment was commanded by Colonel John C. Shandrew and was called into service May 6, 1918. They were mustered out of service at Camp Muller November 5, 1898.

Anderson, Axel E.
Anderson, Charles
Anderson, Elmer Olin
Anderberg, Otto A.
Angier, Carrol W.

Barrett, John
Baum, Clarence C.
Benedict, Fern
Bertelson, John
Boettcher, William F.
Bogert, Edward B.
Bronson, Ole A.
Buckman, Charles W.
Burns, John L.

Campbell, Ernest W.
Carlson, Frank
Casey, Frank
Cates, Robert M.
Champion, John C.
Christianson, Bertie P.
Christopherson, H. C.
Coombs, Louis N.
Cooper, Charles
Crosby, Everett E.
Culp, Loxley
Curran, John C.

Davis, William
Day, Harry W.
Dewey, Rupert C.
Dougherty, Thomas R.
Dunleavy, Edward

Eastman, Aldine C.

Elling, Valentine

Forberg, Charles E.

Galvin, John
Giblin, Joseph F.
Gorton, Milo R.

Hagerman, George A.
Harrison, Alfred E.
Haugland, George
Helgeson, Boyd
Hershey, Hiram R.
Hessler, Charles T.
Hinds, John S.
Hine, Benjamin
Hoar, Irvine
Holm, Theodore A.
Holmberg, Frank A.
Holstein, Herman G.
Houck, James F.

Jacobs, James T.
Jebb, Anthony L.
Johnson, Theodore

Kline, Louis F.
Kyte, Harry J.

Lane, George A.
Larson, Chris
Lawson, Oscar A.
Leidholm, Edward
Lindell, Otto A.
Linnell, Albert T.

Madson, Louis
Marshall, Lewis C.
Masters, George H.
Maynard, William R.
McCabe, Edward J.
McCarthy, William M.
McCracken, T. H.
Mickelson, Louis A.
Miller, Herman F.
Monagahn, Charles F.
Morrison, Joseph G.

Nelson, Albert C.
Nelson, August
Nelson, Nels P.
Nelson, Waldemar W.

O'Hearn, William
Olmstead, William A.
Olson, Paul Herbert
Olson, Thomas
O'Mara, John J.

Palm, Reuben
Parin, Henry C.
Peterson, Frank A.
Peterson, Hans C.
Peterson, John A.
Peterson, Peter M.
Peterson, Victor C.
Pettit, Theodore
Platt, Earl Leroy
Prothers, Charles
Pushar, Forest

Quinn, Joseph H.

Rausch, Peter.
Reha, Louis
Reveling, Erick
Ribb, Olof
Ryan, John J.

Samstad, Walter W.
Sanstad, Andrew
Scart, John O.
Schrag, Elind J.
Schultz, Fred D.
Schultz, Louis
Sodergren, Olof L.
Sorenson, Louis
Steele, John
Stillman, Guy L.
Stockstad, Christian
Stone, Royal A.
Sullivan, Eugene
Summers, Fred
Sundahl, Ole M.
Swanson, Robert W.
Swanson, Richard, W.

Thompson, Morris
Troup, Fred

Weisen, Joseph
Wells, James P.
Williams, Oscar
Wolf, Rufus F.
Worman, Charles
Wynn, Peter

Young, Clarence

THE WORLD WAR

April 6, 1917 — November 11, 1918

In the compilation of this history the aid of the Adjutant General's department of Minnesota and the War Department at Washington was sought in an effort to secure a complete roster of those who responded to their country s call in the World War. It was found that no such record is in existence. The historically minded citizens of the county expressed a desire that the names of these service men and women should be recorded. With that purpose in mind, the compiler searched the files of Meeker County newspapers, secured the aid of the American Legion and the Veterans of Foreign Wars, and presents the following roster with apologies for any names omitted, or any other errors that may have occurred in its compilation. In this effort the writer is indebted to the Legion Posts of the county and other patriotic organizations for assistance rendered. The files of the Litchfield Review and Independent have been an invaluable aid in the work.

WORLD WAR ROSTER

Adams, Arthur
Ailie, Charles W.
Adams, Earl J.
Adams, Sam
Ahlsted, Harry O.
Ahlstrom, Adolph G.
Ahlstrom, Edwin
Amdahl, Conrad
Amundson, Ernest
Amundson, Lawrence
Anders, R. J.
Anderson, Albert
Anderson, Algot
Anderson, Alvin
Anderson, August
Anderson, Augustine
Anderson, Axel
Anderson, Andrew B.
Anderson, Arthur E.
Anderson, Arthur G.
Anderson, Axel W. B.
Anderson, Bernard
Anderson, Bernard A
Anderson, Bert G.
Anderson, Benford M.
Anderson, Carl A.
Anderson, Chas. A.
Anderson, Chester A.
Anderson, Clarence E.
Anderson, Carl E.
Anderson, Carl Oscar
Anderson, Carl W.
Anderson, Clarence O.
Anderson, David
Anderson, Erick G.
Anderson, Ernest
Anderson, Ernest E.
Anderson, Edward P.
Anderson, Edward John
Anderson, Elmer Olin
Anderson, E. S.
Anderson, Elmer W.
Anderson, E. (Nurse)
Anderson, Floyd
Anderson, Frank
Anderson, Fredrick N.
Anderson, Fred W.
Anderson, Henry W.
Anderson, John A.
Anderson, Joseph Emil
Anderson, Melvin
Anderson, Nels
Anderson, Otto
Anderson, Oscar
Anderson, Oscar E.
Anderson, Oscar H.
Anderson, Oscar W.
Anderson, Peter
Anderson, Reuben
Anderson, Rudolph
Anderson, Victor
Anderson, Willie A.
Angier, Lloyd H.
Arbogast, Clarence
Arbogast, Lawrence
Armstrong, George E.
Askeroth, Clarence M.
Asp, Albert
Aspelin, Theodore, Jr.
Bach, Frank
Bach, Leland
Baden, Art S.
Baril, Hector
Bay, William
Becker, Chas.
Becker, Frank
Becker, Fred
Becker, Joseph H.
Becker, Nicholas S.
Becker, William P.
Beckstrand, George
Beckstrand, Irenus
Beerling, Anthony
Beerling, Herman C.
Bergerson, Gulbrand
Bergquist, Arthur
Bergquist, Arvid
Bergquist, John
Bergfalk, Victor
Belin, Lewis E.
Bell, Robert John
Bellquist, Oscar Wm.
Benson, Arthur
Benson, August W.
Benson, Carl
Benson, Edward E.
Benson, Harry Ben
Benson, Harvey C.
Benson, Ida (Nurse)
Benson, Joseph
Benson, Lewis E.
Benson, Victor Ed.
Benson, William Ed.
Berg, Albin N.
Berg, Ellis
Berglund, Alfred
Bernatson, Harry A.
Berry, Roy J.
Besonen, John A.
Besser, Conrad
Bierman Alfred

Bierman, Bernie
Blood, Walter
Boeck, Fred E.
Bokander, August A.
Bokander, Robert
Boquist, John G.
Boren, Carl Herbert
Boren, Edgar Willard
Boren, Fritz Arthur
Boyer, Claude
Boyer, John C.
Boyer, Marion
Booth, Walter N.
Brandley, John E.
Brandley, James I.
Brasie, Frank
Bredeson, Aldrich
Bresden, George C.
Brewster, Edward V.
Breznow, Andrew
Broberg, Claude A.
Broberg, E. F.
Broman, Joseph E.
Brooks, Lloyd A.
Brown, A. J.
Brown, Earl
Bruner, Andrew
Bruner, George
Bruner, Mike C.
Brunner, Sverge
Brynteson, Wm. C.
Buckley, Ed. Lee
Burdick, Alvin E.
Burdick, Charles
Burns, John L.

Caineen, George
Campbell, Patrick J.
Carlson, Bert
Carlson, Conrad
Carlson, Hugo W.
Carlberg C. A.
Carlson, Carl Joseph
Carlson, Frank
Carlson, Gotfred A.
Carlson, Gustaf
Carlson, Gust. M.
Carlson, Harold
Carlson, Helmer
Carlson, Henry Theo.
Carlson, Hilda, Nurse
Carlson, John W.
Carlson, Lowell
Carlson, Maurice C.
Carlson, Oscar
Carlson, Otto Edwin
Carlson, Otto Manuel
Carlson, Percy
Carlson, Reuben
Carlson, Roland

Carlson, William
Carter, Oklahoma
Casey, Peter Joseph
Caswell, Leon
Chellin, Arnold J.
Chevre, Daniel C.
Chevre, Frank J.
Christian, Peter L.
Christenson, Arthur L.
Christenson, H. W.
Christenson, Lars J.
Christenson, Peter L.
Christianson, Emanuel
Clinton, Everett
Cole Malcolm
Coleman, Theodore B.
Collier, Basil
Compton, Lemuel L.
Conson, John J.
Crider, Bert
Crider, John
Crowe, Henry
Crowe, John
Curry, E. R.

Dahlgren, Peter H.
Dahlgren, Otto
Danielson, Victor
Dahlman, Tony J.
Damuth, Fred G.
Daniels, Fred
Danielson, Chas V.
Danielson, Emil
Danielson, Gustaf C.
Danielson, Gust M.
Danielson, Herman E.
Danielson, Dr. K. A.
Danielson, Nels L. F.
Danielson, Paul Arthur
Danielson, Victor
Dart, Ivan H.
Davis, Dale
Davis, Ernest C.
Davis, George W.
Davis, Harry P.
Deneen, David
Deneen, Raymond P.
Dickson, Kenneth
Dille, Paul F.
Dille, W. O.
Dillon, Francis
Dillon, Mark
Dietel, John
Dockendorf, Nicholas
Dollerschell, William F.
Donnay, Anton
Donnay, Henry W.
Donnay, John
Donnay, Math H.
Donovan, Dr. J. J.

Dorge, R. I.
Dornsbach, Otto
Dougherty, Clifton
Drange, Adolph
Draxten, Elmer R.
Draxten, Oscar G.
Draxton, Palmer I.
Driver, Charles

Earley, Albert
Earley, George E.
Edgecomb, Ira J.
Edgecomb, Onnie
Edminster, James
Edquist, E. David
Edwards, Harry S.
Egan, Joseph M.
Ekblad, Edward
Ekland, August
Eldred, Bert
Ellis, Clarence
Ellis, Ervin H.
Ellis, Evan James
Emerson, Chester A.
Engelbrecht, Gust
Englebrekt, Oscar
Erickson, Albert
Erickson, Adolph E.
Erickson, Arthur
Erickson, Arnold
Erickson, Aaron F.
Erickson, Carl Iver
Erickson, Elmer Axel
Erickson, Eugene
Erickson, Henry D.
Evenson, Jens O.
Erickson, John E. T.
Erickson, John H.
Erickson, Lawrence
Erickson, Oscar Arthur
Erickson, Paul Arnold
Erickson, Reuben
Erickson, Victor
Erland, August
Escen, Theodore A.
Estey, George
Evans, Harry C.

Falk, Robert L.
Fallon, Albert
Fay, Francis Arthur
Ferguson, Delbert H.
Fillipe, Albin
Finkin, Nicholas
Fischer, Arthur C.
Fiske, Martin Benhard
Fitzgerald. John
Flemming, Carl Fred
Floren, Alfred
Flynn, John A.

Flynn, Thomas J.
Foley, Leo
Forslin, Nels
Forsberg, Bernard
Forsen, Hjalmer
Forsen, Walter
Fossum, Arthur
Fossum, Johan C.
Fossum, William
Fourre, George
Fourse, Mark J.
Fowler, George
Fraker, Vernon
Franzen, Adolph
Frederickson, August A
Fredrickson, Svend
Freeman, George E.
Fridner, John
Friend, Edgar R.
Fritze, Arthur
Froehling, Joseph J.
Frost, Ferdinand
Frost, Victor

Gallahue, Michael
Gayner, Arthur B.
Gayner, Karl E.
Geislinger, Albert
Gibson, Clarence O.
Gibson, George F.
Gierke, Ernest Carl
Gimderson, George B.
Glad, John
Godzala, Frank
Goemer, Chas.
Gordon, Edward
Granaham, Mark
Gregor, Edward
Grindall, William R.
Grono, Bert
Grotz, Otto
Groskreuts, William
Gulso, Arthur
Gunn, Art
Gunn, Carl E.
Gunn, John
Gunderson, Alvin
Gunter, John Ernest
Gunter, Voice Virgil
Gustavson, W. A.
Gutte, Emil F.

Haagenson, Haagen M
Haapala, Isaac
Habisch, John A.
Haagenson, Ole E.
Hahn, Theodore
Hakkola, Hjalmer
Haley, John A.
Hallberg, Edwin Olof

Halverson, Harry B.
Halverson, LeRoy
Halverson, Oliver B.
Halverson, Wilton Lee
Hammer, Geo. E.
Hammer, Sidney R.
Hammerlund, Oscar L.
Hammerstein, F. R.
Hankey, Raymond T.
Hanley, Jas. A.
Hannula, John L.
Hannan Eddie
Hannan, John Francis
Hannan, Patrick
Hanson, Albert E.
Hanson, Arthur W.
Hanson, C. O.
Hanson, Hans C.
Hanson, John
Hanson, Lewis
Hanson, Oscar
Hanson, Ray A.
Hanson, Roy
Harder, Joseph Carl
Harrie, Chas. F.
Hartman, Emanuel
Hatch, A. J.
Hatch, Harry M.
Haugland, George
Hagglund, **Herbert**
Harper, Benjamin H.
Hauser, George
Hawes, Glen
Hawkins, Thomas E.
Hawkinson, V. E.
Hedtke, Oscar
Henneman, Robert
Heenan, Oscar D.
Hegg, Lloyd Percy
Heil, Louis
Heil, W. L.
Heinricks, Anton
Helgeson, Boyd
Helgeson, Gail
Helgeson, Joseph A.
Hellvig, Albert
Helgeson, A.
Hendrickson, Albert
Hendrickson, Kareluis
Henke, Emil O.
Henke, William
Herman, Arthur J.
Hermian, Oscar D.
Hermola, Isaac W.
Hess, Jake
Hess, Walter Carl
Hibarger, Leslie R.
Hicks, Fred G.
Hicks, Percival
Hillstrom, Carl

Hinck, Harry J.
Hjulberg, Ernest
Hjulberg, Fred
Hoffies, John
Hogan, Robert E.
Hokkola, Hjalmer
Holcomb, Jesse E.
Hollands, Harold
Holm, Emil A. L.
Holm, Ernest G. W.
Holmgren, Leonard H.
Holmgren, William E.
Holmquist, Edward
Holtz, Paul
Horton, Ruth (Nurse)
Horton, Donald
Huro, Walter C.
Housman, Alva R.
Hovey, Harris
Hovey, Lewis M.
Hoyes, Eliza E., Nurse
Huberty, John P.
Huberty, William
Huckenpoehler, B.
Hull, Robert Guy
Hultman, Isaac Ludvig
Humola, John Leonard
Humola, William
Hunter, Dwight A.
Huro, E. W.
Hutton, Isaac F.

Insberg, Arthur L.
Irvine, Perry

Jarl, Frank Gustave
Jebb, Anthony L.
Jebb, Thomas G.
Jensen, Christ
Jepson, David
John, Carl
Johns Jerome
Johnson, Albert
Johnson, Albin E.
Johnson, Alfred
Johnson, Arthur
Johnson, Albert V.
Johnson, Algot Victor
Johnson, Allen E.
Johnson, A. J.
Johnson, Anton E.
Johnson, Arthur B.
Johnson, Bernard
Johnson, Carl Alfred
Johnson, Carl August
Johnson, Carl J.
Johnson, Clarence E.
Johnson, Clarence J.
Johnson, Dewey E.
Johnson, E. A.

Johnson, Edward
Johnson, Edwin E.
Johnson, Edwin W.
Johnson, Elmer J.
Johnson, Enger
Johnson, Ernest
Johnson, Ernest G.
Johnson, Ervin G.
Johnson, Erwin C.
Johnson, Frank V.
Johnson, George R.
Jones, Fred
Johnson, Harry E.
Johnson, Henry E.
Johnson, Henry W.
Johnson, K. A.
Johnson, Luther
Johnson, L. Dewey
Johnson, Ludvig J.
Johnson, Joseph
Johnson, J. Arthur
Jorgenson, Ole
Johnson, Orphie
Johnson, Oscar C.
Johnson, Otto Alexius
Johnson, Oscar Edwin
Johnson, Olaf J.
Johnson, Palmer O.
Johnson, Reuben A.
Johnson, Sidney
Johnson, Victor
Johnson, William
Jones, John Ed.
Jones, Merton

Kaddatz, A. E.
Kalibe, P. A. C.
Kaisalahti, Walter
Kain, Claude
Kaufman, Martin
Kellevig, Thor
Kelsin, Harold P.
Keenan, Emmet
Keenan, Walter
Ketter, Albert
Kinlund, Carl
Kinkade, Clarence
Kinkade, Elliott
Kinkade, John
Kinkade, Ray
Kinlund, Victor
Klein, Leo M.
Kling, Anton G.
Kling, Oscar
Kline, John Elmer
Kline, Louis F.
Knight, James Bert
Knutson, Thomas
Koenig, Paul
Kohls, Emil

Kohls, Herman
Kohen, Joseph W.
Konitzko, Theodore
Konshak, John
Kopplin, Edwin C.
Koskie, Elmer
Kremer, Nicholas J.
Kring, Albert D.
Kruger, John C.
Kruger, Otto
Kulla, Hjalmer
Kulla, Leonard
Kunnuet, Bernard
Kuster, Henry
Kuster, William

Lagergren, Alvin
Lagergren, Oscar H.
Lahti, John
Lambach, Anton
Landeen, Adolph F.
Larson, Anton
Larson, Archie E.
Larson, Alfred E.
Larson, Arthur H.
Larson, Christ
Larson, Edward J.
Larson, Edwin
Larson, Elmer Nils
Larson, Miss G. (Nurse)
Lappa, William E.
Larson, Jady
Larson, John L.
Larson, John W.
Larson, Lars P.
Larson, Lincoln A.
Lassila, Herbert Wm.
Laurwick, Conrad P.
Lawson, Clarence A.
Lawson, Reuben W.
Leaf Arthur
Lee, Elmer A.
Lehtinen, William
Lehto, Hjalmer
Lehto, William J.
Lenhardt, Frederick J
Leonard, Wilhelm
Lepisto, Henry
Lewernz, Albert J.
Lewerenz, Emil J.
Lewerenz, Rob.
Ley, Norbert H.
Lief, William A.
Lien, John
Lien, Louis Alvin
Lies, Henry
Lindahl, Carl
Lindahl, Otto H.
Lindberg, Carl O.
Lindberg, Otto L.

Lindegren, Anton
Lindegren, August W.
Lindegren, John
Lindgren, Marinus L.
Lindgren, Reynold
Lindholm, Fredoph J.
Lindquist, Arthur
Lindquist, Arthur P.
Lindquist, Alex C.
Lindquist, Julius
Lindsey, James Curtis
Lingren, Chas. R.
Linner, Vendell
Loch, Hubert
Loessen, Paul
Lonn, Osc.
Loven, Nels W.
Lund, Harry
Lund, Walfred
Lundahl, Carl
Lundberg, Carl J.
Lundeen, Albin
Lundeen, Rudolph H.
Lundquist, Arthur L.
Luoma, Axel
Lutzke, Albert

Madson, Louis
Maetzold, Ernest
Maetzold, Henry
Magnuson, J. W.
Malm, Herbert V.
Malmquist, Henry
Manuel, Harvey J.
Marquardt, Edward
Marquard, Louis G.
Martinson, Martin Ed.
Martinson, T. A.
Mattson, Alvin R.
Mattson, Charles
Mattson, Olav
May, Joseph
Mayers, Arthur D.
McCann, Mike, Jr.
McCann, William
McCarthy, Arthur T.
McClure, Leslie
McCusker, Joe
McGraw, Bernard
McGrew, Lemuel E.
McKenzie, Elzie
McLaughlin, B. J.
McLaughlin, J. N.
McMonagle, Peter R.
McMullen, Robert
Meis, Peter V.
Mennan, Oscar Dennis
Mentzior, Matthew
Merrick, C. W. H.
Meyers, Ervin E.

Michaelson, Victor
Mickelson, Victor
Mikkelson, Anders
Miller, Clarence H.
Miller, Charles Victor
Miller, Edwin
Miller, John
Miller, Paul M.
Miller, William H.
Minar, H. J.
Minor, Alvin
Mitchell, Charles
Martinson, Harry
Moe, Oscar Gustav
Monson, George Emil
Morse, Frank
Mortenson, Arthur
Mortenson, Albert A.
Mortenson, Ed. M. C.
Mortenson, Guy P.
Mortenson, Morris
Mortenson, Morten
Mortenson, Otto C.
Mortenson, Walter H.
Moser, Matthew
Mullen, John A.
Mulville, William
Mulville, Walter H.
Murnane, John D.
Murphy, Francis C.
Murphy, J.
Myrman, Fred
Myrman, Gustaf M.

Neidermeier, George
Neidermeier, Phillip
Nelson, Adolph
Nelson, Allan
Nelson, Albert V.
Nelson, Ernest Ed.
Nelson, Edward
Nelson, Elmer
Nelson, Elmer A.
Nelson, Emil L.
Nelson, Enoch
Nelson, George O.
Nelson, Harold
Nelson, Harvey
Nelson, Herbert G.
Nelson, Joel N. H.
Nelson, Louis F.
Nelson, Lloyd M.
Nelson, Mabel (Nurse)
Nelson, Nels F.
Nelson, Nathan H.
Nelson, Orville
Nelson, Olof N.
Nelson, Oscar R.
Nelson, Robert W.
Nelson, Sidney
Nelson, Soren

Nelson, Theodore N.
Ness, Melvin O.
Nett, Albert A.
Neu, Michael H.
Neumeyer, Arthur H.
Neusinger, Richard J.
Newcomb, Bert I.
Newman, Henry M.
Nistler, H. N.
Nordstrom, Elmer
Norgren, Albert Carl
Norgren, Frank W.
Norgren, Henry T.
Norin, Axel
Norin, Erick
Nystrom, Walfred

O'Connor, Jay
O'Connor, Thomas R.
O'Keefe, Dave
O'Keefe, Maurice
O'Keefe, William
Okeson, Willie G.
Olson, Albin
Olson, Alvin Chester
Olson, Alvin Oliver
Olson, Allan R.
Olson, Earl W.
Olson, Louis A.
Olson, Nels
Olson, Otto L.
Olson, Oscar Sigfred
Olson, Otis S.
Olson, Paul Herbert
Olson, Sideny A.
Olson, Samuel L.
Olson, Walter B.
Ornberg, Harry N.
Osberg, Walter Otto
O'Shea, William B.
Olson, August S.
Olson, Charlie O.
Olson, Clarence
Olson, Conrad O.
Olson, Earl
Olson, Edgar
Olson, Edward
Olson, Einer E.
Olson, George
Olson, Henry Walter
Olson, Hilding
Olson, John Bernard
Olson, John H.
Olson, Joseph
Olson, Lewis A.
Olson, Lewis Cogswell
Olson, Levi A.
Olson, Oliver N.
Olson, Oscar E.
Olson, Robert
Olson, Rudolph

Oman, Clarence H.
O'Neal, John
Ornberg, Harry W.
Oslund, Arnold
Oslund, P. V.
Osterberg, Gerhard H.
Pallansch, A. F. W.
Pallmer, Carl Albert
Pallmer, Raymond
Palm, Albert
Palm, Reuben
Palm, Simon
Palmer, A. R.
Pancake, John Leslie
Pancake, Lindsay
Parsons, George E.
Parsons, Elmer
Paul, Edward
Paul, Leonard
Paulson, Earl A. F.
Paulson, Nels Oscar
Paulson, David W.
Pearson, A. N.
Pearson, Geo. Edward
Pearson, Harry E.
Pederson, Valdemar
Peifer, Jack
Peipus, Ferdinand
Peipus, Max F. C.
Peitz, Francis J.
Pelto, Hjalmer
Person, Nels Anton
Peters, George P.
Peters, Rudolph C.
Peters, Jess
Peterson, Albert
Peterson, Alfred E.
Peterson, Arthur I.
Peterson, Arthur J.
Peterson, A. N.
Peterson, Bernard
Peterson, David
Peterson, G. Marmus
Peterson, Gustav M.
Peterson, Hans C.
Peterson, Harry A.
Peterson, John Julius
Peterson, Nels A.
Peterson, Oscar
Peterson, Paul B.
Peterson, Peter
Peterson, Soren
Peterson, Walter L.
Peterson, William
Petzel, William C.
Platt, Earl Leroy
Pope, Ray E.
Post, Jack
Prieve, George
Putnam, Dr. F. E.

Putzier, Herbert E.
Putzier, Lloyd Henry
Putzier, Louis

Quist, Ed
Quist, Elmer A.

Rahn, H.
Rasmusson, Rasmus M.
Rausch, Peter
Reinke, Adolph
Reinke, Henry Fred
Reinke, Herman
Reder, John
Richland, George N.
Rick, Charles F.
Ringdahl, Oscar W.
Ringdahl, R. (Nurse)
Risdall, Gerhard R.
Risdall, Julius, G.
Risdall, Melvin B.
Robbs, Ernest
Robertson, Dr. Carl J.
Robertson, Elford J.
Robertson, Dr. W. P.
Robison, Sherrill
Ross, Bert
Ross Ed. Lewis
Rosengren, August O.
Routsinoja, William J.
Robin, Henry Martin
Rothlisberger, Floyd
Rudberg, Arvid
Ruhland, George N.
Ruud, Adolph, M.
Runquist, Stanley
Ryan, Arthur J.
Ed. Ryan
Ryan, Frank
Ryan, Jennings

Sa, Boyd Einer
Saari, Walter
Sallberg, John
Salmela, Arvid
Salmonson, Ray. W.
Samstad, Bennel G.
Samsted, Elmer L.
Samstad, Walter W.

Sandberg, Arthur F.
Sandberg, William
Sanders, John F.
Sangren, Raymond
Sattler, Grover
Sattler, John Joseph
Schaeffer, William
Scherer, Helen (Nurse)
Schilo, Alvis J.
Schilo, Joseph A.
Schlueter, Emil
Schlueter, Leo
Schmidt, William M.
Schmit, Nick, L.
Schmitz, Thomas
Schreiner, Joseph
Schultz, Alfred Robert
Schumacher, Tony
Scott, Lloyd H.
Servine, E. V.
Servin, Alb. Ed.
Servin, Axel
Servin, Herman B.
Settergren, Alex
Settergren, Arthur
Settergren, Harry
Settergren, V. E.
Sexton, Romeo
Shaleen, Arthur
Shaleen, Louis
Sikkala, Hjalmer
Silverberg, Clarence E.
Simmons, Ernest H.
Sisk, Irving
Sisson, Charles
Sisson, William
Sjoquist, Harry R.
Sjoquist, Henry
Smith, Charles K.
Smith, Frank A.
Smith, Martin
Smith, William
Snell, Arthur James
Soder, Elmer C.
Soder, Gilbert O.
Soltow, Ernest Frank
Sorvari, Michael S.
Sovari, W. J.
Standish, James
Steffen, A. (Nurse)

Stein, Walfred
Stelton, George
Stewart, Ira Daniel
Stewart, Fred E.
Strandberg, Joel J.
Straus, Joseph John
Strom, Arthur
Strom, Clarence
Summers, Fred
Sundell, Arthur
Sundquist, Arthur P.
Sveen, Bernard C.
Swanson, Arthur H.
Swanson, Ben
Swanson, Carl E.
Swanson, Carl V.
Swanson, Robert W.
Swanson, Richard
Swanson, Sandie

Tatz, Gustav
Teberg, Ernest J.
Teberg, Lawrence
Tellers, Joseph A.
Tellers, Joseph T.
Teicher, Joe
Templin, C. John
Tiller, William A.
Thielen, Michael
Thompson, Alfred M.
Thompson, Einert
Thompson, Oscar B.
Thompson, John L.
Thorne, Olof
Thurman, Henry
Tintes, Hubert
Tuman, Fredrick
Tvert, Thomas G.
Tviet, T. J.

Valine, Frans
Van, Vleet W. H.

Waataja, Andrew
Waataja, Elmer
Waataja, Richard
Waaterja, Elmer A.
Wahlberg, Oskar
Walls, Walter H.
Wallberg, August E.

Warner, John T.
Warren, Carl E.
Warren, John M.
Wartman, George H.
Wartman, Carl
Wayrynen, J. Ed.
Weeks, Harold
Weimmer, George
Weisen, Joseph
Welch, Amos L.
Wendorf, Frank
Wendroth, Herman W.
Werner, Fred
Westerberg, Hjalmer
Westerberg, Martin
Westberg, Swan H.
Whalen, Thomas D.
Wharton, Roscoe
Wheeler, Arthur A.
Whitaker, Roger
Whitaker, Dr. V. D.
Williams, Alvah E.
Williams Clyde
Williams, Harry
Williams Ray
Wiesanen, Kalb H.
Wiisanen, Hjalmer
Wimmer, Louis
Winter, Mathias
Wolover, Henry N.
Wortz, George Ed.
Wortz, Louis R.
Wreisner, Ade.
Wreisner, Arthur
Wreisner, Hjalmer
Wreisner, Joseph
Wreisner, Richard
Wright, Newell
Wuotila, George
Wuollet, Harry
Wuollet, Leonard

Yerks, Emil
Yerks, Erick
Young, Leon O.

Zabel, Arthur H.
Zimmerman, Leo

WORLD WAR FINANCIAL SUPPORT

Meeker County nobly supported the government in all its varied appeals for financial aid in the conduct of the war. In all the Liberty Loan drives the county exceeded its quota with the exception of the Fifth or Victory Loan.

The total amount raised in the first four loans is as follows:

First, $294,000; Second, $512,400; Third, $843,200; Fourth, $1,185,000; War Savings Stamps, $412,000, an aggregate total investment in government securities of $3,246,600.

In the Fourth Liberty Loan there were 5,300 subscribers which was 30 per cent of the population of the county at that time. The village of Dassel showed a subscription of $90 per person. Litchfield village was a close second with $85 per individual. The average for the entire country was a trifle under $55 per capita. The contribution to various organizations, Y.M.C.A., Salvation Army, Red Cross, and Knights of Columbus totaled $65,000.

THE VICTORY LOAN

The Fifth or Victory Loan fell somewhat short of the quota allotted Meeker County which was $835,000. The subscriptions exceeded $700,000 but the exact figures are not obtainable but it is definitely stated that the following towns and villages subscribed amounts exceeding the quotas allotted: Villages of Dassel, Grove City, and Watkins. Towns of Collinwood, Danielson, Dassel, Swede Grove, and Union Grove.

Sibley Avenue During World War Period
Litchfield, Minnesota

THE END OF THE WAR

The signing of the Armistice took place November 11, 1918. It was the occasion of impromptu celebrations in every town, city, and hamlet throughout the entire nation. Litchfield and the villages of Meeker County were not backward in expressing their joy and satisfaction in the termination of the war.

The Litchfield News Ledger in glaring first page headlines announced the event in their issue of November 14, 1918 as follows:

Peace on Earth
Good Will Toward Men
The Earth's Kingdoms Crumble
and Freedom's Banner Floats
Triumphant Over the World

Hohenzollern Bandits Bend the Suppliant
Knee to Individual Freedom and Progression

Unconditional Surrender is What Royalty
Had to Swallow

Greatest Day in World's History, Surrender on the Lord's Day at 5 p. m. Sunday, November 10, 1918. Firing Ceased at 11 p. m. To be Commemorated Throughout Future Ages.

NELSAN-HORTON POST NO. 104, AMERICAN LEGION DRUM AND BUGLE CORPS

(Martin B. Peterzen, Drum Major and Manager)

The Drum Corps has a deserved state-wide reputation, having given exhibitions at Minneapolis, Duluth, Winona, St. Cloud, Rochester, Brainerd, Bemidji and many of the smaller cities of the state. It has won first honors at the state and sixth and seventh district conventions of the American Legion. Their equipment represents an expenditure of $3,500. Martin B. Peterzen has served as drum major and business manager since its organization in January 1929.

WORLD WAR ORGANIZATIONS

There are five Legion Posts in Meeker County located in the villages of Litchfield, Dassel, Eden Valley, Cosmos and Watkins. The Veterans of Foreign Wars are represented in Litchfield and Grove City. These organizations are an active force in their several communities in teaching the lessons of patriotism and the obligations of all citizens to state, nation and community.

The Nelsan-Horton Post of the American Legion at Litchfield is the oldest patriotic organization growing out of the World War. Its charter bears the date, August 19, 1919. It was named to honor the memory of Orville A. Nelsan and Donald Horton, two of Litchfield's exemplary young men. They enlisted in the United States Marine Corps, April 19, 1917 and continued in that unit of service during their period of the war. They landed in France, August 20, 1917; entered the trenches March 31, 1918 (Easter Sunday) and were transferred to Marne, May 23. They participated in the bloody warfare at Chatteau Thierry.

Orville Nelsan was killed in action June 6, 1918 and his remains were returned to the United States and buried with military honors in Lake Ripley Cemetery.

Donald C. Horton was killed in action, June 23, 1918. The body was returned to the United States and interred in Arlington Cemetery at Washington, D. C.

The Nelsan-Horton Post, in the early period of its organization had a membership of 384 World War Veterans, but due to the establishment of Posts in neighboring villages has an average annual membership of 100. The community takes pride in their memorial (recreational) park on the east shore of Lake Ripley. This is one of the Post's major accomplishments which has received the commendation of the state organization.

POINTS OF HISTORIC INTEREST

There are several points of marked historic interest in Meeker County that have no permanent marking. Among those deserving of such attention are the following: Location of the Forest City Stockade, Location of the First Flour Mill in Minnesota west of the Mississippi river, Kingston townsite; Location of the first white man's cabin in Meeker County, Harvey Township; Location of the Manannah Massacre and the points where Caleb Sanborn, Andrew Olson and Daniel Cross were killed by Indians. A hugh boulder with a bronze plate attached giving a brief mention of its import would be sufficient. In the judgment of the writer this would be a desirable project to engage the attentions of the patriotic societies of Meeker County.

Our Honored Dead

Veterans of the Civil War

"No more the bugle calls the weary one
Rest noble spirits in thy graves unknown.
I'll find you and know you among the
good and true
When a robe of white is given for that
faded coat of blue."

LAKE RIPLEY CEMETERY, Litchfield.

Sol. Almquist, A. J. Anderson, C. L. Angell, H. N. Angier, John Angier, J. B. Atkinson. Dr. J. H. Bacon, O. C. Bissell, George Boner, J. C. Braden, W. H. Branham, E. A. Briggs, E. R. Brooks, Arthur Brown.   O. H. Campbell, George Chapman, J. D. Chapman, William Christopher, E. E. Cole, James Collier, O. W. Collier, John Conson, Frank Crosby, Isaac Crosby.   Frank Daggett, Albert H. DeLong, James Davis, Ransom Davis, Charles Dougherty.   E. M. Eastman, Nicholas Eberts.   A. F. Foster, J. M. Foster, Clinton Frazier, Charles Friend.   C. A. Gilman, Samuel Gleason, John Gordon, William Gordon.   Lars Hanson, John Harper, V. H. Harris, Nelson Hart, J. B. Hatch, Elias Hinds, J. M. Howard, A. E. Howe, T. B. Hull.   C. H. Jenks, R. Milo Jacks, Henry Johnson, Lorenz Johnson.   V. P. Kennedy, William Koch, Aug. T. Koerner, John Knights.   Andrew Larson, James Lawton, S. W. Leavett, John Lockwood, Isaac Loyd.   N. J. March, Simon Mayer, T. W. Main, John Mattson, Henry Mead, W. H. Miller, Joseph Mills, Horace Mullen.   James Nelson.   Alonzo Olmstead, Christian Olson.   L. J. Perry, Alvin Phelps, Orrin Phelps.   Delafield Rowen.   J. B. Salisbury, Carl Schultz, Fred Schultz, Ludvig Schultz, D. A. Shelp, Job Sherman, G. H. Sholes. Van Spence, Charles Staples, Albert E. Stewart, C. H. Stinchfield, J. E. Stuntz.   C. M. Tileston, C. G. Topping.   Robert Vorys, O. B. Vose.   W. J. Willis, C. M. Windle, R. A. Wheeler, J. A. Whitaker, Paris Whiting.

CALVARY CATHOLIC CEMETERY, Litchfield

E. A. Campbell, John Fitzgerald, M. J. Flynn, C. Koenig, William White.

FOREST CITY CEMETERIES

Jacob Brower, James Brower, Austin Brower, Peter Depue.   William Hamilton, W. B. Hammond, C. Hokenberg, Jasper Holmberg C. W. Hubbard.   Charles Keck.   William Leslie.   John Mayers.   Joseph Reynolds.   John Shoutz.   Henry Welch, George Wortz, John Wortz.

CATHOLIC CEMETERY (Darwin): Richard Fourre, Michael Roberts, Peter Stiren.

MANANNAH CEMETERY, Union Grove

John Brown, Thomas Chrystal, Curtis Clark, C. L. Houghton, Louis Koch, James McCarney, Patrick McCarney, Peter McIntyre, Charles Maybee, Edward Murphy, William Porter, John C. Regan, Charles Shepherd, J. W. Torrey, William Towler, Martin Welch, Chauncey Wilson.

ARNDAHL CHURCH CEMETERY: William Hanson, O. K. Nelson, Paul Paulson.

KIMBALL CEMETERY: Adam Brower, Moses H. Crusenberry, Charles Peabody.

NESS CHURCH CEMETERY: Jacob Anderson, Carl Hanson Bye, Even Evenson, L. Jenson, E. Jenson, Amos Nelson Fosen.

EDEN VALLEY CEMETERY

George Arnold, J. L. Chadwick, H. G. Charles, R. G. Charles, Morgan Driver, Rudolph Enderle, John Fick, J. Goble, William Grimmel, J. Groves, G. Hamilton, D. J. Hanscom, James Jones, Mr. Jones, Enoch Leavett, James McIntyre, Albert Nichols, Alb Nichols, Edward Oven, J. S. Reeves, William Rogers, William Shoemate, George Thomas, C. Tschimperle, William Wierner, Asa Wilson, Philander Wixon, F. Zearl.

GROVE CITY CEMETERIES

(Swedish Lutheran) O. M. Linnell.   (Norwegian Lutheran) Carl Waller.

SWAN LAKE CEMETERY, Dassel: Isaac N. Russell, Wells Tuman.

GREENLEAF CATHOLIC CEMETERY: Daniel McGraw, Michael Mcgraw, Ed Goff..

SPRING GROVE CEMETERY, Cedar Mills

Noah Felt, B. J. Hawkins, C. B. Jordan, N. D. Merrill, Andrew Smith.

BURR OAK CEMETERY, Union Grove

Smith Flanders, W. P. Hanson, Abner Marshall, A. G. Petrie, J. J. Stump.

GERMAN LUTHERAN CHURCH CEMETERY, North of Atwater

William Dameron, Valentine Hurr, William Miar, Emmanuel Reyff.

KINGSTON CEMETERY

Simon Brockway, Ozias DeCoster, Henry Freeman, Alex Grove, T. D. Groves, C. Hohenberg, James H. Miller, J. H. Miller, Andrew Simonson, Charles Shea, Dagman, George Robinson, J. C. Thomas, Nelson Turner, John Smith.

ATWATER CEMETERY

M. Broberg, August Davidson, John DeFoe, P. O. Hall, J. Maynard, Hover Mickelson, Charles J. Peterson, Solomon Porter, J. H. Snydam.

HARRISON CEMETERY

Granville Abbott, N. P. Aspinwell, Martin Halverson, Johnson Harris, William Hull, Albert Sperry, David Stuart, C. M. Vandyne

DASSEL CEMETERY

C. B. Dunn (confederate), Alvin Boyer, E. Collins, Presley Chaney, Robert Dalton, R. T. Elliott, William O. Eldred, R. F. Ferguson, Joseph Goding, Edward Gibney, H. Harland, Tayler Johnson, Noah Parks, James Patterson, T. H. Pendergast, Joel Robinson, Luther Tuman, John A. Quick, Samuel Quick, Peter Yorrick.

DARWIN CEMETERIES:

Michael Roberts, Peter Stiren, Richard Fourre, Michael T. Wynn.

Collinwood Cemetery, Thomas Bogart; **Beckville Cemetery,** Charles Johnson; **Arlington Cemetery, Washington, D. C.,** F. V. DeCoster; **Cannon Falls Cemetery,** T. G. Crump; **Lakewood Cemetery, Minneapolis,** Dr. F. E. Bissell; **Watkins Cemetery,** A. D. Spaulding.

Veterans of Spanish American War

LAKE RIPLEY CEMETERY

Ernest W. Campbell, William Davis, Aldine C. Eastman, Charles Forberg, Frank Holm, Theodore Holm, Andy Ingeman, Fred Schultz, Bert Tyleson, Clarence E. Young.

Veterans of the World War

"Take up our quarrel with the foe
To you from falling hands we throw
The torch, be yours to hold it high
If ye break faith with us who die,
We shall not sleep though poppies grow
In Flanders Field."

— John McRae.

LAKE RIPLEY CEMETERY

Ethel Anderson (Nurse), George V. Coombs, Vernon Fraker, Clarence Gibson, George Gibson, Earl Gulso, Roy A. Hanson, L. Dewey Johnson, Claude Kane, Milford H. Kennedy, Vendell Linner, Reynold Lindgren, Archie Larson, Arthur Mortenson, Albert A. Mortenson, Guy Mortenson, Herman Mundt, Arthur Nelson, Herbert Nelson, Carl Albert Palmer, Raymond Palmer, W. P. Robertson, Ray Sangren, William Smith, Alfred C. Skappel, Amanda Stephen-Powell (Nurse), John Storm, Frans Valine, Merrill D. Wanvig, Orville Nelson.

ARLINGTON CEMETERY, Washington, D. C.: Donald Horton.

CALVARY CATHOLIC CEMETERY

Anthony Beerling, John J. Donovan, Ed Flynn, Arthur Ryan, Jennings Ryan, Ambrose J. Flynn.

GROVE CITY CEMETERIES

(Swedish Lutheran), Frank Carlson, Ed Mortenson, Harry Ornberg.
(Baptist) Victor E. Erickson, Hector Baril.

DASSEL CEMETERY

Arthur Benson, *Paul F. Dille, *Theodore E. Dahlgren, James Edminster, *J. Lindhult Fredolph, Herbert Lassila, *Edward Paul, *Albert Servin, H. B. Servin, Louis Shaleen.

LAKE JENNIE CEMETERY: Arthur Settergren, Alex Settergren

CATHOLIC CEMETERY, Watkins

Joseph J. Froehling, Otto Grotz, John P. Huberty, Joseph May, Peter V. Mies, John T. Post, Peter Rausch, Joseph A. Schillo, George F. Stelton, Carl T. Wartman.

Private cemetery joining Catholic cemetery at Watkins: Alonzo Spaulding.

Abandoned cemetery in Section 3, Township 121, Range 30: Simpson Anderson.

Cemetery between Watkins and Eden Valley on Highway No. 55: James W. Polk, Philander Wixon, John Walters.

St. John's Catholic Cemetery, Darwin, Bernard McGraw; **Greenleaf Catholic Cemetery,** Arthur McGraw; **St. Gertrude Catholic Cemetery, Forest City,** Thomas F. Branley, J. A. Flynn, John D. Murname; **Forest City Cemetery,** Sigfrid Oscar Olson; **Arndahl Church Cemetery,** Ernest E. Anderson, Lars Christenson; **Ness Church Cemetery,** Oliver Halverson; **Beckville Church Cemetery,** John B. Fridner; **Salem Cemetery, Cosmos,** Andrew B. Anderson, John Glad; **Swedish Lutheran Church Cemetery, Rosendale,** Arthur I. Peterson; **Spring Grove Cemetery, Cedar Mills,** James Standish; **North Kingston Cemetery,** John Crider; **Manannah Cemetery, Union Grove,** Thomas Hawkins, James Christle; **Ellsworth Public Cemetery,** William Henke; **Lake Arvilla Cemetery,** Elmer Erickson.

TRINITY CHURCH, LITCHFIELD
(Episcopal)

Schools and Churches

SCHOOL HOUSE, DISTRICT NO. 43

EARLY PUBLIC SCHOOLS

The pioneer schools of Meeker County were held in the first instance in private homes and small log structures which were succeeded by crude frame buildings. The furnishings were usually made of native lumber by a local carpenter. Sections of the walls were painted coal black to serve as blackboards. A framed bed of sand served in lieu of zinc under the stove and children buried their ink bottles therein to prevent freezing. The first school building in Litchfield is pictured on page 112. This was termed a subscription school in which the patrons and citizens met the expense of its maintenance. This modest structure is in marked contrast to the present grade and high school building constructed in 1930 at an expenditure of $225,000 exclusive of grounds and equipment.

The improved conditions of the present day are in marked contrast with the educational facilities of the early years. The school houses are of modern construction, well lighted and ventilated and the furnishings are of the best. The teacher has all essential maps, charts and reference books needed in the teaching of the varied subjects. The schools are well graded and the eighth grade graduates are equipped to enter our state accredited high schools without examination. Many of the school houses have a modern heating system, electric lights, piano and telephone and serve as civic centers for the community.

RURAL SCHOOLS

There are six superior state accredited ungraded elementary schools in Meeker County. An accredited school meets the state required standards in equipment, a nine months' term of instruction, an adequate and well kept building and the teachers must have had superior training for their work. The schools complying with these requirements that have won the distinction of being rated among the accredited schools of the state are: Districct 1, Kingston townsite; 2, Forest City townsite; 28, Manannah township; 36, Union Grove township and numbers 50 and 72 in Danielson township.

The schools in the following districts have an enrollment requiring the services of more than one teacher: Number 1, 3 teachers and the following schools are served by two teachers to each school, Districts 2, 43, 52, 60 and 93. The rural schools of the county are under the supervision of the County Superintendent of schools, Miss Ruth Peterson.

HIGH SCHOOLS

There are four state accredited high schools in the county and pupils in the several schools in the county are conveyed to the high schools by buses and all the pupils of the county are provided with equal educational opportunities.

Litchfield High School

The Litchfield school has a staff of forty-six teachers and seven other persons including nurse, secretaries and janitors are carried on the pay roll. Thirty-six school districts and parts of eleven other districts are served by the high school. It compares favorably with the high schools in metropolitan centers. There are more than 1,200 pupils enrolled in the school system.

Grove City High School

The Grove City High School is the pride of the citizens of the village and is a modern structure well equipped to meet the educational needs of the territory it serves. The curriculum includes all the constants outlined by the State Department of Education. The auditorium serves as a civic center for the community and the teachers are active assistants in social and church activities.

Dassel High School

The Dassel High School is a modern structure of an attractive type of architecture and fulfils the needs of the districts served. The curriculum meets all the requirements of the State Department of Education. Their teaching staff is chosen with great care and contribute liberally to the social life of the community and the character building of the youth entrusted to their care.

Eden Valley High School

The present Eden Valley High School building was erected in 1927 but the village high school was established in 1901. Including the grades seven teachers are carried on the pay roll and a full-time custodian is employed. The enrollment is 200 and the 1939 graduating class numbers 24. The course of study meets all state requirements.

ST. ANTHONY PAROCHIAL SCHOOL, WATKINS, MINN.

PAROCHIAL SCHOOLS

Parochial schools exist in Eden Valley and Watkins. The Eden Valley school is sponsored by the Assumption Catholic Church in the Stearns County section of that village and the Watkins school is connected with the Parish of St. Anthony. These schools are very efficient and the faculty consists of Sisters of Charity especially trained for their work. Their course of study qualifies the pupils for entrance to the high schools of the county.

The Church of St. Philip at Litchfield established in 1931 the Institute of St. Philip's which gives a free kindergarten course to children of all denominations. Their course in music is open to the public with a moderate tuition charge. The religious course is open to the children of Catholic faith without charge. The Institute is in charge of five Sisters of the Order of St. Benedict.

Protestant

TRINITY PARISH
Protestant Episcopal Church

Trinity Church was founded 69 years ago at which time it was an adjunct of the Gethsemane (missionary parish) of Minneapolis. The first service was held February 13, 1870 and was conducted by Reverend D. B. Knickerbocker who later became Bishop of Indiana. In June of the same year Reverend T. G. Crump held services in the Masonic Hall.

Trinity Church was incorporated, April 10, 1871 at a meeting held in the Masonic Hall with Rev. T. G. Crump presiding.

The parish is greatly indebted to the liberality of friends for the beautiful church in which to worship. J. C. Braden gave the lots on which the church is located. Among the donors are numbered, Mrs. Ellen Anchmuty, of New York; Mrs. E. D. Litchfield, of London, England and others. These donations amounted to about $8,000. A parish school and rectory were constructed and Rev. T. G. Crump, affectionately called Parson Crump, conducted the first school which was eagerly patronized by Litchfield parents. Parson Crump was endowed with the missionary spirit and held services at intervals in the villages of Meeker and neighboring counties.

Trinity parish was admitted into union with the church council in 1871 and became self sustaining in 1891. Rev. Crump's rectorship covered a period of nineteen years of faithful service. He was succeeded by Rev. Pinkham who conducted services occasionally in the Swedish language which prompted a number of citizens of Swedish birth to affiliate with Trinity Church and many became active members. Rev. D. A. Trofteen, at a later date, established a Swedish Mission that led to the organization of the Emanuel (Swedish) Episcopal church and the erection of a church building. In 1928 there was a consolidation with Trinity Church.

Rev. Pinkham's pastorate terminated in 1892. The present rectory was built during the rectorship of Rev. W. E. Harmann which covered the period from 1918 to 1937. The parish is indebted to Bishop Keeler in the work leading to the erection of the rectory.

Trinity Parish is justly proud of its sixty-nine years of faithful Christian service and equally proud of two of its sons who entered the ministry; Rev. Elmer Lofstrom (son of Mr. and Mrs. A. H. Lofstrom) who, at the time of his death, was professor of New Testament Languages and Exegesis at the Seabury Divinity School in Faribault, Minnesota.

Rev. Elmer M. Lofstrom (son of Mr. and Mrs. A. E. Lofstrom) was baptized, confirmed, ordained and married in Trinity Church. He is serving at present as Rector of the Episcopal church at Cody, Wyoming.

Rev. Elmer E. Johnson came to Trinity Parish in May 1937 from the Diocese of Duluth where he was in charge of the Crookston field. Mr. Johnson is a native of Minnesota, having been born at Eagle Bend where he graduated from high school and later attended Carleton College and graduated 1930 from Seabury Divinity School. Previous to coming to Litchfield Rev. Johnson had served the missions at Paynesville and Glenwood and the field of International Falls, Warroad and Northome.

PRESBYTERIAN

The Presbyterian Church at Litchfield is the only existing church of that denomination in Meeker County. A temporary organization was effected January 2, 1870 under the direction of a committee from the St. Paul Presbytery.

For several months previous to this meeting citizens of that faith had gathered in the newly erected school house where services were conducted by Rev. D. B. Jackson.

The permanent organization was established March 10, 1870 with the following charter members: A. N., Mrs. Eusebia, Rachel A. and Isabella Grenier, Henry and Mrs. Mary L. Hill, Henry Wilson, Miss Martha Gibson and Rev. D. B. Jackson, pastor. The following trustees were elected: Henry Hill, A. N. Grenier and H. A. Runions.

Reverend D. B. Jackson was a concientious, Christian worker and laid the foundation for effective religious service among his members in the Litchfield community.

The present church edifice was erected in 1871 at a cost of $4,000 and a parsonage was subsequently built at an expenditure of $1,400.

Rev. D. B. Jackson was succeeded by Reverends W. C. Harding, Prescot Fay, A. J. Buel who was followed by Rev. J. S. Sherrill whose pastorate extended from 1876 to 1887 during which time the church continued to grow and prosper. He was followed in 1888 by Reverend D. E. Evans at which time the church had a membership of 94 and gave great promise of future growth and usefulness. Rev. H. M. Pressley was his successor who gave way in turn to Reverends G. C. Pollock and Sidney Stone who was succeeded in 1903 by R. C. Mitchell during whose pastorate the church was remodeled and a pipe organ was installed. He was followed in turn by H. G. Lacey, J. F. McLeod and B. M. McCullough, when in 1926 Rev. Barackman was called to the pastorate during whose period of service the manse was erected. P. C. Voris was his successor in 1931 and his ministry was terminated by his death June 14, 1934 and he was followed by the present pastor, Rev. H. H. McLeod.

THE BAPTIST CHURCH
Grove City

The Baptist Church was organized October 13, 1866 with fifteen charter members. The lot on which the church and cemetery is located covers a ten acre tract of land presented the society February 28, 1868.

A church was erected the same year. The church grew in numbers and in 1880 the present church edifice was erected, remodeled in 1899 and an addition constructed in 1915. There has been no interuption in services during subsequent years.

The first pastor was Rev. Anders Ekbom. The present pastor is Rev. William Ault.

THE CHURCH OF CHRIST

The Church of Christ often called the Christian Church was initiated at Litchfield by L. Y. Bailey (a teacher in the village school) in a series of discourses held in the school house during the summer of 1870. He was later ordained as a minister of the Christian Church.

In 1871 the church society was duly organized with L. Y. Bailey and wife, Chauncy Butler and wife, O. B. Knapp and wife, C. J. Rowley, Mrs. J. V. Branham, Jr., V. H. Harris, G. B. Lyon and others. They rented Asher's Hall where services were held prior to the erection of the church in 1873 at an original cost of $3,000.

Mr. Bailey continued to serve the church without compensation during his entire residence in Meeker County. He was succeeded by Elder Grant who served the church for about a year. Following his period of service there was no regular pastor for several years until April, 1882 when Elder E. W. Knapp took charge, followed in turn by Elder R. C. Bryant and a brief interval of inactivity when the church was without a pastor.

In March 1884 Rev. Louis A. Pier was installed as pastor and the church took on new life. He was a man of marked ability and greatly endeared himself to the members of the church and the community at large. During his pastorate the parsonage was erected.

Rev. Pier terminated his services as pastor in 1894. During the years that have elapsed the church was served by numerous pastors.

Rev. Marshall, the present pastor, is a graduate of the Minnesota Bible University (class of 1930). He was installed as pastor in January 1927. In addition to serving the congregation of the Litchfield church he serves the Christian Church in Dassel, and holds a two-weeks' meeting for some church in the brotherhood without a pastor at least once in each year.

At the present time the Litchfield church is entirely free from debt, has a membership of one-hundred and a Sunday school enrollment of seventy-five. It is generally hoped that Rev. Marshall will continue to be the leader for many years to come.

CHURCH OF CHRIST
Dassel Village

The oldest church edifice in Dassel village is used at the present time as a house of worship by what is known as the "Church of Christ." This church was erected in 1874 by the Congregationalists and maintained as such until 1885. From 1885 to 1889 it was used as a house of worship by the Christian denomination and the pulpit was supplied by Rev. Louis A. Pier, pastor of the church at Litchfield. Rev. Pier was a man of fine character and good ability. He was the founder of the Litchfield Saturday Review and later became the first president of th Christian College at Excelsior. He later severed this connection and moved to California.

During subsequent years the church was used at different intervals by the Baptists and Church of God. Since October 17, 1933, there have been regular church services. Rev. E. W. Marshall, pastor of the Litchfield Church of Christ, supplies the pulpit.

CHURCH OF GOD
(Eden Valley)

The Church of God was organized February 16, 1899 with 47 communicants. The elders elected were William Hardy, Jacob Williams; Deacons, Frank Marshall and Alfred Welliver. Lizzie C. Hanscum was chosen clerk. Elder Thoms was called as pastor and delivered his first sermon, April 23, 1899. In 1900 the present church edifice was erected. The present pastor is Rev. Jerry Cooper.

THE TRONDJHEIM CHURCH
Acton Township

The extinct church which was organized in 1861 was one of the oldest church organizations in Meeker County and at the time of its organization had a congregation of 236 men and women. The church building was moved to Atwater in 1885 and the spiritual needs of the Trondjheim community are guided by the Atwater church. The Trondjheim Church tract of ten acres is used as a church cemetery.

NESS NORWEGIAN EVANGELICAL LUTHERAN

The Ness Norwegian Evangelical Lutheran was the first organized church in Meeker County and during its earlier years served the settlers in a territory having an area of 15 to 20 square miles. Among the first interments in the church cemetery were the victims of the Acton Massacre of August 17, 1862. The first Christian service of this denomination was held in the home of O. H. Ness in the fall of 1858.

A church organization was effected October 28, 1867 with 25 charter members. On October 31, 1864 a meeting was held at the home of Iver Jackson and a tract of 40 acres in section 20, Litchfield town was purchased from Henrik Thoen for a consideration of $100. In 1870 a parsonage was built at an expenditure of $700 which was destroyed by fire in 1885. Ten acres of this tract had, previous to purchase, been set aside as a cemetery.

The present church edifice was erected in 1874 at an initial cost of $2,600. In 1917 or 1918 the parish was divided and the Ness Church was without a regular pastor until 1930 when it entered into a joint call with the Zion Church of Litchfield and the Bergen Church near Glencoe, McLeod County and chose Rev. Carl J. Field as their pastor and spiritual guide and he continues to serve these congregations at the present time.

The church organization numbers some twenty-five families and one hundred members of these families are under the spiritual guidance of Rev. Carl J. Field and the church officials.

ARNDAHL LUTHERAN

The Arndahl Norwegian Lutheran Church located in section 33 Acton town was organized at a meeting held at the home of Rasmus Nelson in section 34. The first pastor was Rev. T. H. Dahl (1869-1873).

Reverend J. Trelstad, the present pastor, has served the congregation since 1920. He was educated at the Red Wing (Minnesota) Academy and College and the Luther Seminary from which institution he was graduated in the class of 1920.

The Arndahl church communicants who have entered the ministry are Adolph Dokken, pastor of the church at Carter, Wisconsin; R. L. Falk at Maskel, Nebraska; James Falk at Rosholt, South Dakota and E. A. Evenson at Tioga, North Dakota.

In the cemetery which forms a part of the church grounds rest the mortal remains of the territorial pioneers: N. K., Peter and R. K. Brown, Soren Nelson and Birger Anderson and the Civil War veteran, William Brown.

The three acre site of the present church and cemetery was donated by Rasmus Nelson. The present church edifice was erected in 1874 and John E. Stark and John E. Johnson were awarded the contract and the building was completed the same year. During the pastorate of Rev. Trelstad the church has been modernized by the installation of a reed organ, piano, new pews and electric lights.

SWEDISH LUTHERAN
Grove City

Seventy years ago, when Minnesota was a bleak prairie dotted with tangled woods and overrun by redskins, and when Grove City was Swede Grove, a dozen pioneer families gathered at the home of Peter Lund for the purpose of carrying on the work of the Lord in the wilderness. Thus, on October 29, 1868, the Swedish Lutheran Swede Grove Congregation had its beginning.

The new congregation held its first meetings at the homes of the members, but the next year Rev. P. Beckman was called to serve as the first pastor. The services were held one Sunday each month in the section house which belonged to the railroad company. However, in 1873, three acres of land were purchased, and the first Lutheran church in Swede Grove (a small, white frame building) was constructed.

In 1874, the congregations of Atwater, Litchfield, Beckville and Swede Grove decided to combine and call Rev. Peter Dillner as their pastor. However, in 1878 the four were divided into two parishes, and in 1883 Rev. L. J. Lundquist took charge of Swede Grove and Atwater. During his stay, the total membership at Swede Grove grew to two hundred persons, and in 1885, the Sunday school was organized with J. E. Dime as the first superintendent.

Numerous changes in pastors and territory served by the church has taken place and many notable improvements made during the period from 1886 to 1929. The present church edifice was erected in 1923 during the pastorate of Rev. M. Levander. Dr. Pearson accepted the call to Grove City in 1929 and is the present pastor.

NORWEGIAN LUTHERAN

The Norwegian Lutheran church of Grove City was organized December 31, 1876 at a meeting held in the Swedish Lutheran church in Grove City as the Manannah church of that denomination. The pastor present at the organization of the meeting was Rev. H. G. Stubbs and the officers chosen were S. O. Thoen, secretary; Johannes Lyng and Thomas Olson. The meetings prior to the erection of the present church edifice were held in private homes and on one or more occasions in the barn of one of the parishoners.

The congregation numbers 138 communicants which with their families and others affiliating number over two hundred. The present pastor is Rev. Gronlud, the successor of Rev. E. R. Weeks whose pastorate covered a period of 23 years (1915-1938) during which time he endeared himself to the citizens of Grove City, irrespective of church membership.

SWAN LAKE LUTHERAN CHURCH

Dassel town was originally known as Swan Lake township.

The Swan Lake Lutheran Church was organized at the home of Louis Nelson in Section 6, Dassel town, October 14, 1873.

Rev. Fr. Peterson, pastor of the church at Cokato, was chairman and A. E. Boren, secretary. The legal name adopted at this meeting was The Swedish Evangelical Lutheran Congregation of Swan Lake Town, Meeker County, Minnesota. The S.P.&P.R.R. deeded to the church as a free gift the ten acres described as follows: The NE¼ of the NE¼ of the NE¼ in Section 5, Township 119 Range 29. A church building was located on this tract in 1874, a portion of which served as a cemetery. A detailed history of this church and its upward struggle is published in the Jubilee Album of the Lutheran Churches of the Dassel and Swan Lake communities. The present church edifice was erected in 1899 and numerous improvements have been made in its construction during subsequent years including a full size basement.

The church is now an auxilliary adjunct of the church in Dassel, the pastor being Rev. F. Wm. Hanson of the Dassel church.

FIRST LUTHERAN CHURCH
Dassel Village

The First Lutheran Church of Dassel was organized February 13, 1873 in a log house owned and occupied by Sven Harling in Section 3, Collinwood town in what was known then and now as the Steelsville community.

The official minutes of this meeting are signed by Rev. J. G. Lagerstrom, Pastor of the Mooer's Prairie church in Wright County, as chairman, and Daniel Johnson as secretary.

A log church was built in Section 11 in Dahlman's woods and a burial ground was established. Rev. Lagerstrom of the Mooer's Prairie church served as the first pastor assisted by Mr. A. Olson, a lay preacher at Mooer's Prairie.

In 1877 the Steelsville congregation united with the Dassel community in church relations. From this time forward there was a strong upward movement in the growth of the church culminating in the erection of the present church edifice in 1886. The present pastor is F. Wm. Hanson, graduate of Augustana College and Seminary at Rock Island, Illinois.

FIRST LUTHERAN CHURCH
Rev. A. H. Franzen, Pastor
Litchfield, Minn.

As early as 1861 Rev. E. Norelius held services in pioneer homes in the present Litchfield territory. Ten years later Rev. P. Beckman, of Kandiyohi County held services in Litchfield every sixth Sunday. He was followed ten years later by Rev. G. Lagenstrom, pastor of the church in the town of Stockholm, Wright County who made regular visits to Litchfield and organized, August 28, 1873, the first Lutheran church.

The present church edifice was erected in 1884 and the Luther Hall was erected in the form of an addition to the church in 1912.

The church has celebrated three anniversaries: Fortieth, June 23-24, 1913; Fiftieth, August 26-27, 1923 and Sixtieth, July 9, 1933. Rev. J. G. Linner published an historical sketch of the church in 1913 and a Jubilee Album was published by Dr. G. Rast in 1923.

Societies

The Ladies Aid was organized in 1875 when thirty ladies were embraced in the organization. Among the leaders were Mrs. Andrew Nelson, Mrs. A. Palmquist and Mrs. J. P. Scarp. The sixtieth anniversary celebration of the Aid was held in 1935 at which time it was disclosed that they had raised $21,364.43 which had been expended for improvements to church property; benevolences and home, conference and synodical missions.

The Luther League had its inception in the organization of a Girl's Sewing Circle in the early nineties. At a later date the young men of the church became interested and the Christian Young Peoples Society was formed March 13, 1903 and the name changed in 1911 to the Luther League. The League has contributed to the needs of the church and in 1933 installed the new electric fixtures.

Other existing organizations are the Woman's Missionary Society, organized in 1919 and its auxiliary, the Junior Missionary Society. The Men's Club was organized in 1916.

The congregation has 371 communicants and 119 children are identified with the church. Since 1905 the Ostmark Lutheran Church in Forest City town has been included in the parish.

During the World War the church roll carried the names of 34 young men inducted into service and two young ladies.

ZION CHURCH

The Zion Norwegian Evangelical Lutheran church of Litchfield village constitutes one of the three churches comprising the Ness parish. It had its inception in 1885 when 30 individuals were under the spiritual guidance of a chosen pastor. This condition continued until 1892. In 1887 a church was built at a cost of $1,000 which was later sold to the German Lutheran Church Society. In 1892, due in part to a change in the residence of the officiating pastor, church services were discontinued until 1907 when services were held at infrequent intervals for some period of time.

The Zion Church was organized in the latter part of May, 1920 at a meeting held in the home of G. A. Jorgenson, now occupied by Lars Roberg. At this meeting those present pledged $325 toward meeting the expense of the organization. A few weeks previous to this gathering Rev. Haatvedt was urged to establish a Sunday School which was deemed by him as an impossible task but a Sunday School was started in 1920 at Greenleaf. Rev. M. O. Silseth was installed as pastor in June 1920 by Rev. B. K. Bolstad and a Sunday School was organized a few months later.

In June 1921 the Sunday school was reorganized with Mrs. M. O. Silseth as Superintendent.

The church was reorganized at this meeting and the following constituted the official board: Chairman, T. T. Barka; Secretary, Christopher Sather; Treasurer, C. J. Stephenson; Trustees, Ephram Johnson, G. A. Jorgenson and John Tuseth. The church was established in its present home August 17, 1930. The church served twelve families following the adoption of the constitution and for a period of years the services were conducted in the Norwegian language but at present the English language is used almost exclusively.

The present church edifice was constructed in 1890 by an Independent Swedish Lutheran group and was later owned by the Emmanuel Episco-

OF MEEKER COUNTY

palions from whom it was purchased by the Zion congregation for $2,500. This indebtedness has been paid and the church has no outstanding obligations.

Rev. Carl J. Field, the present pastor is a graduate of the Waldorf Academy and Junior College of Forest City, Iowa and St. Olaf's College at Northfield, Minnesota and a two-year course at the Lutheran Bible School and Maywood Seminary in Chicago and later graduated (class of 1930 from Luther Theological Seminary in St. Paul.

ST. PETER'S LUTHERAN CHURCH
Ellsworth Township.

Religious services were held as early as 1865 by preachers of the German Lutheran faith. An organization was perfected in 1889 and for three years services were held in the school house in District 66. The present church structure was erected in 1892 and the first pastor was Rev. H. Brown. The present church services are held each Sunday alternating in the use of the English and German languages. The Sunday school has an average attendance of thirty or more and is conducted in the English language. Thirty-five families are represented in the membership. The cemetery, which is located opposite the church, is one of the best maintained in Meeker County and is the final resting place of some very eminent pioneers.

GERMAN EVANGELICAL
Section 25, Harvey

The church was erected about 48 years ago and was for years served by pastors from Albion in Wright County and Eden Valley. Church and Sunday school services are held on alternate Sundays. There are 22 or more members. The church is served by Rev. Victor Grupe of Maple Lake, Minnesota.

COSMOS LUTHERAN CHURCH
Cosmos Township

The First Lutheran church of Cosmos was organized May 18, 1893 under the name of Swedish Evangelical Lutheran Salem Congregation. It was in the home of Andrew Gustafson that the organization meeting was held and he was the first Sunday school superintendent and Mr. and Mrs. Gustafson were the donors of the church and cemetery grounds.

During the period 1893-1896 services were held in the Union Church three miles north east of the present location. In 1896, the present building was erected and the same was dedicated in the autumn to the Lord's service at which time the congregation had met the major portion of the church debt. Erick Erickson was the first organist.

Among the pastors of the longest tenure of service were E. O. Chelgren (1911-1917); A. F. Seastrand (1917-1928) and the present pastor, J. Gottfrid Larson since 1928.

It was the privilege of the writer to have known Rev. Emil Chelgren in his youth when he was enrolled as a pupil in the Collinwood public school of which the writer was the teacher. He was a young lad of exemplary habits and excellent character well fitted in every way for his chosen work.

OSTMARK LUTHERAN CHURCH
Forest City Township

The Ostmark Lutheran Church was organized in 1893 and the church erected in 1911. It was struck by lightning and burned in the spring of 1912 when it was rebuilt. There are regular services each Sunday and the Sunday School has an average attendance of thirty-five. The pastor is Rev. H. Franzen of Litchfield.

ROSENDALE LUTHERAN CHURCH
Danielson Township

The Emanuel Lutheran church was originally an annex of the Swedish Lutheran church at Atwater. A chapel was built in 1891 but the desire of the Rosendale community to become an independent organization resulted in a called meeting held March 7, 1892 at which time a distinct and separate unit was established. Rev. J. A. Frost served as chairman. Among the leaders in this movement who continue their work of service to the church are Emanuel Gustaf Lindstrand, Mr. and Mrs. C. A. and Victor Holmgren, Axel Glass and Mr. and Mrs. O. P. Wilner. C. A. Holmgren for 27 years has given free janitor service. Mrs. Amos Johnson has served as organist 26 years. The little chapel of 1891 is a part of the present church building.

During the passing years the church has met and surmounted many difficulties. For twenty-five years the congregation had no parish connections and the calling of a pastor was necessary at each annual meeting but in 1917 parish connections were established to include the congregations at Beckville and Cosmos. Since that time these congregations have had the same pastoral guidance, Rev. A. F. Seastrand serving from 1917 to 1928 and Rev. J. Gottfrid Larson, the present pastor since that date.

KINGSTON FINNISH APOSTOLIC LUTHERAN CHURCH

This church was organized January 24, 1898. The following directors were chosen: John E. Matsen, Peter Pelto, M. A. Leppa and Matti Leppa, John Heikel and Andrew Kurtti. The first pastor was Rev. Henry Nurmi.

Shortly after the organization was perfected they purchased the vacant Swedish Lutheran Church located on the present site of the Town Hall. This building was moved to the location of the present church. A few years thereafter this building was too small to accommodate the congregation and the present church was erected. Services are held each Sunday and the pulpit is supplied at present by Rev. Arvid Hurula, the resident pastor.

The services are in the main held in the Finnish language with occasional services in the English.

FINNISH EVANGELICAL LUTHERAN CHURCH
(Kingston Township)

The Finnish Evangelical Lutheran Church was organized in 1904 and for a long period of years the Presbyterian church which occupied the site where the creamery now rests was used as their house of worship. In 1925 the present church edifice was erected in Section 10. The pastor is Rev. Tamminen.

The church services are held in the Finnish languages, but the Sunday School classes are conducted in both the English and Finnish languages. Miss Bertha Haapajoki is the efficient Superintendent and the school has continued to grow in interest and attendance.

ST. PAUL LUTHERAN CHURCH
(Eden Valley)

The St. Paul's Lutheran Church was organized June 5, 1911. Rev. M. W. Weseloh was the first pastor who was succeeded in 1912 by Rev. W. Melahn whose pastorate terminated in 1917 and he was followed by M. C. Goetsch. In 1922 he gave place to C. H. Lueker who served until 1925 and Rev. J. H. Klausmeier became his successor. Rev. F. E. Pasche arrived in 1929 and is the present pastor. Rev. Pasche is a German scholar of note, is the author of a number of books published in both the German and English languages and is one of two citizens of Meeker county listed in "Who's Who in America."

PEACE LUTHERAN CHURCH
Cosmos

The Peace Lutheran Church was organized May 15, 1923 with 23 members and was established to serve the Americans of German descent in the Cosmos community. Rev. H. Krull was the first pastor during whose term of service (1823-1926) the present church building was erected. The present pastor is Rev. E. J. Kaiser. The congregation, served, numbers nearly three hundred of which 227 are communicants. Their Sunday school has an enrollment of one hundred.

LAKE JENNIE METHODIST

Lake Jennie Methodist Church was organized in 1878. The present chapel was erected in 1892 and was dedicated by Presiding Elder John Stafford. The pulpit is supplied at present by Rev. Burns of Hutchinson, Minnesota. The pulpit was supplied for a long period of years by Roy Case, a lay preacher of exceptional ability and the surivival of the church during all these years is largely due to the zeal and effort of Rev. Case and his estimable wife. The pulpit was also filled by Rev. McBee, a resident pioneer preacher of the Lake Jennie community.

CROW RIVER M. E. CHURCH

The Crow River Methodist Episcopal Church organization is the outgrowth of a series of Methodist camp meetings held in the early seventies on the Doll farm at the present location of the church edifice. The spiritual life of the community in these early years was fostered by the following families: Petries, Carpenters, Hoars, Marshalls, Hubbards, Leamings, Hosfords, Flanders, Clarks, Caswells, Wrights, Browns, Swifts, Ryckmans, and Dolls.

The ladies of these families were the real leaders in the activities that led to the organization of the church. The present church grounds were presented by Mr. and Mrs. Marcus Doll and the church was erected in the late seventies.

The church activities have been furthered by a reorganization of the Ladies Aid Society in 1905 and it is largely due to their effort that services have been held during the passing years.

The building was remodeled in 1930 by the construction of a basement and an addition to the front of the church. At present church services are held on alternate Sundays with Reverend Charles Pavey of Paynesville as pastor and Sunday school is held each Sunday, Mrs. Leon McIntyre is the superintendent and the average attendance is forty.

LITCHFIELD METHODIST EPISCOPAL CHURCH

The Rev. John Robson preached his first sermon on the Forest City Circuit, of which Litchfield was a part, in January 1857, and in April of the same year the first Sunday school was organized, with W. H. Dart as the first Sunday school superintendent. Rev. Thomas Harwood was appointed to the new circuit in the fall of 1857.

August 1, 1860 a Board of Trustees was appointed to hold the property of the organization in Litchfield. The work was much hindered during the next few years, due to the Civil War and the Indian outbreak in Meeker County.

A quarterly conference was held October 24, 1870 and the name of the circuit was changed from Forest City to Litchfield which suggests that during the decade the Litchfield church had become the more prominent. J. H. Fasig was appointed pastor. The names of W. H. Dart and Rufus M. Eastman were among the early official members of the church, early members to the organization being Henry Boynton, Ruth Boynton, Eldora Boynton and James Sawter.

A new building was erected in 1872, dedicated in the spring of 1873 on the present site of the church property. Church officers at this time included R. L. Hershey and J. L. Lovitt, stewards; James Austin and W. H. Dart, class leaders..

The church building was improved in the late 90's under the pastorate of Rev. L. Dodds; the lecture room was enlarged during the pastorate of Rev. Crawford Grays about 1918; an extended choir loft during the pastorate of Rev. Burns in 1933. During the present pastorate of Rev. J. S. Kettlewell the church was raised, a new basement put under the entire structure containing recreational room, kitchen, class rooms, lavatories and furnace room, a new heating plant, and the superstructure renovated throughout the interior and the outside of the building repainted. The church has a membership of 375 with a Sunday school enrollment of 175; Ladies Aid Society with 75 members and Missionary Society with 20 members.

THE DANIELSON M. E. CHURCH

The Danielson Methodist church is located in section 18 Danielson town and was organized in 1890 at which time Rev. Farrell, pastor of the Atwater church was the spiritual leader. A two acre tract of ground had been secured of which the larger portion is used as a church cemetery.

The church was built the same year at a contract cost of $780.60 by O. Gunderson. The building was sold in 1902 for $275 and replaced by the present structure in 1902 at an expenditure of $3,000. Rev. Wagner was the pastor during the period of its construction. The church was dedicated May 30, 1902 at which time Bishop Joyce delivered the message.

The church is served at present by Rev. K. A. Stromberg, of Atwater and services are held each Sunday. The Sunday school has an enrollment of about 40 and is under the superintendency of Miss Esther Hanson.

COVENANT MISSION

The Evangelical Covenant Mission church of Dassel was organized August 15, 1879 with twenty charter members. Rev. J. G. Sjoquist was the first pastor and served as chairman of the church board. The officers constituting the governing body of the church were the following trustees: John Norgren, Sr., was the secretary and treasurer, E. Sherwick and E. Rundquist. The present church edifice was erected in 1909 and dedicated November 21, 1909. The present pastor is Rev. C. Edwin Anderson, a graduate of Concordia college and seminary.

The same year (1879) that the Covenant Church was organized marked the establishment of the present public cemetery. Mr. Norton donated one-half acre of land in the southeast corner of the present cemetery as a burial ground and the first interment was that of his wife, who died the same year. The conveyance was made to the trustees of the Covenant Church. Later another half-acre was purchased through the sale of lots. John Norgren for a period of several years had the management of the cemetery. The acreage was subsequently increased by purchase of about ten acres.

Since 1915 and for several years previous thereto there was a noticeable improvement in the maintenance and beautification of the cemetery and under the present supervision of E. Gust Erickson it has become one of the best maintained and beautiful burial plots in Meeker County.

SOUTH KINGSTON MISSION CHURCH

Fifty or more years have come and gone since religious activities began to take form and shape among the Scandinavian people in Kingston town.

Their first church was built in 1886 near Lake Arvilla at which time it was an annex to the church in Dassel and was served by the resident pastors of that village.

The Kingston Covenant Church was formally organized in 1896 with twenty-eight members.

The cyclone of July 27, 1932 completely destroyed the church and the present chapel was erected the following year on the same site and was dedicated August 6, 1933.

For more than thirty years the church was served by the highly gifted pastor of the Dassel church, Rev. J. B. Sjoquist, but in 1915 a vacancy in the pastorate occurred by his removal to California. Rev. H. M. Olson became his successor and entered upon his duties in January, 1916, and with the exception of a five year period (1921-1925) has remained the resident pastor. He has by his kindly manner and neighborly spirit endeared himself to the entire citizenship of Kingston town.

BETHANY MISSION COVENANT
Litchfield

The Bethany Mission Covenant Church was organized nearly seventy years ago in the town of Greenleaf.

Some time later several of the families belonging there moved to Litchfield. They soon felt the need of organizing a Covenant church here. This was done on March 4, 1912 with a membership of seventeen. The congregation met for services at the Adventist and Swedish Methodist churches until 1923 when they built their own church. The first board members were: Gustaf Anderson, chairman; J. W. Williams, secretary; C. E. Nystrom, Aaron E. Anderson and J. W. Williams, directors; Ferdinand Peterson and C. E. Nystrom, deacons; and Ellen Williams, organist.

At the present time the church has a membership of forty. Walter Anders is the chairman; Lloyd Chellin, secretary; Charles Nystrom, treasurer; Chris Olson, Emil Nystrom, Levi Holmgren, trustees; and Clarice Nystrom, pianist.

The different branches of the church are: the Sunday school, Young People's Society, Ladies Aid and Master's Ten.

Rev. Victor Mars, who has attended the Northwestern Bible School of Minneapolis and Moody Bible Institute of Chicago, is the pastor of the church at the present time.

Other Churches

Nazarene Church

The only churches of this denomination in Meeker County are located in Litchfield and Corvuso. Services are held each Sunday. The combined membership numbers eighty and eighty or more pupils are enrolled in the Sunday school.

The Church Society was organized by Rev. R. S. Taylor, district Superintendent for Minnesota. The present pastor is Rev. Martin Leih, a native of Holland and the son of a minister of the Dutch Reformed Church of that country. Previous to entering upon his work in the Litchfield District he served as pastor of the church at Glenwood, Minnesota and had spent four years as an evangelist. The members are tithers and contribute one tenth of their income in the furtherance of Christian work. In 1938 a parsonage was built at an expenditure of $4,500.

A Norwegian Methodist Church is numbered among the older churches of Litchfield. Rev. K. A. Stromberg, of Atwater is the present pastor.

She Seventh Day Adventists were in early years an active organization but at the present time have no resident pastor. Services are held at varying intervals at the Litchfield church.

The Evangelical Church, Eden Valley

The present Evangelical Church building was erected in 1886 at Eden Valley.

The Lake Jennie Covenant Mission Church is located in Section 20 and was organized in 1886. The present pastor is Rev. Victor Mars.

Lamson Free Mission Church is located in Section 36. First pastor, Rev. Levi Coleman. Present pastor, Rev. Philip G. Thorn.

The first protestant religious service in Meeker County was conducted by John Robinson (Methodist) in November 1856. In 1857 religious service was held in a room above Whitney's store in Kingston village by Reverend J. C. Whitney. There are a few obsolete church edifices in Meeker County where Sunday school is the only regular service.

Catholic

It was in the plain cabin home of John Flynn in Forest City town that Rev. Father Alexius said the first mass in Meeker County in 1857 and two years later Father Benedict administered the last rites of the church to that worthy gentleman who had greatly endeared himself to the pioneers, irrespective of religious creed. He has been memorialized by one of the windows in the Church of St. Gertrude.

ST. GERTRUDE CATHOLIC CHURCH
Forest City

The present church edifice was built in 1867. John Dougherty and others hauled the lumber from St. Cloud. It was located north of the stockade and was moved in 1897 to its present location since which time it has been remodeled and enlarged. The church is at present served by Rev. Father Donovan of Darwin. Services are held each Sunday. The membership embraces about eighty families. The cemetery which is a part of the church grounds is one of the oldest in the county and contains the marked graves of many of the sturdy territorial pioneers. Among the burials in this cemetery is the grave of John Dougherty, who assisted in the interment of the victims of the Acton Massacre. Among the oldest residents of the Forest City townsite is Mrs. Anna Crusoe. She came with her parents from Sherburne County to Forest City town in 1869.

ST. JOHN'S CHURCH
Darwin

About the year 1867, Rev. Father Burns, a priest of the order of St. Benedict, was in charge of the Forest City Parish. He was anxious to found a college and selected Darwin as the location. He persuaded the officials of the St. Paul and Pacific Railfay to donate Block 21 as a site for the institution and the deed to this property was recorded November 12, 1869. Two years later the higher authorities of the church saw fit to establish certain boundaries within which the Benedictines were to confine their labors. Darwin was not included in these boundaries and Block 21 was transferred to Bishop Grace and at a later date the tract of land upon which the church and parochial residence is located was given to the parish. This gift prompted the construction of the present church which was completed and the first Mass was celebrated by Father McDermott December 8, 1878 and the church named, The Church of St. John the Baptist.

Father McDermott served the church at Forest City and Darwin and the mission at Manannah for four years. The present pastor is Father Donovan.

Two sons of the parish of Darwin, entered the priesthood. Father Ambrose McNulty (deceased) and Father McRaith. The following daughters entered the holy sisterhood: Sisters Evangelist (Bridget McNulty), Emerantia (Margaret Casey), Josephine (Bridget McRaith), Clementia (Ellen Curry) and Agnella (Gertrude Curry).

ST. PHILIP'S CHURCH
(Litchfield)

The Saint Philip's Catholic Church of Litchfield was organized as a unit of the Catholic parish at Forest City in 1871 by Rev. Father Arthur Hurley serving as pastor of both churches until 1873. The first church building dedicated for that purpose was a room in the parsonage which was arranged to serve as a chapel in which Mass was celebrated. In 1875 Rev. Father John McDermott became pastor. He was a man of strong convictions on the use of liquor and organized a Father Matthew Temperance Society, the first total abstinence society in Meeker County. It was during his service as pastor that lots were purchased for the erection of a church. In 1882 Father Patrick Kinney became pastor and served until 1885, when he was succeeded by Father H. McDevitt.

In 1886, the universally loved priest, Father Boland was placed in charge of the parish. His pastorate covered a period of nearly fifty years during which time the church grew and prospered. He died December 25, 1932. His death was mourned by the citizens of the county irrespective of their church affiliations. He was succeeded by Rev. Father Doran who served until 1938 when the present pastor, Rev. Father Joseph O'Neil became his successor. He served as a chaplain during the World War.

The St. Philip's parish has given to the holy priesthood Father James Ryan (son of James and Mary Ryan); Father Patrick J. Ryan (son of Patrick and Hannah Ryan) and Father Roger Connole (son of John and Agnes Connole).

The parish has established a conservatory where instruction is given in vocal and instrumental music and a kindergarten has been established. The facilities they afford are offered to the community irrespective of religious creed.

The social and fraternal relations of the membership rest in a number of religious societies, among which is the Knights of Columbus whose membership is limited to adult males of the Catholic faith. At present this lodge has a membership of sixty-five and meetings are held semi-monthly.

The present church was erected in 1922 at an expenditure of $65,-000. The present parsonage was erected in 1887 at an initial cost of $4,000.

CHURCH OF OUR LADY
Manannah

The church of "Our Lady" was organized by Rev. Father John McDermott, of Darwin in 1876, at which time a portion of the present edifice was erected. The site was donated by Anthony Kelly of Minneapolis. The church was finished during the pastorate of Father Kinney and was included in the Litchfield parish. The parochial residence was erected in 1885.

The parish of today is an independent parish and is in charge of Reverend James R. Coleman. He serves the St. Columbanus Church in Greenleaf township, one of the oldest organizations in the county. The present church edifice was erected in 1889. The site occupied by the church and cemetery is a twenty acre tract and was donated by Louis Maher and Michael McGraw.

ST. JOHN'S CHURCH
Sec. 34, Cedar Mills Township.

The church was organized in 1892 at which time it was served by Pastor H. Braun of the parent church at Acoma, McLeod County who in the early years served all the German Lutheran congregations of the Wisconsin Synod in Meeker County until they were able to establish self-maintaining societies and have resident pastors.

In 1894 a church school was built and Rev. Ph. Bechtel became their first pastor. The church was erected in 1896 and in 1909 a pipe organ was installed. Rev. Bechtel was succeeded in 1928 by Pastor William Petzke and in 1932 the present pastor, Rev. A. C. Krueger, was called. The church school is taught the present year by Raymond Duhlmeier.

CHURCH OF THE ASSUPMTION
(Eden Valley)

The Church of the Assumption was organized in 1894 by Rev. Fr. J. Bastian and the present church edifice was erected the same year. It is built of native brick from a yard adjacent to the village. December 4, 1894 the church was dedicated by the pastor of the diocese, Rev. Msgr. J. P. Bauer. Rev. Fr. A. Kastigar, of Watkins ministered to the needs of the congregation until the appointment of a resident pastor, the Rev. Fr. N. J. Al Pfeiffer who continued as pastor from 1899 to 1934. He was succeeded by the present pastor, Rev. Fr. Peter Gruenes, a native son of the Eden Valley community. The church has a modern parsonage. The parochial school building was erected in 1901 and blessed by the Bishop, January 1, 1902.

ST. PETER'S CATHOLIC
(Eden Valley)

St. Peter's Catholic Church was built in 1904. The first pastor was Rev. Father McDermoth. In 1912 Father O'Callaghan became pastor and during his pastorate an addition to the church was built and the parish house erected. The present pastor is Reverend Father Cogwin.

BOARD OF COUNTY COMMISSIONERS
(IN SESSION)

Left to right, standing: C. R. Patterson, George Hannula. Seated: James Campbell, Frank Ecker, Orville Dille, Frank Dollerschell, William Schulte.

CAMPBELL, JAMES (son of James and Emma Russell-Campbell) was born in Duddeston, Warwick County, England, May 9, 1871. He was left an orphan at seven years of age and was reared in the home of Mr. and Mrs. George Paterson, farmers residing in the vicinity of London, Middlesex County, Ontario, Canada. He was educated in the rural schools and at the age of eighteen was placed on his own resources and located at Sarnia, same province, where he became an apprentice to a harness maker and at the end of that period was employed at his trade in the province of Manitoba and later in North Dakota.

Mr. Campbell came to Meeker County and located in Litchfield and opened a harness shop in 1893 and for 45 years continued in the business until March, 1939. During these years he has taken an active interest in promoting the development of the village. He has served as a member of the village council and Board of Education. In 1932 he was elected County Commissioner of the first district (Townships of Acton, Darwin, Litchfield and villages of Grove City, Darwin and Litchfield) which position he holds at present, and serves as chairman of the board.

Mr. Campbell married, May 4, 1897, Jean Miller (daughter of David and Catherine McDougal-Miller) born, August 8, 1875. Children, Florence I. (Mrs. Marlin H. Booth) born August 23, 1900. They are the parents of Beulah and Arlene. Geneveive (Mrs. H. C. Sharpe) born September 5, 1904. They are the parents of James Campbell.

SCHULTE, WILLIAM (Son of Henry and Margaret Loeffers-Schulte) was born in Cedar Mills township, February 28, 1879. Mr. Schulte was educated in the public Schools of his native township and has been engaged from boyhood in farming. He owns and operates a farm of 120 acres in section 29, Cedar Mills township. He has served as township treasurer six years, assessor two years and has been treasurer of school district 69 for the past seventeen years. In 1930 he was elected County Commissioner of the second district (townships of Cedar Mills, Cosmos, Danielson, Greenleaf and Cosmos Village) which position he holds at present.

Mr. Schulte married, September 24, 1902, Martha Hass (daughter of Albert and Emma Heller-Hass) born October 24, 1876. They are the parents of Clara, born June 3, 1916.

DILLE, OLIVER V., of Swedish and Norwegian descent, (son of Peter O. and Christine Person-Dille) was born in Collinwood township, February 14, 1887. He was reared on a farm and educated in the public schools. With the exception of three years residence in Minneapolis, he has engaged in farming and at present operates a farm of 100 acres in Section 15, Dassel township. He served for 11 years as Clerk of Dassel township and has also served as a member of the Dassel High School Board of Education. In the election of 1932 he was elected County Commissioner of the Third Commissioner District embracing the village of Dassel, Dassel Ellsworth and Collinwood townships, a position he continues to hold.

Mr. Dille married, June 18, 1919, Eleanor Johnson (daughter of J. A. Johnson and Elizabeth Erickson-Johnson) born October 30, 1888 in Kingston township. They are the parents of Donald, Roland and Elaine.

ECKER, FRANK (son of Carl and Louisa Behnker-Ecker) born May 17, 1887 at LaCrosse, Wisconsin. The family came to Meeker County in 1896 and located on a farm in Kingston township. Mr. Ecker was educated in the public schools. He has served as a member of the town board six years and thirteen years as a member of the school board in District 33. He owns and operates a farm of 120 acres in section 26, North Kingston township. He was elected County Commissioner of the fourth district (townships of Kingston, Forest City, Forest Prairie and Watkins Village) in 1938.

Mr. Ecker married in 1911, Emma Sternberg (daughter of Fred and Anna Schaffer-Sternberg) born November 5, 1891. They are the parents of four living children.

DOLLERSCHELL, FRANK (son of Gustaf and Ericka Ross-Dollerschell) was born in Cottage Grove, Washington County, Minnesota, April 20, 1890. He came with his parents to Meeker County in 1898 and they eventually located on a farm in Harvey township. Mr. Dollerschell was educated in the public schools and has been engaged in farming since early boyhood. He has served as township supervisor three terms, member of the school board, District 71, several years and for a period of eight years was president of the Forest City Creamery for eight years. He is at present, the owner and operator of a farm of 120 acres in section 12, Harvey township. He was elected County Commissioner of District 5 (Swede Grove, Harvey, Union Grove, Manannah and Eden Valley village) in 1918 in which position he continues to serve.

Mr. Dollerschell married, February 20, 1912, Anna Jording (daughter of Christof and Johanna Richter-Jording) born October 3, 1881. Children: Lucille, born October 18, 1915 and Russel, born, August 31, 1920.

HANNULA, GEORGE W. (son of John Albert and Hilma Prunki-Hannual) was born in Cokato, Minnesota, July 7, 1901. He graduated from the Dassel, Minnesota High School in 1919. He was Assistant Cashier of the Hamlin County Bank at Hayti, South Dakota from 1920 to 1922 when he returned to Meeker County and served as clerk in his father's hardware store at Kingston and in 1932 following the death of his father he became the manager of the business. He was elected County Auditor in 1938 by a majority of 1,349 over his opponent.

Mr. Hannula married, November 25, 1926, Carrie D. Nelson (daughter of Arvid and Olga Gustafson-Nelson) born April 4, 1906. They are the parents of Shirley, born February 23, 1928 and Gerald, born August 24, 1931.

PATTERSON, CHARLES R. (son of Peter and Mary Woodman-Patterson) was born in West Townsend, Vermont, August 3, 1885. He was reared on a farm. He graduated from Leland and Gray Seminary (1906) and in civil engineering from New York City University in 1911. He entered upon the work of his profession in Idaho and Oregon on irrigation projects and later was engaged on railroad projects in Canada. In 1917 he came to Minnesota and entered the employ of the state highway department. From 1917 to 1933 he was engaged in highway work in Sibley County and in 1933 he located in Litchfield here his services were engaged as county Highway Engineer, his present position.

Charles H. Patterson married, November 20, 1918, Frances Lorenz, born August 20, 1887. They are the parents of Bernard, born in Gaylord, Minnesota, August 18, 1923.

COMPLIER OF MEEKER COUNTY HISTORY

LAMSON, FRANK BAILEY (son of Levi and Adelaide Bailey-Lamson) was born Mt. Carmel, Connecticut, October 14, 1867. He was left motherless in infancy and was reared by his maternal grandparents, Mr. and Mrs. Frederick A. Bailey with whom he moved to Sherwood, Wisconsin in 1869. Their home was on a small farm, thirteen miles from a railroad. At the age of 13 he became dependent on his own resources and securing a place to work for his board attended Ryan High School at Appleton, Wisconsin.

In 1884, Frank accompanied his grandparents to Dassel, Minnesota and located them in a crude frame house, seven miles south of Dassel, on the east shore of Lake Jennie. He became the sole support of his grandparents and uncle for several years. He taught rural and village schools for seven years in Meeker, Chisago, McLeod and Wright counties. Upon his retirement as a teacher he has had a varied career, editor and publisher of the Cokato Observer (Enterprise); Buffalo (Minnesota) Standard; county auditor of Wright county, Minnesota; Postmaster of Buffalo, Minnesota, twelve and one-half years; deputy county auditor of Wright and later Beltrami county, Minnesota; assistant Sergeant-at-Arms of the State Senate, 1897 session; secretary of the Minnesota Progressive Republican League, 1911; secretary of Chambers of Commerce at Bemidji, Minnesota: Marshfield, Wisconsin; Moberly, Missouri and Peru, Indiana.

Frank B. Lamson

During his residence in Peru, Indiana, he served as secretary of the Miami County Historical Society (1927-1935) and took a leading part in the development of their museum which has been publicly designated as one of the greatest points of interest in the State of Indiana. When Mr. Lamson was located at Moberly, Missouri, he originated and promoted the establishment of the Mark Twain Park at the author's birthplace in Florida, Missouri, and served one year as secretary of the Missouri Mined Coal Association. Mr. Lamson is the compiler and publisher of the Lamson Genealogy (1635-1908) and has compiled and published numerous county histories.

Frank B. Lamson was married January 1, 1890 to Anna S. Nordine (daughter of Andrew and Anna Christopherson-Nordine) born April 24, 1867 in the province of Vermland, Sweden. Mrs. Lamson has shown unusual ability as an artist in oil. She has been a worthy helpmate of her husband and a devoted mother to her four living children.

Clarence McKinley (adopted) born in Minneapolis, Minnesota, September 10, 1891. Clarence Lamson is a successful business man at New Lisbon, Wisconsin where he is engaged in the furniture and undertaking business. He married Mrs. Alda Kromroy-Peuse. They are the parents of Warren Lamson, who was born November 4, 1916 and married, July 3, 1939, Kathryn J. Drought.

Frank Vernon, born in Buffalo, Minnesota, June 28, 1899, received his education at the Universities of Minnesota and Missouri. Before accepting his present position in the Advertising Department of the Consolidated Edison Company of New York, he served as advertising manager of one of their subsidiary companies, the New York & Queens Electric Light & Power Company for ten years. He married, November 5, 1926, Mary Deputy, daughter of Manfred W. Deputy, ex-president of the Bemidji Teacher's College, Bemidji, Minnesota. Mary Deputy-Lamson is a landscape architect of national reputation. She received her BA and MA degrees at Indiana University and a Master of Landscape Architecture from Smith College.

Ruth Marion, born March 27, 1906, graduated from the Moberly, Missouri High School and completed her education by attendance at William Woods College, Fulton, Missouri, Ball's Teacher's College at Muncie, Indiana and Manchester College, North Manchester, Indiana. She married, December 1, 1928, Earl M. Bear, son of Howard and Mae Monroe-Bear, born November 16, 1907, at Madison, Indiana. They are the parents of Betty Jean Allan (adopted) born at Terre Haute, Indiana, December 19, 1928 and Richard Cecil born at Plain City, Ohio, December 20, 1937. They reside at present in Cincinnatti, Ohio, where Mr. Bear is in the employ of the Singer Sewing Machine Company.

Edmond Herbert, born November 21, 1908, is a graduate of the Moberly, Missouri, High School class of 1926 and of civil engineering, Purdue University. He is at present employed in California as an Engineer Inspector of Public Works. He was married February 29, 1936 to Helen Roth, daughter of Omer H. and Anna R. Todd-Roth, born November 9, 1913, at Loogootee, Indiana.

Walter Harold, died in infancy.

THE MARCH FAMILY

The progenitor of the March family in America was Hugh March, one of a band of Puritans, under the leadership of Rev. Thomas Parker, who led his flock from Newberry, England and established in 1635 the Newberry colony at the mouth of the Merrimac river in Massachusetts.

Hugh March was a skilled mechanic. He built the famous Blue Anchor Tavern at Newberryport which has been taken over by the Historical Society of that city. The membership embraces the descendants of the first sons and daughters of the original settlers of old Newberry. Frank M. March is a life member of the Society.

Hugh March became the ancestor of the American branch of the March family. The ancestral strain of the Meeker County family descended through five generations in the following order (Hugh, 1; Captain Hugh, 2; Joshua, 3; Lieut. John, 4, and George, 5) to Nelson J. of the sixth generation. Lieut. John, fourth, in the line of descent from the emigrant ancestor was a soldier of the Revolution. He was at this time a resident of Walpole, New Hampshire. His son George became a resident of Ackworth, New Hampshire and was the father of Nelson J., the founder of the Minnesota branch of the March family.

NELSON J. MARCH (son of George and Hannah Nelson-March) was born July 11, 1828. He grew from childhood to youth in his native environment. At the age of fifteen he went to Boston and six years later to New York and in 1852, he journeyed to Illinois, and engaged his services with a railroad company, establishing his headquarters in the cities of Springfield and Bloomington.

In August, 1855, he came to Minnesota where he followed the trade of carpenter in St. Paul.

When the Civil War broke out Mr. March engaged his time in the recruiting of men for service in the Union army until July 1862 when he was appointed Provost Marshal for the Second District and served as such until his release from duty in July 1865.

Mr. March purchased 160 acres in Section 14, Cedar Mills township, Meeker County. He engaged in farming and in January 1863 he established his family, consisting of his wife and sons, Frank and Nelson D. in their new home. He continued to operate the farm until 1874 when, having been elected sheriff of Meeker County he moved to Litchfield to assume the duties of his office which covered the period from 1874 to 1878 inclusive. He had disposed of the Cedar Mills farm in 1876 and shortly afterward purchased 240 acres in Section 30 of the same town, which he owned and operated until 1885, when he sold the same and having taken a tree claim in Spink county, South Dakota in 1880 and purchased lots in the village of Mellette he was for a few years a resident of that state. He returned to Meeker county in 1885 and purchased a farm of 80 acres in Section 1, Litchfield township. Nelson J. March Married, May 13, 1862, Mary J. Morrison (daughter of Moses and Mary Cressy-Morrison) born May 25, 1842. They were the parents of Frank M.; Nelson D.; George K.; Charles H. and Mary N.

Nelson J. March died April 28, 1913.

Mary Morrison-March died October 26, 1932.

The children of Nelson J. March became closely associated with the growth and development of Litchfield and Meeker county. They were a loyal band of brothers. The individual interests of each member of the family became the common interest of all the Marches and March Brothers became a synonym for family loyalty.

THE MARCH BROTHERS
(Hudson Bay Expedition)

Back row: left to right, Charles H., Frank M., Nelson D. and George K. March. Front row: left to right, Ralph M., Douglas H. and Harry, sons of Nelson D., and Harry Wells, son of Charles H. March.

The illustration represents the March brothers and their male children on their return from an expedition to Hudson Bay in March, 1921 to inspect their land holdings at Hudson Bay harbor and the feasibility of establishing a townsite.

FRANK M. MARCH was born October 22, 1863 in St. Paul, Minnesota. He was educated in the Litchfield schools and in 1883 he engaged his services as a teacher in Ellsworth and Collinwood townships.

In 1885, Frank found employment as a clerk in the general merchandise store of his uncle, Captain A. H. Reed, of Glencoe, Minnesota. He left his employ in 1889 and established himself at Pierre, South Dakota, where he engaged in the mercantile business. He disposed of his interests at Pierre and in 1894 went to Zumbrota, Minnesota, and organized the Security State Bank and soon thereafter established his family in this chosen field of his activity. During the period of his residence he was recognized as one of Zumbrota's leading citizens and was thrice elected mayor, a position he was holding when he organized the bank at Lake Park, Minnesota.

In 1901, the March Brothers organized the Manitoba Land Investment Company and brother Frank became their representative in disposing of their vast acreage of Canada lands in the provinces of Manitoba and Saskatchewan and in numerous promotion activities in this huge virgin area. He established his headquarters and residence in Winnipeg until 1910. He then went to Spokane, Washington, where he organized the National Bank of Commerce and in 1917 disposed of his interests and retired from active business. In 1925 he returned to Litchfield and engaged in varied activities.

Mr. March is at present a resident of Morris, Minnesota, but he remains a citizen of Litchfield and Meeker County in his loyalty to all matters pertaining to its growth and development.

Frank M. March married, June 17, 1901, Emma F. Wadsworth (daughter of Henry and Fidelia Gilbert-Wadsworth) born, December 20, 1866 in New Haven, Connecticut. She died August 24, 1913 leaving two children:

Fidelia Wadsworth was born August 4, 1892 at Pierre, South Dakota. She married, October 4, 1917, at Litchfield, Minnesota, Roy A. Bowers. They reside at Eugene, Oregon and are the parents of five children: Fidelia, born July 30, 1918; March, born November 29, 1919; Patricia, born July 18, 1922; David, born August 9, 1924; George Keith, born April 28, 1931.

Mary Wadsworth was born at Pierre, South Dakota, May 17, 1894. She married at Minneapolis, Minnesota, April 12, 1921, John T. Lyons, who died August 8, 1928. Their children are: Barbara, born January 15, 1924; Marilyn, born May 22, 1927; Joan (deceased).

NELSON D. MARCH was born in St. Paul, Minnesota February 26, 1866; died April 5, 1931.

He was educated in the Litchfield schools and entered upon the study of law and was admitted to the bar. He opened a law office and became recognized by his numerous clients as a safe counselor in all matters affecting their several interests. He never sought public acclaim or public honors but did not shirk civic duties and responsibilities. He served as county attorney, city attorney and mayor and as a member of the Board of Education. He was conservative in the discharge of his official duties.

Mr. March had a wide acquaintance with the legal fraternity of this section of the state and merited and received their confidence, respect and friendship.

Nelson D. March married, December 21, 1899 Nellie Olive Hanson, daughter of Peter E. and Rachel Halverson-Hanson) born February 3, 1871. This union was blessed with four children:

Harry N., born in Litchfield, Minnesota, January 7, 1901. He married, September 14, 1931, Helen Steinkruger. They are the parents of Hugh born February 8, 1935 and Martha, born June 8, 1936.

Ralph M., born in Litchfield, May 26, 1902. Married Eveline Engeseth. No children.

Douglas H. born January 30, 1903. Married, June 13, 1933 Geneva Bachman. They are the parents of Daniel Nelson, born January 23, 1937.

Marian Lucille, born Litchfield, February 6, 1909. Married, July 3, 1937, Millard Mans, born May 31, 1907.

GEORGE K. MARCH was born in Cedar Mills township, July 26, 1868. In 1874 the March family established their home in Litchfield where George was educated in the public schools, graduated from the high school and attended Curtis Business College in Minneapolis. He taught rural schools in Acton and Danielson townships and then engaged in a varied business career. He was more or less closely associated with his brothers in their varied business experiences which ultimately resulted in financial success. These various occupations may be listed as follows: general merchandise and operator of a cattle ranch at Pierre, South Dakota; automobile and road contracting in the state of Washington with location at Spokane in 1912 where he resides at present. He retired from active business in 1935. George K. March married, October 1898, Helen Sammus of Pierre, South Dakota. No children. Mrs. Helen Sammus March died December 31, 1919.

CHARLES HOYT MARCH was born on a farm in Cedar Mills, Meeker County, Minnesota October 20, 1870. He attended the Litchfield schools and Curtis College, studied law and was admitted to the bar. He formed a partnership with his brother, Nelson D. March, and practiced at Litchfield, Minnesota. The partnership continued until the death of Nelson D. March April 5, 1931. He was appointed Colonel on the staff of Governor Knute Nelson and also by Governor Clough. At the time of the Spanish American War he organized the Fourth Regiment National Guard and was made its Colonel. He was elected President of the Farmers and Bankers Council of Minnesota and Vice Chairman of the Minnesota Safety Commission which had charge of war preparations during the World War. This commission was given full power by the legislature which can only be done in the time of war. He was a delegate to three Republican National Conventions and Chairman of the delegation at two different conventions. At the convention in Cleveland, held in 1924, the Minnesota delegation unanimously voted for him as their choice for Vice President. President Coolidge appointed him as a member of the powerful Federal Trade Commission, and he has been twice elected Chairman of this Commission. His appointment was unanimously confirmed by the United States Senate. President Roosevelt reappointed him for a seven-year term and again the United States Senate unanimously confirmed him. When the news reached Litchfield that he had been appointed by President Coolidge, a banquet was tendered him by the citizens of his native county which was very largely attended. He served as mayor of Litchfield and as president of the library board. He was always a leader in all progressive movements, both political and in industrial matters. Mr. March is one of two Meeker County citizens listed in Who's Who in America and has recently been prominently mentioned as a possible republican presidential candidate in the campaign of 1940.

Charles H. March married, February 28, 1899, Aimee W. Wells (daughter of H. H. and Clara Wolf-Wells) born at Morris, Minnesota. Children:

Cora, born December 20, 1899. She married C. L. Christenson, Dean of the Agricultural Department of the University of Wisconsin. They are the parents of Charles and Christian (twins) born December 31, 1931.

Harry Wells, born January 31, 1902.

Charles H., Jr., born July 21, 1912, married, August 31, 1936, Nancy M. Neef.

MARY (MAYME) MARCH was born July 1, 1874. She was educated in the schools of Litchfield, graduating from the high school in 1894. During these years she was a student of Mrs. S. A. Heard in piano music. In 1894 she enrolled as a student at Stanley Hall, Minneapolis, in elocution, vocal and piano music and in 1896 gave piano instruction in her home city of Litchfield. Miss March married Robert Burns Benedict, September 19, 1906, and they established their home in Mayoak, British Columbia, Canada until 1911. They moved to Oklahoma City in 1915 where they continued to reside until his death, June 21, 1925. She resides at present in Spokane, Washington.

THE HARVEY DOUGHERTY'S

Mr. and Mrs. Thomas O'Doughertay and their family of seven children, five sons and two daughters and his brother John, a widower with six children, four boys and two girls constituted an overwhelming majority of the population of Harvey township in the year 1856 when they staked their claims to lands in sections 22 and 15.

The heads of these families, Thomas and John, were born in Dunneghall, Ireland. They came to America in 1840. They were at Jolliet, Illinois when hearing of the fertile woodland and prairie bordering the Crow River in Minnesota they took to the somewhat vaguely blazed trail to seek a new home in the unbroken wilderness. Their caravan in addition to the members of the families consisted of one team of horses, seven yoke of oxen, twenty-two cows and a small flock of poultry. They were six weeks in making their journey, when fording the Crow River at or near Kingston, they reached the land of their dreams and proceeded to Forest City where they found surveyors engaged in platting the townsite. They arrived July 14, 1856 and halted for a brief period to bid welcome to the arrival of Sarah Jane Dougherty, who was born in one of the covered wagons. The group of settlers at Forest City joined with the Doughertys in congratulating the proud parents on her arrival and the owners of the townsite deeded a lot in the embryo city to the little maiden. Soon after this important episode in Meeker County history the Doughertys staked their claims to what became the future and permanent home of Thomas and John O'Doughertay (brothers) and their families of children.

Mr. and Mrs. Thomas O'Doughertay

THOMAS O'DOUGHERTAY

O'DOUGHERTAY, THOMAS, was born in Dunneghall, Ireland in 1816. He emigrated to America in 1840. Catherine Ward a native of the same country was a passenger on the same vessel and a friendship was formed that resulted in their marriage one year later. Mr. O'Doughertay was a tailor by trade and soon found employment in New York City and later in Syracuse, New York. In 1856 he was residing in Joliet, Illinois at which time he was the father of seven children. They staked their claim to the N½ of the NE¼ of section 22, Harvey town in the summer of 1856 and building a shelter house of prairie sod began the labor of developing their wilderness home. Their two boys, aged 12 and 14 and the mother were very helpful in the hard labor that followed but they made rapid progress and in 1862 they were quartered in a log house and had constructed crude but comfortable shelter buildings for their stock and poultry. They had seemingly overcome their greatest difficulties and were on the highway leading to a greater degree of competency. Hopes of a better future were destroyed when in August 1862 the Indian outbreak occurred and they were forced to abandon their home and seek safety in the Stockade at Forest City. They had succeeded in driving two cows to Forest City the day following the housing of the wife and children in the stockade. While engaged in the effort they were making to drive their stock to a point of refuge they were closely pursued by a band of Indians, the herd of cattle was scattered and Mr. Dougherty and his son John had a narrow escape from capture and probable death by the savages.

They spent the winter of 1862 in a rented shack in Stearns County and returned to their home farm in the spring to find their home partially wrecked, their shelters for stock destroyed by fire and their herd of cattle killed or stolen.

With undaunted spirit and courage Thomas O'Doughertay and family faced and overcame these disasters and in the years that followed increased their land holdings by homesteading 160 acres of land in section 22. The log house had given place to a comfortable frame dwelling and the family enjoyed many of the luxuries of life.

Mr. O'Doughertay was recognized as a kindly hearted and generous man and was familiarly known in his circle of acquaintance as "Uncle Tommy" and his kindly advice and words of cheer gave wholesome aid to many a desponding neighbor and friends. His good wife was equally beloved and she was one of those kind motherly women who rejoiced with the success and sympathized with the sorrows of all her neighbors and the memory of her many acts of kindness continue to dwell in the minds of those whose parents she befriended. Their union was blessed with nine children all of whom lived to maturity except Edward who died at eleven years of age. The children in order of birth are John, James B., Mary Ann, Thomas W., Domnick, Catherine, Patrick Henry, and Sarah Jane.

Thomas O'Doughertay died February 8, 1890. Mrs. Catherine Ward-O'Doughertay died December 14, 1900 and was born August 29, 1820.

There are seventeen living descendants of the territorial pioneers, Mr. and Mrs. Thomas O'Doughertay.

DOUGHERTY, SARAH JANE (daughter of Thomas and Catherine Ward-O'Doughertay) was born in a covered wagon in the townsite of Forest City, July 15, 1856. She married, October 7, 1896, John Joseph Dougherty (no relation). This union proved one of true happiness giving the lie to the old adage,—"Change your name and not your letter you change for worse instead of better."

John Joseph Dougherty was born in Ireland February 6, 1858. He came to America in 1888 and for forty-three years was engaged in railroad work, serving as a section foreman and later as a caretaker of the Great Northern Station in Minneapolis. He retired on a pension February 6, 1929 and died February 6, 1938.

Mr. and Mrs. Dougherty became the parents of Thomas W. Dougherty, born in Litchfield, Minnesota, November 25, 1877. He graduated from the law department of the University of Minnesota and became a practicing attorney in Wisconsin and later in Dakota. In 1936, he located in Montevideo, Minnesota where he is connected with the Ford Automobile Agency and gives loving and tender care to his aged mother with whom he shares an attractive bungalow home.

Sarah Jane Dougherty

Mrs. Sarah Jane Dougherty is a frail and somewhat delicate lady of refinement. She retains all her faculties and enjoys recounting the experiences of her long and useful life. The writer will long remember his visit to her attractive home and the courtesies extended by mother and son.

John Dougherty (the eldest son of Thomas and Catherine Ward-O'Doughertay) was a lad of 19 years at the time of the Indian outbreak at which time he left St. Paul and found employment on a Mississippi River steam boat (The War Eagle). He later went to Little Rock, Arkansas where he married Ellen McKenzie. He died leaving an infant son, who died in childhood.

James B. married Elizabeth Dowdell. Mary Ann Married Thomas Wheeler and became the mother of ten children, five boys and five girls. Thomas W. married Mary Dowling and became the father of ten children. Domnick married Hannah Finnegan and had two children. Patrick Henry married Catherine Dowling and had two children. Catherine married Hugh Dowling, no children. Sarah Jane.

The John Dougherty (brother of the Thomas family) gradually disposed of their land holdings in Meeker County and the family became somewhat scattered in their places of residence. Of the four sons and two daughters who should be numbered among the earliest residents of Meeker County and the township of Harvey, there are said to be one hundred and fifty living descendants. There are seventeen who reside in Meeker County as follows: Mrs. Mary McAloon and her three children: Rose, John and Mary C.; John Dougherty and his four children: Margaret, Frances, John and Robert; Dennis Dougherty and his seven children: Dorothy and Marie (twins), Joseph, Frances, Thomas, James and Donald. The pioneer ancestors bore the name O'Doughertay but the present generation has modernized the name and spell it Dougherty.

John O'Doughertay

DOUGHERTY, THOMAS W., son of Thomas and Catherine Ward-Dougherty, was born in Illinois and was only four years of age when his father located in Meeker County. He spent the remaining years of his life in the township of Harvey and became one of its most prosperous citizens, owning at the time of his death nearly a section of Land.

He married, June 1874, Mary Dowling. They were the parents of the following children in order of birth: Edward F., born August 4, 1875, married, resides in Hollywood California, no children. Thomas I., born December 1, 1877, unmarried. Sarah, born March 30, 1880; died, October 2, 1925. John R., unmarried, born July 1, 1882, and with his brother Thomas successfuly operates the home farm. Catherine, born September 28, 1884; died August 30, 1902. Hugh F. born February 26, 1887; died September 2, 1887. Marian

Mr. and Mrs. Thomas W. Dougherty

Esther died, March 15, 1908.

Grace M. is a teacher and resides at the Curtis Hotel, Minneapolis.

Frank E. is a practicing attorney in Fairmont, Minnesota and was elected State Senator of his district in 1938. He is married and is the father of three children: Francis, William and Patricia.

Thomas W. Dougherty died in 1902 and his wife, Mary Dowling-Dougherty, died in 1937.

Lest We Forget

BIOGRAPHY

—

THE BIOGRAPHICAL SKETCHES THAT FOLLOW TELL THE STORY OF THOSE WHOSE LIFE OF SERVICE HAS LEFT ITS IMPRINT ON THE SEVERAL COMMUNITIES IN WHICH THEY LIVED AND SERVED. . . . . . .

"To live in hearts we leave behind is not to die"

THOSE WHO LIVED AND SERVED

JOHN OSBORN

KNUTE JOHNSON

ADAM BROWER

MRS. CYLA ELLIOTT

REV. A. G. McBEE

OLE NORDINE

MAGNUS JOHNSON

MADISON DELONG

CONTRIBUTED BY DASSEL (MINNESOTA) DISPATCH

MEEKER COUNTY PIONEERS
Dassel Community

There are individuals of character and worth in every community who have left their imprint on the social, moral or commercial development in their field of action.

JOHNSON, MAGNUS, a native of Sweden, came to America at the age of 19 and in 1902 purchased a farm in Section 17, South Kingston town. From boyhood he had been deeply interested in the problems of government. He became a forceful political leader and in 1914 was elected to represent Meeker County in the State legislature. He was an unsuccessful candidate for governor in 1922 but at the special election of 1923 to fill the vacancy in the U. S. Senate occasioned by the death of Hon. Knute Nelson he defeated Governor J. A. O. Preus by a majority of 94,000. By sheer force of character he had raised himself from the humblest stages in life (common laborer, lumber jack, tiller of the soil, chopper of wood and milker of cows) to the highest position in the gift of his adopted state, membership in the U. S. Senate. An unparalleled record in the political history of America.

JOHNSON, KNUTE, was reared from childhood to manhood in the Dassel community and became its most eminent citizen. It was largely due to his efforts that Dassel has become known as The Seed Corn Center of the Great Northwest. He was a civic leader and active in religious work.

OSBORN, JOHN, was a native of the Empire State. He located in Dassel in the early seventies and became the first lumber dealer in the village. He was among the pioneer rural school teachers of the county and was a man of strong Christian character.

BROWER, ADAM, a native of Indiana and a veteran of the Civil War, came to Meeker County in 1867 and settled on a farm in Kingston town. He operated a saw mill in Dassel village for a brief period. He was Meeker County's first brickmaker.

DELONG, MADISON, a native Virginian, homesteaded land in Section 34, Dassel town which includes a portion of the village of Dassel. He was a sturdy and reliable character and served as County Commissioner of Meeker County for several years.

McBEE, Rev. A. G., was born in the historic town of Harpers Ferry, Virginia. He came to Meeker County in 1877 and purchased a farm in Collinwood town. He became a circuit rider of the Methodist denomination and ministered to the religious needs of sparsely settled English speaking settlements in Stearns, Meeker and McLeod counties.

ELLIOTT (HUNTLEY) Mrs. CYLA L., became a resident of Dassel village in 1876. She lived a useful, self-sacrificing life. She was active in the civic, social and religious life of the community and was generous beyond her means. She was a prominent member of the W. R. C., D. A. R. and Royal Neighbors.

NORDINE, OLE E., was reared from childhood to manhood in Dassel town. He was leader of the Dassel Band for several years and served as County Commissioner, 1902-1912.

SCHULTZ, MARTIN, a native of Germany, came to America in 1851 and in 1876 purchased the Washington Lake Water Power Mill which he successfully operated for twenty years. He acquired and merited the confidence and good will of his patrons and enjoyed a wide acquaintance throughout a large portion of the county.

NORRIS YOUNG TAYLOR

TAYLOR, NORRIS YOUNG (son of George and Matilda Leonard-Taylor) was born in Vermillion County Illinois, October 8, 1850.

The progenitor of the Taylor family in America was Richard Taylor who came to Virginia in 1608 and is presumed to have been a lineal descendent of King Edward the Third of England. Richard's wife, Dorothy, came to America in 1620. George W. Taylor, the father of Norris is of the 8th generation from the emigrant ancestors.

Norris Y. Taylor's boyhood was spent in the county of his nativity, but at nineteen years of age, because of lung trouble, his family physician advised him to go to Minnesota. In the spring of 1870 he took passage on a Mississippi river boat, going north. He worked at several towns along the river and finally landed at Stillwater in August 1870, where he worked for several weeks in a saw mill. From there he went to St. Paul where he met and began work with some government surveyors. In 1873 he was appointed Deputy United States Surveyor General which position he held till 1877, surveying most of the White Earth and Leech Lake Indian Reservations. During the summer months of these years he continued with his studies at Duluth, St. Paul, and the University of Minnesota.

In 1877 having completely recovered his health he came to Meeker County, where he had in 1874 purchased a farm of 246 acres in Section 17, Ellsworth Township (now owned by the family of the late State Representative August Smith.)

In 1880 he accepted the Superintendency of the George L. Seeney, Noble's County farm, and the following year transferred his services to the management of the Horace Thompson estate and continued in the service of the executors for three years. At the expiration of this period, he returned to Meeker County and resumed the operations of his Ellsworth Township farm. Very early in the farming operations he became interested in dairying and maintained a herd of pure bred Jersey cattle, the remnants of which became the nucleus for the herd which his son George now has on his dairy farm near Forest Lake, Minnesota.

Norris Y. Taylor

The complete knowledge Mr. Taylor had gained in the United States Land System and his acquired skill as a surveyor led to his election as County Surveyor of Meeker County, in 1888, which position he held from 1889 to 1924.

From this time forward Mr. Taylor's service in his chosen profession left its impress on the county and the entire state, measured by the accomplishments resulting from his efforts. In 1895 he was the author of a bill to have all the government corners marked with iron monuments. He was also the author of a bill requiring surveyors to record all surveys.

Mr. Taylor was married May 3, 1881, to Fina Shuart (a native of Geauga County, Ohio, and daughter of William and Mary Ann Morse-Shuart) born August 16, 1850. Four children were born of this union: George S., Dairyman, Forest Lake, Minnesota; Wilfred B. Attorney, Grand Rapids, Minnesota; Marion, Asst. Auditor, State Bank, Litchfield, Minnesota; Jessie E., Assistant County Superintendent of Schools, Hennepin County, Minneapolis, Minnesota.

In 1892 he moved with his family to the south shore of Lake Ripley which place was their home during the remainder of his lifetime. Norris Y. Taylor died June 23, 1929. Fina Shuart Taylor died December 30, 1922.

In an obituary address delivered at the annual meeting of the Minnesota Federation of Architectural and Engineering Societies held in Duluth, February 14 and 15, 1930, the following tribute was paid him by Charles A. Forbes, Division Engineer of the Minnesota Department of Highways:

"It is perhaps in connection with this society that Mr. Taylor has rendered his greatest service for the advancement of his profession. He was among the first to move for its organization, and, very fittingly, became its first president.

We who knew Mr. Taylor for so many years will miss his amiable personality, his delightful reminiscences and his observations of the little things in nature, his prophecies concerning some of the perils of indiscriminate drainage in Minnesota and his abundant old-fashioned Southern hospitality. His memory will long be cherished in the annals of this Society."

CAMPBELL, ERNEST WELLS (son of Otho H. and Isora Creath-Campbell) was born at Kingston, Minnesota, November 19, 1869. After a residence of three years in Kingston, the family moved to Litchfield, which was their home for two years, when they located in Manannah. In this little village, situated on the banks of the Crow River, Otho Campbell became the owner and operator of the Manannah flour mill and there Ernest spent his boyhood years.

Later the family established their permanent home in Litchfield. Ernest was graduated from the Litchfield High School in 1891, after which he entered Yale University at New Haven, Connecticut, where he took his degree in law. After his admission to the bar he returned to Litchfield, where he practiced his profession until his death.

At the outbreak of the Spanish-American War in 1898, Ernest assisted in recruiting Company C of the Fifteenth Minnesota Regiment and served as First Sergeant and later Second Lieutenant until the Company was mustered out in 1899.

During his years of residence in Meeker County, he became closely identified with the civic, financial, political and religious life of the County seat village. Mr. Campbell served as County and City Attorney and was Mayor of Litchfield for four consecutive terms. So well did he serve in this capacity that the voters were reluctant to release him from public life.

He was for a period of years Vice President of the Bank of Litchfield and when the State Bank of Litchfield was organized became Vice President of that institution. At the time of his death he held the office of Referee in Bankruptcy and was the oldest Referee in point of service in the State. He was also President of the Meeker County Bar Association, Vice President of the Minnesota Tax Payer's Association; Chairman of the Boy Scouts' Court of Honor; a member of the Library and Hospital Boards and of the Executive Committee of The Good Cheer Club.

Mr. Campbell was an active member of the First Presbyterian Church of which he was treasurer for thrity-five years and was actively interested in the work of the Sunday School.

He was married March 7, 1900 to Marion R. Roraback (daughter of Uriah and Harriet E. Roraback) born February 3, 1872. They were the parents of Myra Catherine, born October 4, 1902. She married Harlan M. Quinn April 12, 1932. They are the parents of Harlan Marshall Junior and Marion Margaret Quinn.

Ernest W. Campbell died January 11, 1933.

The Litchfield Review in commenting on his death paid him the following tribute: "It was one of his tenents that every man owes to his community and to his Church a portion of his time and service and some of his means. He paid these debts and earned a high place among his fellow men as an unselfish community builder."

RODANGE, LOUISE BRANHAM (daughter and grandaughter of the distinguished pioneers to whom this history is dedicated) was born in Forest City, August 1866. She graduated from the Litchfield High School, class of 1885, and from the State Teachers College in Mankato, Minnesota in 1889. She taught in the Litchfield and Minneapolis public schools.

Mrs. Rodange became a leader in the civic, literary, musical and social life of Litchfield and Meeker County and was well and favorably known in the cultural ladies' organizations of her native state. She organized the Federated Womens and Music Clubs and the Molly-Stark Chapter of the D. A. R. She was first State President of the Federated Music Clubs of Minnesota. She was active in civic affairs serving as chairwoman of the Meeker County Republican Committee (1928-1932) and in 1932 was a delegate from Meeker County to the county, district and state conventions and in 1932 an alternate delegate to the National Republican Convention. In all her public activities she was tactful, diplomatic and efficient and greatly endeared herself to all who became associated with her in the administration of her duties.

Louise Branham married, June 26, 1893 Peter Rodange (son of John and Margrethe Nichols-Rodange) born February 1, 1868. They became the parents of Marguerite (Mrs. John J. Sullivan) born in Litchfield, June 22, 1894. They reside in

Louise Branham Rodange

New York City and have one child, John, Jr., born April 2. 1924. Mrs. Louise Branham-Rodange passed away at the home of her daughter in New York City February 10, 1937 and was laid at rest in Ripley Cemetery, Litchfield, Minnesota.

TRIBUTE BY A FRIEND

Louise Branham Rodange was a woman richly endowed by nature. Possessed of great kindliness of heart and gentleness of manner. She was for many years a leader in civic and social life. Her loyalty to her friends was outstanding. Her faith in mankind unfailing. She spoke ill of no one and was always ready to defend those who were maligned. "Lovely in youthful comeliness; lovely all her life long in comeliness of heart."

ALBERT H. DELONG, a native of St. Lawrence County, New York, was one of the outstanding heroes during the Indian outbreak of 1862. He served as a scout during this troublous period and was a member of the Sibley expedition.

HENRY McGANNON, a native of Jennings County, Indiana, came to Meeker County in 1859 and located in Section 34, Litchfield township. At the time of the Acton Massacre he joined his neighbors in visiting the scene of the tragedy. They armed themselves with pitchforks and scythes to resist a possible attack by Indians.

NELS ELOFSON, was living in Section 33 Swede Grove township at the time of the Acton Massacre and assisted in the interrment of the victims. He visited Sweden in 1870 and returned the following year with 300 emigrants from his native land.

LEAVITT, SILAS W., of colonial-Scotch ancestry, (son of Joseph and Hannah Cotton-Leavitt) was born on a farm near Laconia, New Hampshire, November 11, 1843.

At the age of 19, Silas enlisted in Co. A., 50th N. H. V. I. He took part in the siege and capture of Port Hudson. Due to impaired eyesight, resulting from an attack of measles and malaria, he was discharged from service in October 1864. He located in Boston, Massachusetts for a brief period where he was employed at clerical work.

Following his marriage in 1868 he and his bride journeyed overland by railroad, team, and boat to Chicago. They remained there for a short time before establishing themselves at Mendota, Illinois where they engaged in the mercantile business. Their first child, Edith May (deceased) was born in Mendota.

Mr. Leavitt came to Meeker County and the Register of Deed's files contain a record of his purchase of 133 acres in Section 17 Town of Ellsworth described as Lots 2 and 3 and SW¼ of NW¼. T. 118, R. 30. On this farm he built his own cabin. He hauled the lumber from St. Cloud in an ox-cart. On this trip he was chased for miles by a pack of wolves and was obliged to part with provisions of food to insure their escape. Mrs. Leavitt, was with him seated in a rocking chair in the rear of the cart with Edith May sitting in her lap. These experiences doubtless prompted the removal of the family to Litchfield the same year when he engaged in the grain business and in 1871 was elected Clerk of Court of Meeker County, serving twelve years.

S. W. Leavitt

Mr. Leavitt became active in the commercial and civic affairs of the village. He engaged in the retail lumber business and organized the Meeker County Abstract and Loan Company. He served as president of the Litchfield Board of Education for twenty years and when Company H. of the First Regiment of the Minnesota National Guards was organized in February 1883 he became Captain of the Company and continued in command of the same until its disbandment in 1889. At this time the members of the company presented him with a handsome gold watch and chain which he cherished as one of his most priceless possessions.

Mr. Leavitt served Meeker County in the state senate, sessions of 1891 and 1893 where he became an intimate friend of Ignatius Donnelly. During his legislative service he was active in promoting improved methods of taxation, inheritance, and income taxes. In 1900 he was appointed a member of the commission to investigate the need of a State Board of Control and when the same was created he became its first chairman, serving as such for eight years. During this period he resided in St. Paul. In 1918 he established his home in Minneapolis where he associated himself with his son-in-law, James C. Matchitt in the publication of "The Northwest Insurance," a trade journal. He served as business manager until 1934, when he retired from active business due to the death of Mr. Matchitt. Mr. Leavitt at his death, March 11, 1939, was the last surviving member of Frank Daggett Post G.A.R. No. 35 of Litchfield. During Mr. Leavitt's life in Litchfield he was a real factor in promoting its growth and development.

Silas W. Leavitt was married August 24, 1866 to Mary Dyson-Chapman, a native of Worcester, Massachusetts. Mrs. Leavitt died December 30, 1932. Mr. and Mrs. Leavitt were the parents of four children, two of whom died in childhood. The surviving children are: Grace W. who married James C. Matchitt; children, Marion, Myrtice, and Ridley.

Marion H. married Edward B. Robertson; children, Ruth, Leavitt, Burr, Denel, Douglas, and Mary Katherine.

NELS E. HANSON, is numbered among the territorial pioneers of Meeker County and was an early resident of Swede Grove township. He was an active participant in the stirring events of that bloody month of August 1862 and was among the defenders of Forest City at the time of the Indian attack, September 4, 1862.

EVEN EVENSON

EVENSON, EVEN (son of Hans and Christine F. Anderson-Evenson) was born in Norway November 21, 1844. The parents were territorial pioneers who made their first trip to America in 1852 and settled for a time in Rock County, Wisconsin and in 1854 they returned to their native land and remained until 1857 when they again came to America and in 1860 to Meeker County and established a home for the family on a 160 acre farm in Section 8, in Greenleaf township.

Even Evenson was the eldest in a family of five children. He was approaching his eighteenth birthday when the news reached him of the Acton Massacre. He joined a fearless group of settlers that visited the Baker and Jones homes and viewed the bodies of the victims. Here he remained until after the burial. On Wednesday of the same week he joined the family in seeking refuge first in Kingston and two weeks later at Forest City. He was doing guard duty on that memorable morning of September 4 when the attack was made on Forest City and fired the second shot in defense of the settlers.

In 1863 he was employed in Anoka and in the fall of that year he enlisted in Company I, Second Minnesota Cavalry. The regiment was assigned to frontier duty and escorted Captain Fisk's immigrant train to the Idaho gold fields. He was mustered out of service in 1865 when he returned to the family homestead where he continued to make his home during the remainder of his useful and eventful life.

Mr. Evenson became one of Meeker County's most conspicuous citizens. He filled various offices with credit and in 1870 was elected member of the Board of County Commissioners which position he occupied continuously until 1879, serving the last four years as chairman. In 1886 he was the candidate of the republican party for representative in the legislature and received the largest majority of any candidate in Meeker County with one exception.

Mr. Evenson was married November 1869 to Helen Danielson, daughter of Nils Danielson, a territorial pioneer who established his home in Danielson town and whose name has been perpetuated by the naming of the town to honor his memory

Mr. and Mrs. Evenson were the parents of seven children: Robert E., deceased, Henry Nicholas born October 24, 1871, Carl Richard born December 17, 1873, Robert B. born July 27, 1877, Elmer Emanuel, born August 13, 1879, Anna Bertha, born September 25, 1881, Nels Oscar, born April 13, 1884. Mrs. Helen Evenson died October 4, 1905. Even Evenson died, April 27, 1911.

MOSES, SALINA JANE (wife of Frederick A. Bailey and daughter of Joshua and Abigail Lee-Moses) was born in Harwinton, Connecticut, November 2, 1810 and died January 11, 1892. She was laid at rest in the Dassel cemetery.

Frederick A. Bailey (son of John and Sarah Corbine-Bailey) was born at Thompson, Connecticut, February 24, 1809. At the age of fourteen he was apprenticed to a carpenter and worked seven years for board and lodging in learning his trade. At the termination of this period he was paid $100 and began life for himself. He was regarded as an expert carpenter. In partnership with his brother, Charles, he built the Colonial Congregational Church building in Bristol, Connecticut which continues to be the leading house of worship in that city. He died in 1894 and his grave joins that of his wife.

Mr. and Mrs. Bailey were the parents of three children, George, Claude and Adelaide (Mrs. Levi Lamson). They reared three other children: Salina Jane Thomas, a niece, who married Charles Hayes, a first cousin of Ex-President, R. B. Hayes; Nellie Judson-Blood (adopted) and Frank B. Lemson, son of their daughter, Adelaide, who graduated from Hudson River Institute, class of 1860, and was teaching at Snow Hill, North Carolina, when the Civil War compelled her return to her home at Mount Carmel, Connecticut. (See page 33.)

THE NORDINE FAMILY

Left to right: Seated, Mary, Mr. and Mrs. Andrew Nordine, Andrew, Jr. Standing, Anna, Elizabeth, Lena, Ole, Huldah and Alfred

NORDINE, ANDREW, a pioneer Scandinavian farmer of Dassel township, was born in Bogens Kappell parish, Vermland, Sweden, November 13, 1826. In October 1853 he married Anna Christopherson, who had been born in the parish of Lekvatten, January 18, 1833.

In April 1868 they set sail for America with a family of five children: Andrew, Mary, Caroline, Ole and Anna. Andrew, the oldest child, was 14 and Anna, the youngest daughter, spent her first birthday on the ocean.

Andrew Nordine arrived in Minneapolis with only a $5 gold piece in his pocket. At that time Minneapolis was a small city of less than 13,000. He found work in a saw mill and a few months later moved with his family to a farm in Carver County and in 1869 to Meeker County, where in 1874 he purchased a farm with his savings: Lot 5, a fractional 80 acre tract of land in Section 36, Dassel Township. The land was wild and heavily timbered but with the help of his two sons, Andrew Nordine, quickly brought his land into cultivation and built a log house and outbuildings. Eighty additional acres of land were acquired and modern frame buildings took the place of log structures as the family prospered.

Andrew Nordine was an intelligent, capable and prosperous farmer a kind and understanding husband and father . . . a good citizen and neighbor, proud of his American citizenship and extremely loyal to the land of his adoption. Anna Nordine, his wife, was a capable and industrious housekeeper, an excellent cook, and her home churned butter sold at premium prices in the village.

The Nordine home was for many years the temporary refuge for many friends and relatives who followed them to Minnesota from Sweden . . . serving them as shelter until they were able to establish themselves in the new country. No wayfarer, regardless of creed or race, was ever refused food or lodging.

Four children, Alfred, Elizabeth, Huldah and Carl, were born to the Nordines in this country. In all there were five sons and six daughters: eight of whom lived to maturity in Meeker County. Andrew Nordine, Sr., died at his Collinwood home, June 5, 1896. He was survived by his wife, who died at Dassel, May 25, 1915.

HARRIS, VIRGIL H., son of Daniel and Martha Dowling-Harris, was born May 14, 1840 in Hanover, Licking County, Ohio.

Mr. Harris was of colonial ancestry, his paternal great grandfather was a native Virginian whose son Daniel later became a citizen of Mecklenburg, North Carolina and was an active participant in the movement resulting in the Charlotte, Mecklenburg County, North Carolina declaration of independence from English rule, May 20, 1775, preceding the Declaration of Independence adopted by the colonies, July 4, 1776.

Ephram Harris, son of Daniel, and grandfather of Virgil was a close associate of Daniel Boone and in company with him penetrated the then wilderness of Ohio and homesteaded a tract of land bordering Licking River in the county of that name. The son, Daniel, after reaching maturity purchased a farm in the same county where his son Virgil was born.

Virgil Harris, the subject of this sketch, in 1848 accompanied his father (a tanner by trade) to Dayton, Ohio where the father followed his trade for about a year when he died leaving a family of five children of whom Virgil was the eldest.

Virgil remained with his mother, Martha Dowling-Harris, who removed to Licking County, Ohio and two years later moved to Marion County, Ohio, the home of her parents and subsequently married John Baker.

Virgil H. Harris

In 1852 when 12 years of age Virgil Harris went to Macon County, Illinois where for a period of four years he found employment as a herder of 4,000 sheep. In 1859 he returned to his native state of Ohio and although not of legal age cast his first presidential vote for Abraham Lincoln.

In May 1862 he enlisted in Company B. 111th Ohio Infantry and at the close of the war was discharged as an Orderly Sergeant June 28, 1865, whereupon he attended college in Indianapolis, Indiana and also at Ashland, Ohio for a period of nearly two years.

Mr. Harris married, December 25, 1868, Lizzie Hill, daughter of John and Catherine Hill, who were pioneers of Marion County, Ohio. For two years following his marriage Mr. Harris engaged in farming in Marion County. In 1871 he took up his residence in Litchfield and in company with S. Y. Gordon opened a meat market and two years later a drug store.

Mr. Harris was a republican in politics and was honored by election to various village and county offices: Alderman, recorder, mayor, county commissioner and was Judge of Probate at the time of his death.

He was a member of the Frank Daggett Post G. A. R., holding the third office in rank in the Department of Minnesota

Mr. and Mrs. Harris were the parents of four sons: Bert (deceased), John, Maro and Ernest.

Virgil H. Harris died October 14, 1910. Lizzie Hill-Harris (his wife) died September 7, 1917.

CASEY, PATRICK, a native of the county of Tipperary, Ireland, was born in March 1816. He grew to manhood in the Emerald Isle and reached the mature age of thirty-two years when, in 1848, he sailed for America and landed at the port of New York, January 22, 1849. He remained in the future metropolis of America for a short time before proceeding to Allegheny County, Pennsylvania, where he remained for a period of six years. It was here he met and married, July 8, 1851, Hannorah McRaith. He bade his family good bye and left the Keystone State in the spring of 1856 in search of a permanent home for his family, which at that time included his wife and three children. He reached Manitowoc, Wisconsin and from there went by way of Chicago to Dubuque, Iowa and proceeded by steamboat to St. Paul, Minnesota. When he reached there he contacted Captain Hayden and his corps of surveyors, William and Michael O'Brien and Patrick Condon. He joined them in the month of May, in a direct trip to Meeker County. They had an ox team and wagon, loaded with four barrels of flour belonging to Hayden. They reached the "Big Woods" June 1 and were sixteen days in their journey of thirty-five miles to the Kingston townsite where they arrived June 16, 1856. Two days later he staked his claim to land in section 33, Darwin township where he established what became his permanent home during the remaining years of his eventful life. With the aid of his comrades they built their log cabin homes.

Mr. Casey cleared a one acre tract of land and paid Captain Hayden $35 to plow the ground and then returned to Pennsylvania to pilot the family to their future home. He had barely reached his destination when he learned that his claim had been "jumped" by a brother-in-law of Captain Hayden which prompted him to make an immediate return, leaving his family behind him. He found his cabin unoccupied and took immediate possession. He spent the winter in company with Condon in his neighboring cabin. They had ample provisions and did not suffer want. With the coming of spring he sent for his family and met them in St. Paul and guided them to their new home where they arrived, May 9, 1857. They raised a scant crop of potatoes that season but in 1858 they sowed one bushel and one-half of wheat which produced a yield of forty bushels which he threshed by flail. During the years 1858-1862 more land was cleared and brought under cultivation, his family had been increased by the birth of two sons, he had 35 or more of head of cattle and the family witnessed the dawn of approaching prosperity.

The afternoon of August 18, 1862 the family learned of the Acton Massacre and immediately fled to Kingston for refuge and two days later to Clearwater, from which point the wife and children were sent to Minneapolis while the father returned to his cabin home to care for his stock. He left six cows in the care of his neighbor, John Peiffer and drove 27 head of cattle to uncertain markets. He then went to Minneapolis where he remained until 1865 when he returned with his family to the Darwin farm. The State of Minnesota reimbursed him in part for his financial losses in the sum of $300 and the Caseys began life anew and at the time of his death, August 10, 1894 he had become one of Meeker County's most prosperous and highly respected citizens. Mrs. Hannorah Caasey died January 2, 1911.

There were twelve children born to this worthy couple: Bridget, born, April 16, 1853; Mary, August 31, 1854; Patrick, April 18, 1856; Daniel, April 3, 1858; John, March 24, 1861; Edmund, December 24, 1862; Margaret, August 20, 1865; Thomas, January 20, 1867; Ellen, February 3, 1869; Hannorah, June 27, 1870; Joanna, May 14, 1872 and James, February 9, 1874.

The family and their descendants were and are devout members of the Roman Catholic Church and have taken an active part in the development of Meeker County. Patrick Casey, Sr., the territorial pioneer, was, politically, a democrat. He served his township as chairman of the town board of supervisors and town treasurer.

There are 90 or more living descendants of Mr. and Mrs. Patrick Casey in addition to their four living children: Thomas; Margaret (Sister Emerantia); Hannorah and Josephine.

OLSON, ANDREW, born in Norway, July 28, 1828 was living on his farm in Section 25, Acton town at the time of the Indian outbreak and with his family found refuge in the stockade at Forest City and assisted in its construction. He was present during the Indian attack of September 4, 1862. September 22, 1862 he accompanied Nels Danielson, Berger Anderson and Ole Amundson to their farmsteads to harvest their grain and care for stock. While engaged in salting his cattle he was killed and scalped by a band of Indians. He was buried on his farm but later his body was reinterred in the Ness cemetery in Litchfield township and a monument was erected at his grave. He was survived by his wife and three children: Sibert, Christine (Mrs. G. H. Snndahl) and Marie (Mrs. Charles H. Hammer.)

WEILER, MATHIAS E., (son of Peter and Margaret Braden-Weiler) was born in Luxemburg, Stearns County, Minnesota, May 6, 1863. The father, Peter Weiler, was a native of Gr-D. de Luxemburg, one of the small independent countries of Europe. He came to America in the early fifties and established his residence in the township of Luxemburg where his son Mathias was born. He was a locksmith by trade but engaged in farming. Mathias Weiler, his son, spent his boyhood years on the farm and later attended the State Teachers College at St. Cloud where he qualified himself to engage his services as a teacher. At the age of 16 he taught the rural school in his native township and the following year taught a rural school in Darwin township.

In 1880 he engaged his services as a clerk in the general store owned by Marcus Maurin in Cold Spring, Stearns County where he remained for four years. In 1887 he came to Eden Valley and entered the employ of Theisen and Schoen, general merchants. Mr. Weiler entered into partnership with his brother-in-law, Joseph Friedman in 1891 and established the well known firm of M. E. Weiler and Company. They used the slogan: One Price Big Store. The firm prospered and the store was enlarged and ranked among the largest and best stocked stores in Meeker County. Mr. Weiler became recognized as one of the real leaders in the upbuilding of Eden Valley.

Mr. and Mrs. Mathias E. Weiler

In 1907 he became president of the State Bank of Eden Valley and continued as president for a period of 21 years at which time the bank was reorganized under the corporate name of the State Bank in Eden Valley and he became Chairman of the Board of Directors. Mr. Weiler took a deep interest in civic affairs serving as Mayor of the village, president of the Eden Valley Telephone Exchange and established a brick yard near the village which furnished much of the brick used in the construction of public, church and business buildings. He was a devout member of the Catholic church and contributed liberally toward its support and in Company with Joseph Friedman presented St. Peter's Church with the grounds on which the church is located.

Mathias E. Weiler married, June 1, 1886, Mary Friedman (daughter of Nicholas and Marie Young-Friedman) born January 4, 1864 in Cold Spring, Stearns County, Minnesota. Her father, Nicholas Friedman was a soldier in the Civil War and died at Marietta, Tennessee soon after his enlistment. Mr. and Mrs. Weiler were the parents of two children: Dennis who died in infancy and Rose A. born October 5, 1901.

Mathias E. Weiler died, January 5, 1929; his wife Mary Friedman-Weiler died April 6, 1937.

PETERSON, OSCAR, a native of the province of Smoland, Sweden, came with his parents to Meeker County in 1855 and to Meeker County in 1876 where the father purchased a farm of eighty acres in Section 3, Collinwood township. Oscar developed the farm to a high state of productivity. He had a good education in his native language and acquired a knowledge of English superior to that of his pioneer neighbors. He had a natural talent in the writing of poetry in the Swedish language and composed the introductory poem in the Jubilee Album of the Dassel Lutheran Church. He enjoyed controversial debates on political issues and Norgren's Store was the forum for earnest debates with his neighbors. He died July 6, 1928.

NEILSON, NEILS L. (son of Anders and Martha Neilson-Sellan) was born, March 12, 1851 in the parish of Bergenstift, Bergen, Norway. The family moved to Loofoden (western coast of Norway) in 1853. Neils spent his boyhood years in this fishing port and what more natural than his becoming a sailor and fisherman.

In 1868, the Neilson family sailed for America. During their six weeks' voyage, a terrific storm arose and young Neilson joined the ship's crew during the remainder of the voyage. They landed at the Canadian port of Quebec from whence the family journeyed to St. Peter, Minnesota, arriving there July 4, 1868. They left St. Peter in 1869 in a covered wagon, drawn by oxen, and established their home on a farm in Lake Elizageth township, Kandiyohi County.

In 1879 they sold the farm and came to Meeker County and father and son purchased individually a combined acreage of 160 acres in section 36, Danielson Township.

Neils L. Neilson was a public spirited citizen and took an active interest in church, school and political affairs, serving as postmaster of the extinct Dickson post office, member of the school board (District 70) and township supervisor.

Mr. and Mrs. Neils L. Nielson

Mr. Neilson married, September 1876, Paulina Hansina Hanson, who was born near Tromso, Norway, June 4, 1851, and came to America with her parents in 1863. Mrs. Neils Neilson was of a deeply religious nature, a descendant of the sturdy Norsemen. Three of her cousins were famous walrus hunters and captains of ships at Spitzbergen, Norway, engaged in this hazardous vocation. One of the cousins, Captain Hans Christian Johannesen, made constructive arctic observations, which proved of great value to the famous explorer, Nordenskjold, in his trip thru the North East Passage and across Siberia to the Orient. Captain Johannesen accompanied the explorer on this trip and was in command of one of the ships and is mentioned by Nordenskjold as the first man to sail as far as the Lena river. Another cousin of Mrs. Neilson (Larson by name) was a member of the Norwegian Storthing (Parliament). Mrs. Neilson inherited many of the characteristics of her Viknng ancestry in meeting the hardships of pioneer life.

In 1916, Mr. and Mrs. Neilson established their home in Litchfield where they spent the remaining years of their life. Mr. Neilson died December 15, 1927 and was buried under Masonic auspices and laid at rest beside his wife in Ripley cemetery, who preceded him in death, May 11, 1924. They were the last surviving charter members of the Lake Elizabeth Methodist Church.

The living children are: Alfred H. born September 25, 1877; Dora M. (Mrs. Hugh Angier) June 18, 1881. Lester E., November 30, 1889. He is an attorney and for the past 22 years has been in the employ of the United States Treasury Department in St. Paul and Washington, D. C. He is a veteran of the World War and an author of legal publications. Nathaniel H., April 6, 1891, married Verne Olson, one child, Nathaniel, Jr. The family reside at Detroit Lakes, Minnesota where Mr. Neilson is employed in the U. S. Treasury Department as an official investigator. Etta M. (Mrs. S. C. Peeples) born, Janutry 26, 1893, children Audrey, Richard, Bruce and Pauline. They reside in Salt Lake City, Utah.

The deceased children are: Martin L. born June 17, 1879 died January 22, 1904; William C. born August 13, 1883, died June 26, 1922. Married Amanda Pearson, children: Lloyd and Lois Ruth. Arthur O., born May 20, 1885, died March 11, 1905; Ella E. born October 24, 1887 died January 23, 1908.

PETERSON, EDWARD P. (son of Olof and Johanna Ockerson-Peterson) was born near Vasa, Goodhue County, June 9, 1855. The Peterson family came to Meeker County in May 1867. The father homesteaded 80 acres in section 30 Harvey town where the son grew from boyhood into manhood. Edward assisted in the work of developing the farm and attended the public school and later the Litchfield High School from which he graduated with the class of 1873 and also spent one year at the Minnesota University.

At the age of nineteen he began teaching in the rural schools of the county and followed that profession for three years and at the conclusion of this period of service he joined his brother H. I. Peterson as a part owner of the Litchfield Independent. Mr. Peterson severed his connection with the Independent in 1880 and engaged in the study of law in the offices of the well known law firm of Campbell and Spooner and in 1883 was admitted to the bar and engaged in the private practice of law, opening an office in Litchfield.

His honest methods in dealing with his clients secured for him a lucrative practice. He did not often engage in the trial of cases in district court. His practice partook of that of a consultation attorney and a settlement of differences between conflicting interests outside of court. Mr. Peterson was considered one of Minnesota's best authorities in Probate practice in which he specialized.

Edward P. Peterson

During the years of his active life in Meeker County he served the village of Litchfield as President of the council, President of the Board of Education and village attorney. He served one term as County Attorney. He was elected State Senator in 1910, re-elected in 1914 and again in 1922.

Mr. Peterson was married in 1886 to Jennie Crowe (daughter of George and Jane O'Brien-Crowe) born in Ireland in 1860. Children: Marie (Mrs. T. L. O'Hearn) and Frances (Mrs. Wm. Kretchmar). Mrs. Jennie Crowe-Peterson died in 1909.

Edward P. Peterson died Saturday, February 21, 1931. At the time of his death the legislature was in session and a resolution was passed by the senate extending condolence and sympathy to the bereaved family and a committee consisting of Senators Victor Lawson of Kandiyohi, Herman Schmechel of Renville, and C. J. Putzier of Meeker County represented the Senate at the funeral.

NORGREN, LOUIS M. (son of John and Karen Larson-Norgren) was born in the province of Varmland, Sweden, February 19, 1864.

The father, John Norgren, with his wife and five children, came to America in 1866 and purchased a farm near Hancock, Carver County, Minnesota. In 1873 the family came to Meeker County and located in Kingston town, where the father purchased a half interest in the saw and flour mill at East Kingston. In 1875 he disposed of his interests to his partner and established his home in Dassel, where he engaged in the general merchandise business under the firm name of J. Norgren and Company. The firm was highly successful and Mr. Norgren was a leader in every effort to develop the Dassel community. He was noted for his great generosity and gave liberal credit to the early pioneers, financing many of them until they had a self-sustaining business. Immigrants newly arrived from Sweden received a warm welcome at the Norgren household and were aided financially when necessary. Mr. Norgren and his wife were charter members of the Mission Church, donated the lots on which the church was built, and also gave an acre of land to the Cemetery Association. They later met with serious reverses due to Mr. Norgren's connection with Peter Johnson in promoting a Swedish tile stove factory in Dassel Village.

Louis M. Norgren

Louis M. Norgren, his son, grew from boyhood to manhood in the Dassel community and served as a clerk in his father's store. He had a strong, magnetic personality, and was recognized as one of Dassel's most popular young men. Later he became a partner in the reorganization of his father's merchandise business, operating with his brother, John, under the firm name of Norgren Brothers.

On January 1, 1901, he was married to Huldah W. Nordine (daughter of Andrew and Anna Christopherson-Nordine) born April 9, 1877. A daughter, Violet Marian, was born December 3, 1903, and a son, Louis Lyndon, on May 16, 1905.

Louis Norgren was active in politics and served as Mayor of Dassel and in 1906 he was elected Register of Deeds for Meeker County and established his home in Litchfield. He served in this position three terms; at the conclusion of this period of service in 1913 he again took up his residence in Dassel village and opened a shoe store, which he operated at the time of his death, July 12, 1923.

The Dassel Dispatch, in commenting on his death, paid him the following tribute: "He was one of the best known men in the Dassel community and had a host of friends who loved him for his many fine qualities. He was an intelligent thinker and a deep student of public affairs. His integrity, sound judgment and honesty were never questioned. He was a good citizen and an upright man."

His widow, Mrs. Huldah W. Norgren, resides in Los Angeles, California, as does his son, Louis Lyndon, who is employed as teller in the Security First National Bank of that city. His daughter, Violet, at present residing in New York City, is the wife of Monroe Boston Strause, nationally-known baking consultant and lecturer; they have a daughter, Marilyn Barbara, born May 21, 1938.

ANGELL, CLARK L. (son of Nicholas and Asenath Nott-Angell) was born in Jefferson County, New York, May 25, 1838. The parents were natives of Vermont. The father served in the War of 1812 and the mother, from her home near Plattsburgh, New York, witnessed the naval battle between the British and Americans on Lake Champlain. Nicholas Angell died at the age of 61 and his widow came to Minnesota and died at the home of her daughter, Mrs. Olive Fuller in Rockford, Minnesota, at the age of 88.

Clark L. Angell was reared in the Empire State but in 1855 he journeyed westward and engaged in the development of the farm owned by his mother, acquired by the use of government bounty warrants awarded her husband as a soldier in the war of 1812 in effecting removal. The certificate of title is in the possession of the Angell family and bears the signature of President Buchanan.

Mr. Angell enlisted in the fall of 1861 in Co. A. 3rd Minnesota Infantry and served one year, when due to sickness he was discharged and returned to Minnesota. He became a student of photography and traveled thru Minnesota and North Dakota but in 1869 he came to Litchfield, Minnesota where he erected a home and became a permanent resident of the county seat where he established an art gallery, the first in the county. Mr. Angell was a

Clark L. Angell

prominent factor in the development of the village and exerted a marked influence in county affairs. He was public spirited and gave freely of his time and became a leader in public enterprises. He was a charter member of the Frank Dagget G. A. R. Post and Golden Fleece Lodge No. 89, A. F. and A. M.

Mr. Angell married, July 3, 1864, Nancy Ball (daughter of Joseph and Sarah Haylett-Ball) born in Prescott, Ontario, Canada. Five children were born of this union:

Alice, born at Rockford, Minnesota, December 7, 1865; Married Charles F. Lamb (deceased). One child, Newell (deceased).

Hiram (deceased) born November 29, 1867.

Otto (deceased) born June 7, 1871.

Clark, born June 7, 1871. He married September 12, 1899. Kate Austin (daughter of Mark and Mary Austin of Ellendale, North Dakota) born in Wisconsin in 1873.

Two children were born of this union; Louis, born July 1900, married, June 27, 1923, Christine Baumgartner. They are the parents of Clark and Hiram. Mary, bo.n September 25, 1902; married, March 3, 1926 Captain G. A. Tacot and has one child, Charles. Louis died in childhood.

Clark Angell, Sr., died June 16, 1907. Mrs. Nancy Ball-Angell died February 2, 1929.

SALISBURY, J. B. was born in 1824, of Holland Dutch descent. He was a native of New York and was a skilled surveyor of land. He had one year's service in the Mexican War and was at the City of Mexico when the war closed. He came to Meeker County in 1855 and while engaged as a surveyor in establishing township lines in the county, he was greatly pleased with the section of country in Kingston town and in 1855 he staked a claim in sections 18 and 19 and the following year he moved his family from his home in Scott County, Iowa. He brought all his goods with him and it took him nearly an entire month to make the journey. To one large wide tracked wagon were hitched four yoke of oxen and to another wagon a team of horses. Much of the time consumed on this trip was spent in clearing a road thru the "Big Woods" there being no other road than a blazed trail so narrow that one team could barely get thru. This trail for years was known as the "Old Territorial Road."

Mr. and Mrs. J. B. Salisbury

The cabin home he erected on his arrival was one of the first houses erected in the county. The family at this time consisted of self and wife (Margaret Weymer-Salisbury), one son, Frank L., his father-in-law, Jacob Weymer, his wife and two sons, Jacob, Jr., and Joseph. At the time of the Indian outbreak, he left the farm and went to Kingston village which he helped to fortify. All the refugees for a time spent their nights in the grist mill which was being used as a fort. One month later he enlisted in the "Mounted Rangers" or First Minnesota Cavalry and served thru the Indian troubles and then re-enlisted in Hatch's Independent-Battalion of Minnesota Cavalry and served during the duration of the war. The family spent these years in their former home in Iowa but in 1866 he was united with his family in his Kingston home. In 1868 he was elected to represent his district in the legislature and in 1870 was elected County Surveyor and served as such or as deputy for a long period of years. Mr. and Mrs. Salisbury were the parents of eight children.

HANSON, BENGT, was born in the province of Skona August 6, 1825. He left his native country enroute for America in October 1857. When they reached Hamburg, Germany, they were detained for 20 days before embarking for their overseas voyage. The family consisted of Mr. and Mrs. Hanson and three children, Emma aged 3; Carl and Nels, (twins) less than one year of age. They landed in New York, July 3, 1858 and proceeded westward via Dunkirk, New York and Toledo, Ohio and finally arrived at Chicago. There was no depot at the latter place and his goods were dumped on the ground and the family were obliged to walk three miles through muddy streets to another railroad line where in the absence of passenger cars they rode in box cars Prairie Du Chein and from there they boarded a boat for Carver, Minnesota. Mr. Hanson purchased a team of horses and wagon and leaving his family behind explored the unsettled country in adjoining counties but did not find an appealing location. Mr. Hanson then took the trail to Meeker County and purchased 130 acres of land in section 23 Litchfield Town. Mr. Hanson prospered in his new home and gradually increased his acreage to a farm of 1,000 acres and became one of the most substantial citizens of Meeker County. The Ripley Cemetery was formerly part of his holdings.

During the Indian outbreak the family found refuge in the stockade at Forest City where their daughter Caroline was born, September 4, 1862. During the outbreak the Indians stole his team of horses. Mr. Hanson gained the confidence and respect of the citizens of Litchfield town, evidenced by the fact that he held the office of town supervisor for more than twenty years. Bengt Hanson married in October 1853, Elna Larson and they became the parents of eight children.

Emma, born, December 10, 1854, married Olof H. Peterson. She died leaving one daughter, Minnie (Mrs. Berg).

Carl J. G. and Nels C. G. (twins) born in Hamburg, Germany May 14, 1857. Nels C. G. married June 30. 1887, Emma C. Lindberg and Carl J. G. married, November 4, 1886, Clara L. Ahlstrom.

Alfred Emmanuel, born July 30, 1859, died December 15, 1898.

Caroline, born in the Forest City Stockade, September 4, 1862, married March 13, 1884, Andrew Johnson. She died June 6, 1916 leaving a family of four children: Oscar A., Mabel, Florence (deceased) and Dewey.

Esther, born April 4, 1865, married P. P. Isaakson. They are the parents of Carl, May, Evelyn and Hannah.

Edla Victoria, born May 30, 1874, married Christian Christianson.

Mrs. Bengt Hanson died, April 5, 1892. Bengt Hanson died in 1902.

HOAR, DAVID B., a territorial pioneer and descendant of the prominent Hoar family of Massachusetts came to Meeker County in 1857 and in 1861 purchased a farm of 160 acres in Section 34, Union Grove township which was later increased to a farm of 320 acres. He was living on the farm when the news reached him of the Acton Massacre and he and his wife and other near relatives made a hurried trip to Manannah townsite from which point the members of his family went to Monticello. Mr. Hoar remained and joined other settlers in the perilous adventures of that period. He and his wife, formerly Melissa Bryant, experienced all the difficulties of the early pioneers in Meeker Couny but weathered all obstacles and achieved a comfortable independence. In 1877 their crops were destroyed by grasshoppers. During the early years, farm products brought little cash to the home treasury. Wheat sold as low as 35 cents a bushel, eggs, 5 cents per dozen and butter 5 cents a pound. They raised a family of eleven children and their sons Ambrose and Forest reside on the home farm and are highly respected citizens of Union Grove township.

JOHNSON, HERMAN S., (son of Swan and Marie Johnson) was born August 27, 1872 and died December 26, 1935. He was reared to manhood on his father's farm in Collinwood town where he attended the district school and later graduated from Gustavus Adolphus College at St. Peter, Minnesota, class of 1899. He then engaged in teaching and was principal of the Grove City Schools in 1905-06 and was elected County Auditor the same year, serving three terms when he accepted the position of Deputy under his successor, A. O. Palmquist, serving for 5 years when he resigned this position to become cashier of the Citizen's State Bank. He severed his official connection with the bank in 1923 to become editor and manager of the Meeker County News which position he filled with great credit until August 1933 when due to impaired health he was obliged to abstain from all public service.

During his lifetime he was active in the religious, social and civic life of the community. He married in 1908, Bertha Lenhardt (daughter of Michael and Margareta Lenhardt) born August 14, 1880. They are the parents of Ruth, born, April 7, 1910, who married Russel M. Johnson, of St. Paul and by this union have one child, Stephen Russel, born October 7, 1937.

ANGIER, JOHN R. (son of Roland and Mary Marsh-Angier) was born in Porter County, Indiana, February 12, 1845. In company with his parents he came to Minnesota in 1859. They established their home in section 10, Greenleaf township. They found a temporary refuge at Forest City following the Acton tragedy and later at Clearwater. When the danger period had passed they returned to their home and resumed their farming operations.

John R. Anger enlisted, February 15, 1865 in Co. M, First Minnesota Heavy Artillery and was stationed at Chattanooga, Tennessee and at the close of the war served as an orderly to the captain of his company. He was honorably discharged October 9, 1865.

In 1866 Samuel Gleason, a Civil War Veteran, and his family located on the farm adjoining the Angiers. The Gleason family were originally from Ontario, Canada. They had moved to Wisconsin in 1851 and two years later to Waseca, Minnesota where they were living at the close of the Civil War. Their daughter, Arletta, (whose mother was Lucy Winter-Gleason) was born in Ontario, Canada, February 8, 1851.

Mr. and Mrs. John R. Angier

The Angier and Gleason families became close friends and neighbors and what could have been more natural than the marriage of John R. Angier and Arletta Gleason which was solemnized April 19, 1870. They resided on the Angier farm for two years, then moved to Eau Claire, Wisconsin and two years later returned to Meeker County and established their permanent home in Litchfield where Mr. Angier was employed in carpentry work. He died, August 18, 1924 and his wife Arletta Gleason-Angier died June 29, 1925. They were the parents of four children:

Alice Ethel was born February 4, 1871 and married, June 26, 1890, Clarence Perry (deceased) children: Maud (Mrs. D. F. Williams); Laura (Mrs. Earl Berkey) and Earl who died January 6, 1937.

Harold E., born August 4, 1872, married November 29, 1894, Ada Freeman. Children: Arthur, Alpha (Mrs. Russel Baughn); Dora (Mrs. Wallace Morlock) and Lois who died at the age of 12.

Carroll W., born, September 14, 1877, married, June 15, 1910, Miranda Bottomley. He died December 25, 1937, leaving three children, Constance Jean (Mrs. Gordon McDonald) and Elizabeth.

Hugh I., born March 29, 1880. He married, May 1, 1909, Dora M. Nelson (daughter of Neils and Hansina Hanson-Neilson) born June 18, 1881. Mr. and Mrs. Hugh Angier established their home in Cook county, Minnesota in perfecting a homestead claim and in 1913 came to Litchfield where he has been employed since 1920 as an R. F. D. carrier.

Mr. and Mrs. Hugh Angier are the parents of three living children: Robert B., born March 24, 1917 and his sister, Ethel Luella, born September 2, 1919 are students at Hamline University and Doris Viola, born August 1, 1921 is a 1939 graduate of the Litchfield High School.

BOLAND, REV. FATHER P. J. (son of Patrick and Winnifred Boland) was born in Waltham, Massachusetts, April 19, 1858. At the age of five he accompanied his parents to Minneapolis, Minnesota where he acquired his early education. He then enrolled as a student in St. Francis Seminary, Milwaukee and later in St. John's College at Collegeville, Minnesota, where he completed the theological course and was ordained a priest of the Catholic Church, July 26, 1882. His first pastorate was at Hastings, Minnesota, where he remained for several years when he was assigned to the Litchfield Parish June 21, 1886, as the successor of Rev. Hugh McDevitt, and continued to serve during the remaining years of his life, a period of forty-five years, rarely equalled or exceeded by any other servant of the Master. At the beginning of this period of service his field extended westward to points beyond Willmar, and south almost to Hutchinson.

Rev. Fr. P. J. Boland

In 1911, he celebrated the twenty-fifth anniversary of his Litchfield pastorate. The program of exercises was an event of import in the annals of the County Seat City. Solemn High Mass was celebrated in the morning by Rev. Boland followed by the Anniversary Sermon by Rt. Rev. Father James O'Reilly, D. D., Bishop of Fargo. In the evening a complimentary banquet was tendered him in the G. A. R. Hall at which toasts and addresses were given by Litchfield Pastors, visiting clergy and prominent citizens of the village. The keynote of all these varied addresses was the faithfulness of his labor, the influence radiating from his exemplary life and his interest in all community activities of a worthy nature.

Father Boland established himself in the minds and hearts of the citizens in the field of his labor and his friends were legion. No other citizen of Litchfield was more highly esteemed.

He took an active interest in athletic sports, enjoyed hunting and fishing and camp life in general.

He passed away at the home of his brother, William Boland, of Waverly, with whom he spent the Christmas day of 1931, in fellowship with him and others of his relatives. He retired for the night to open his eyes again in the spiritual world. The body was interred in St. Anthony Cemetery in St. Paul.

His last public address was given before the Litchfield Senior and Junior High School body about one week previous to his death.

This illustration portrays the memorial erected to him in St. Philip's Church cemetery in Litchfield. The inscription reads as follows: "To the Memory of Father Patrick Boland. Ordained, July 25, 1882. Sacredo In Aeternum." Monument dedicated July 25, 1932. Note—This sketch of Father Boland is contributed by his intimate protestant and catholic friends.

DAGGETT, Frank E., whose name was given to the Litchfield Grand Army Post was at the time of his death among the most eminent citizens of Meeker County. He was a native of Vermont. He was an abolitionist of the sternest type and shortly after attaining his majority was a citizen of Kansas where he was a close associate of John Brown and in harmony with his plans to create an insurrection among the southern negroes. He fully intended to accompany Brown on his Harpers Ferry expedition which took place in his absence to visit his mother in her Vermont home.

He served during the Civil War as a private in the First Vermont Regiment, the Sixth Minnesota Infantry and later attained the rank of Lieutenant in the 117th U. S. Regiment (colored) assigned to the Army of the Potomac. He was taken sick and compelled to resign in 1864. He again resumed work as a journalist printer and in April 1872 in company with W. D. Joubert he came to Litchfield and they established the Litchfield Ledger. He achieved state wide fame as a journalist and served as clerk of the House during several sessions of the legislature and at one time was Grand Commander of the Department of Minnesota G. A. R. He died October 14, 1876 at the age of 39. In reference to his death the St. Paul Dispatch paid the following tribute: "As a man he was noble, just and true, a devoted generous friend, a magnanimous foe." W. D. Joubert, his partner on the Litchfield News Ledger, commented as follows: "A man in all the elements that go to make a man. To know him was to respect him and to respect him as one of the noblest works of God." H. I. Peterson in chronicling the death of his competitor in the field of journalism said of him: Independent—enemies he had none. Friends all."

DUNN, CHARLES B., of colonial Dutch descent, was a native of New York, born October 14, 1831. He left home at an early age and found employment following the tow path on the Erie Canal. Later he was employed (1896) in railroad work and was a member of the construction crew that laid the rails for the St. Paul and Pacific railway thru Meeker County. He became in the later years of his life a citizen of Dassel village and served as street commissioner and promoted the establishment and development of the Railroad park in that village. He was a prominent Mason and at the time of his death, March 30, 1925, was the oldest Shriner in the United States.

LINNELL, O. M., a native of Sweden, came to America with his parents in 1852. He served during the Civil War in Company C., Seventh Minnesota Infantry and participated in the stirring events of the Indian outbreak in Minnesota. He was one of the command stationed at Mankato to guard the 38 Indians prior to their execution. He came to Meeker county in 1876 and owned a farm of 520 acres in Acton town and served as a representative in the legislative sessions of 1881 and 1883. He was a worthy member of the Swedish Lutheran church and was a strong supporter of restrictive legislation to advance the cause of temperance.

JORGENSON (JOHNSON) HALVOR, was born in Kongsberg, Norway, May 12, 1837. During his youth and early manhood he was employed by the Norwegian government in their operation of a silver mine in the vicinity of his birthplace. At the age of twenty he came to America and secured employment in saw mills and logging camps near Stevens Point, Wisconsin. Here he wooed and won, in 1866, Mary Runninger, born in Tellamarken, Norway, August 21, 1839 and shortly after his marriage accompanied by Mr. and Mrs. Halvor Christianson and other friends journeyed to Minnesota. They came in a covered wagon hauled by a team of oxen. They spent thirty-one days in reaching Meeker County and established their home for the winter in the town of Acton. The following year Mr. Johnson homesteaded 80 acres in section 14, Swede Grove town and constructed a sod house for their home which was replaced the next year by a log structure.

Mr. Johnson was blessed with a worthy helpmate, Mrs. Johnson joined her husband in extending neighborly help to the influx of Scandinavian settlers. She was a practical nurse and midwife and many men of sixty years of age, now living, were cared for in their infancy by this good wife and mother. Mr. and Mrs. Johnson, during their years of tireless effort, expanded their holdings to a farm of 400 acres and in the later years of Mr. Johnson's life enjoyed all of the comforts and luxuries merited by their years of patient toil.

Mr. Johnson died August 3, 1925. Mrs. Johnson lived to the age of 99. The living children are George, Carrie, Denna, Fred and Louis.

LENHARDT, ERHARDT, a native of Saxony, Germany, was born April 5, 1844 and in 1873 came with his family to America and the same year to Meeker County where he formed a partnership with Louis Poetzer and established the first and only brewery in Meeker County which was located on the north west shore of Lake Ripley in Litchfield township. The business proved profitable and the partnership was at a later date dissolved and Mr. Lenhardt became the sole owner and was numbered among the substantial business men of Litchfield.

Mr. Lenhardt was public spirited and was in the forefront in every movement to advance the interests of the Litchfield community (see pages 114 and 116). He was a charter member of the St. Paul's German Evangelical Lutheran Church and contributed liberally to its support and was the leading contributor in the purchase of the bell which through the years has called the people to worship in this sanctuary.

Mr. and Mrs. Lenhardt became the parents of four children: Minnie (Mrs. William Shoultz); Edmund M.; Emelia (Mrs. John Shoultz); Rose (Mrs. Frank Viren).

Mr. Lenhardt died February 14, 1929. Mrs. Charlotte Flashet-Lenhardt died June 1911.

Edmund Lenhardt was born January 31, 1876 in Litchfield township. He was educated in the public schools. He spent the early years of his life in his father's service and in 1914 became the manager of the Lenhardt Hotel and following his father's death purchased the hotel and continued to own and operate the same up to the time of his death.

Erhardt Lenhardt

Edmund was a man of quiet disposition and kindly nature, extremely loyal and helpful to his friends. He was a great lover of horses and in his younger years was deeply interested in out door sports and belonged to one of the ball teams known throughout the county. He was a liberal contributor to all worthy projects.

Mr. Lenhardt married March 20, 1912, Leona Shoultz (daughter of Louis and Marie Boehlke) born February 7, 1882. Children: Helen, Jane (Mrs. Percy Agnew) and Joan.

The Shoultz family were natives of Germany. They located on a farm adjoining the townsite of Waverly in 1868 and erected a log house and conducted a boarding house for laborers engaged in laying the railroad tracks through the village and among their patrons was James J. Hill, the president of the road. They resided in Wright County until 1893 when the family came to Litchfield and operated the American House (hotel) for a period of years, retiring from active business in 1910. Louis Shoultz was a veteran of the Civil War and participated in some of its most stirring engagements including the memorable battle of Gettysburgh. The Shoultz family were among the early settlers of Wright County and resided on a farm in the vicinity of Waverly.

Edmund Lenhardt

PUTZIER, CHARLES J. (son of Mr. and Mrs. John Putzier) was born in Greenleaf township, Meeker County, October 10, 1865. He grew to manhood on his father's farm and was educated in the public schools. In 1886 he began farming on his own account and owned and operated a farm of 484 acres. He was highly successful and was numbered among the best and most prosperous farmers in the entire county.

When James J. Hill was presenting pedigreed sires of varied breeds of cattle in Great Northern territory, a survey was made of farms in the vicinity of Litchfield, Hill's representative visited the Putzier farm, its orderly appearance and the care given the farm machinery and livestock impressed him so favorably that he offered to place one of the sires with Mr. Putzier. The plan of distribution required a contract obligation whereby an agent of Hill was to have supervision over the care of the animal and enforce the terms of the contract. Mr. Putzier refused entering into any contract and in forceful language stated that Jim Hill couldn't dictate to him how he should run his farm or care for his livestock. In the absence of a signed contract the sire was placed on the Putzier farm and was cared for according to the terms of the unsigned contract. It is believed, by well informed parties, that this was one of very few cases in the state where Hill placed one of his pedigreed sires on a farm without a signed contract.

Charles J. Putzier

In the later years of his life Mr. Putzier took an active interest in public affairs, serving as president of the Citizens State Bank and director of the Meeker County Farmers' Publishing Company. In 1926 Mr. Putzier was the Farmer-Labor candidate for State Senator and was elected and reelected in 1930. Previous to his death, February 15, 1934, he met with serious business reverses but did not forfeit the respect and esteem of the citizens of Meeker County. The funeral was largely attended and he was laid at rest in Ripley Cemetery.

Charles J. Putzier married, October 10, 1888, Minnie Manthey. There were six children born of this marriage, Hazel (Mrs. Albert Helwig); Donald; Lewis; Louise (Mrs. Walter Haag) Glen and Raymond.

Donald Putzier, his eldest son, was born and reared on his father's farm and received his education in the public schools. Upon reaching his maturity, he leased a tract of 160 acres of land in Montana and engaged in farming. He returned to Litchfield in the fall of 1918 and entered the service of the Minar Motor Co. and in 1930-1932 he assisted his father in the operation of his farm. He then secured his present position as manager of the bulk station of the Standard Oil Co. in Litchfield. Donald Putzier married, July 18, 1907, Agnes Schlenz (daughter of Charles and Mary Busse-Schlenz) born October 22, 1895. They are the parents of David, Willard and Jean.

JOHN WHALEN and JOHN FLYNN came through the big woods in the spring of 1856 and forded the Crow river near Kingston. The water was shoulder deep. They found it easier to get into the river than to get out. Whalen drew himself out by a root and Flynn was then rescued by Whalen.

They brought their bread from St. Anthony and after selecting their claims they started on their return trip for their families. They had one small loaf of bread, two weeks old, which was wrapped in a handkerchief and used at night for a pillow. It was stolen by some person during their first night's slumber and they were without food during the remainder of their journey. They stayed at Monticello one night and were charged $6 each for supper, breakfast and lodging on a bed of shavings. They returned with their families and reached their claims October 22, 1856.

WEBER, JOHN (son of Peter and Sebillia Karl-Weber) was born in the Grand Duchess of Luxemburg, Germany, September 13, 1839 and died January 18, 1911. Jeanette Ferris of German descent who became his wife was the daughter of Peter and Anna M. Arendt-Ferris and was born in Reading, France May 20, 1849 and died May 29, 1911.

John Weber came to America in 1867 and remained in New York City for two years and then located in Chicago and was employed in both of these cities as a highly skilled and experienced worker in the shaping and lettering of building rock. He was in Chicago at the time of the disastrous fire of 1871 and had many thrilling experiences. Following the fire, he came to Meeker County and purchased a forty acre tract of land in section 9, Darwin township. He operated the farm and accepted employment at varied periods as a stone mason.

Mr. Weber became a fully naturalized citizen of the United States October 29, 1904. His Darwin home was a rough frame building. The ceiling of straw was supported by poles and rafters and the floor was native soil. All the furniture was home made. On January 6, 1873 in company with his neighbor, Peter Steren, he made a business trip to Litchfield. At three o'clock in the afternoon a blizzard was brewing and they started for home. The intensity of the storm increased to such an extent that at times they were unable to see the horses. They began to despair of finding any refuge when the team halted at a straw shed on the William Mass farm where with their team of horses they found a safe shelter. They spent three days and three nights in the shed before the storm abated to such an extent as would permit Mr. Weber, who was deeply concerned for the safety of his wife and baby, to proceed on foot to his home. A mountain of snow completely covered the house but with frantic and exhaustive labor he effected an entrance and found his wife and child had met with no serious results and the severe experiences through which they had passed were overshadowed with happiness by their reunion. Mrs. Weber had used the pole rafters, straw and all the furniture with the exception of the bedstead for fuel to save the life of herself and child from freezing. From this time forward the family grew and prospered, Mr. Weber increasing his land holdings from 40 acres in 1871 to 400 acres in 1909 at which time Mr. and Mrs. Weber established their home in Litchfield.

Mr. and Mrs. John Weber were married December 25, 1871. There were nine children born of their union, three of whom died in infancy. Their surviving children were: Peter, born December 12, 1872; married, January 8, 1900, Elizabeth Binsfield (daughter of Mr. and Mrs. Michael Binsfield) of Cold Springs, Minnesota.

Mary, born November 24, 1880, died June 17, 1900.

Theresa, born October 4, 1878; married Jacob Pallansch. She was the mother of two sons who died in infancy. Mrs. Pallansch died May 15, 1932.

Henry, born May 24, 1886; married Ostober 6, 1908, Elizabeth Mathiew and they became the parents of three children: Frank, born at Litchfield April 28, 1913; Genevieve (Weber) Mattila born at Litchfield September 28, 1910; Celestine born at Aitkin June 25, 1916. Mr. and Mrs. Weber reside at Aitkin, Minnesota where he is engaged in the drayage business.

Elizabeth, born August 11, 1883; married February 26, 1908, William Miller (son of Mr. and Mrs. Philip Miller of Eden Valley. Children: Edward, born at Litchfield November 3, 1908; Leo, born at Litchfield October 5, 1910; Evelyn, born at Litchfield February 8, 1913; Dorothea, born at Litchfield September 6, 1915, deceased; Franklin, born at Litchfield, died in infancy; Lawrence, born at Litchfield, July 31, 1918; William, Jr., born at Litchfield September 28, 1924. Mr. and Mrs. Miller reside in Litchfield, Minnesota.

Nicholas, born April 16, 1875; married June 25, 1904, Anne Wolf (daughter of John and Margaret Lammel-Wolf) of Pearl Lake, Minnesota. They are the parents of Bertha (Weber) Finnegan, born at Litchfield, April 29, 1905; Alvina, born at Litchfield March 4, 1908; Clarence, born at Litchfield, February 1, 1916. Mr. and Mrs. Weber reside in Litchfield where Mr. Weber has been engaged in the farm machinery business since 1926.

McGOWAN, MARY (daughter of Thomas and Catherine McDonald-McGowan) was born in Ireland May 17, 1864 and died April 28, 1920. The parents, natives of the Emerald Isle, came to America in the late sixties and, October 6, 1864, preempted the N½ of the SW¼, Section 14, Darwin township. They experienced all the privations of the pioneers of that early period but surmounted all their difficulties and achieved a comfortable independence. Thomas McGowan died about 1870 and his good wife was called to her final rest April 28, 1920. The original homestead is owned by the McGowan heirs.

Mary McGowan, in her girlhood developed marked talent as a seamstress and entered the employ of Mrs. Kelly who conducted a millinery and dressmaking shop in Litchfield and subsequently Mary opened a shop of her own which she conducted up to the time of her death.

Mary and Elizabeth McGowan

Miss McGowan was very energetic and possessed good business ability. She was extremely loyal to her family, evidenced by the fact that she cared for and assisted in educating three of her sisters and a brother. She was the owner of the building and home now owned and occupied by her sisters, Sadie and Elizabeth, her successors in the same line of business. The McGowan Millinery Shop is one of the oldest business establishments in Litchfield.

McGOWAN, ELIZABETH, sister of Mary, was born in Darwin township, May 3, 1870. She was educated in the public schools and graduated from the State Teachers College in Winona. She engaged her services as a teacher for a period of fifteen years. In 1903 she was elected County Superintendent of Schools for Meeker County and enjoys the distinction of being the first lady to hold that position in the county. Her services were endorsed by reelection to the office.

PETERSON, MRS. LINA DUNN (daughter of Mr. and Mrs. Charles Dunn was born in Winona, Minnesota, June 5, 1864. In 1869 she came to Meeker County with her parents who located in the Dassel community. She attended the Chaney School and the first school held in Dassel village and in the early years of her maturity became a leader in the social activities of the village of Dassel and later in life became prominent in community activities. She served as president of women's clubs and was well known in Eastern Star circles thruout the county. She was a charter member of the Griswold chapter of that order which she served as secretary for thirty-four years. She served the village as justice of the peace for several years and took an active interest in politics and became an ardent worker for the Farmer-Labor party in the county and state. Mrs. Peterson was keenly interested in journalism and worked as a local reporter for the Meeker County News and Dassel Dispatch. Mrs. Peterson was regarded during her life of service as being among Meeker County's most eminent women.

Mrs. Lina Peterson

Angelina Dunn married, September 2, 1884, Peter Peterson and became the mother of three children, two of whom died in infancy. She died January 19, 1934 and was laid at rest in the Dassel cemetery at which time she was survived by her daughter, Mrs. Gus Carlson and three granddaughters, Phylis, Audrey and Avis Carlson.

WORTHY OF REMEMBRANCE

In the life of every community there have been persons of quality and worth who have had the best interests of their community at heart. In the early days of Meeker County, amid its pioneering hardships, it needed this type of leadership. We call to our mind a few of these pioneers.

In Acton there was Peter Lund who took the leadership in piloting his neighbors to Forest City, following the Acton Massacre and contributed to the development of the Acton Community.

DANIEL JACKMAN, the first settler in the township of Cosmos and a leader in the organization of the township.

EMELIUS NELSON was the most beloved citizen of Danielson township and was the pioneer in the development of the Danielson Cooperative Creamery.

HENRY and HARLOW AMES (brothers) were among the substantial citizens of Dassel township. They owned and occupied the first frame house in the Dassel community and Henry opened and operated a brick yard near Litchfield and supplied the brick used in the construction of the first unit of the Lenhardt Hotel.

SWAN JOHNSON was one of the most eminent citizens of Collinwood township, a sincere Christian, a loyal citizen of his adopted country and a man of commanding influence in civic and educational affairs of the township.

EPHRAIM A. BRIGGS, a veteran of the Civil War, and an attorney by profession was richly endowed by nature and education to become one of Kingston's most influential citizens and a leader in the development of the Kingston community. He was for years engaged in the mercantile business.

DR. V. P. KENNEDY, Civil War veteran, established his home in 1856 on the claim originally entered by Dr. Ripley on the shores of the lake that bears his name. He was a skillful physician and in 1860 was elected a member of the state legislature. He owned and operated the Cedar Mills (water power) flour mill (1867-1869) and later became a practicing physician in Litchfield village.

CHARLES E. CUTTS located in Forest City in 1856. He served Meeker County as County Treasurer and State Senator during the sessions of the fourteenth, fifteenth and sixteenth sessions of the Minnesota legislature.

NATHAN CASWELL was regarded as the most eminent citizens of Manannah township in pioneer days. He was an active leader in public and educational affairs and no Meeker County citizen has been more closely identified with the official history of Meeker County and the township of Manannah.

BRITT, E. O. was one of the first settlers of Harvey town. His mother, Charity Tibbits-Britt was born in Litchfield, Maine, April 3, 1773. She preempted 160 acres of land and was living in 1888 at the advanced age of 103 years.

WAYLANDER, NELS, a native of Sweden came to America in 1852 and to Meeker County in 1857 and established his home in section 4, Acton township as a homesteader and in later years added to his acreage and became one of the prosperous farmers of that town. He was one of the first group of settlers to visit the scene of the Acton butchery and took a prominent part in the defensive activities of the settlers during the Indian outbreak.

CONTRIBUTED BY LITCHFIELD INDEPENDENT

PORTER, DANFORD was born December 24, 1812 in Warren, Vermont where he was reared on a farm and received a limited education in the public school. His paternal ancestor, William Porter came to America in the May Flower. Danford developed an interest in hunting and trapping and for a long period of years he derived his main support by selling the pelts of fur bearing animals. This vocation prompted him to make numerous changes in location. At thirty years of age he moved to Illinois where he preempted forty acres of land near the village of Richmond and in 1856 he established his residence on a farm near Janesville, Wisconsin and the following year came to Meeker County and homesteaded 80 acres in section 12, Ellsworth township where he continued to reside the remaining years of his life.

During the years of his residence in Darwin township he took a keen interest in public affairs and, under his leadership, School District No. 24 was organized and he became a member of the school board. In addition to his farming operations he continued to hunt and trap the fur bearing animals which were very numerous in the vicinity of his home. He was a crack shot with a rifle and when the bottoms of his cane seat chairs became useless he shot loons and used their hides to bottom his chairs.

Danford Porter married (1845) Sarah Streeter, daughter of a Baptist preacher in London, England who was banished from that country due to his being a dissenter from the church of England. Rev. Streeter came to America and served Baptist churches in the state of New York. Mr. and Mrs. Danford Porter became the parents of William; Harry; Edwin H.; Lucy (Mrs. Frank Wheeler); Derwin and Addie who married Caleb Sanborn, the son of Hiram Sanborn who was massacred by the Indians in September, 1863. (See page 70).

Edwin H. Porter, son of Danford, resides on the Porter homestead with his wife and son, Derwin. He has reached the age of 85 years and continues to occupy a portion of his time in the lighter tasks about the farm. Mr. Porter operated a threshing machine in Meeker County for years and has a wide acquaintance in the county. He married first, March 20, 1889, Louise Thompson (daughter of Loren and Sarah Vincent-Thompson) of Kingston township and they became the parents of Sadie (Mrs. O. B. Werner) of Los Angeles, California and Demi L. Mrs. Louise Thompson-Porter died October1 5, 1910 and Mr. Porter married, second, Dora Olmstead and they are the parents of Derwin and Elizabeth (Mrs. Archie Curtis) of Litchfield.

EASTMAN, ENOCH M., one of Meeker County's Grand Old Men, was born of Colonial ancestry at North Conway, New Hampshire, February 13, 1835. One hundred years had elapsed since his paternal ancestor landed in America. In childhood years his parents moved to Aristook County, Maine. Mr. Eastman became a carpenter and builder and in 1856 in company with his brother Rufus came to Meeker County and took up his residence in the Kingston townsite. He took an active part in guarding the settlers from Indian attack in the outbreak of 1862, and was a Civil War veteran. During his entire life he was an uncompromising Republican.

In the pursuance of his trade as carpenter and mover of buildings he had more than a local reputation. He built the Methodist and Presbyterian churches in Litchfield and moved with an ox team the major portion of the buildings in Forest City to Litchfield.

The Litchfield community feted him on his ninety-seventh birthday in a banquet gathering at the Lenhardt Hotel. He died the following month, March 29, 1932. He married, in 1869, Eugenia Belfoy, daughter of Frank Belfoy, the founder of Meeker County's first newspaper. There were four children born of this marriage.

TURCK, PAUL, in company with his brothers, Philip, John and Jacob, came to Meeker County in 1864. They were natives of Germany. Paul Turck was present when the township of Harvey was organized and was the first to suggest that the town be named Harvey to do honor to the memory of James Harvey, a hero of the Indian outbreak and county clerk of Meeker County (1863-1867). The friends of J. B. Atkinson urged that the town be named to honor that very worthy pioneer. A vote was taken and Harvey triumphed over Atkinson.

Biography

-o-

The abbreviated biographies of the men who have achieved success in their varied walks of life are designed to serve a manifold purpose.

Those who have contributed to the publication of these biographies have made possible the issuance of this history.

Many of our leading educators regard biographical study as the most developing subject offered the youth of today. The local biographies listed should make a direct appeal to the youth of Meeker County.

We do not presume to include in our brief sketches all the men entitled to be classed as community leaders. This has been rendered impossible for varied reasons.

HALVERSON, H. L. (son of Ole Halverson Thoen and Gunhill Kittelson-Thoen) was born February 14, 1859 on the home farm in Section 19, Litchfield. Both of his parents were territorial pioneers and suffered all the trials and privations of those early years. The father assisted in the burial of the victims of the Acton Massacre. The family found refuge at Forest City. Their home was burned by the savages.

Mr. Halverson, the subject of this sketch, spent his boyhood and youth in assisting his father in the operation of the farm. He had very little schooling but at the age of 20 he went to Battle Creek, Michigan and enrolled as a student in the Normal Department of the Battle Creek College from which he graduated in 1882. He returned to Meeker County and for five years taught the rural schools in Districts 7 and 8 in his home county. In 1888 he took charge of the home farm and in its operation became intensely interested in the problems connected with farm management. During this period he served as clerk of school District No. 8 and for a time was secretary of the Acton Telephone Company. In February, 1897 he was elected secretary-manager of the Litchfield Creamery.

Mr. and Mrs. H. L. Halverson

In 1908 Mr. Halverson disposed of his farm and located in Litchfield village.

He concentrated on the solution of farm problems. The farmers engaged in marketing their live stock were more or less at the mercy of local and traveling stock buyers and the prices accepted and paid were resulting in a marked loss to the farmers, Mr. Halverson became the leader in establishing the Litchfield Live Stock Shipping Association and became its Treasurer and Manager at the time of its organization in which position he continued until 1935 when he established his home in California. (A detailed story of the success and development of this organization will be found in the chapters relating to the success of this organization under the chapter relating to the agricultural development of the county.)

Mr. Halverson is deservedly called the "daddy" of the Cooperative Stock Shipping Associations that came into existence throughout the United States and Canada. The success attending the operations of the Litchfield Association resulted in many inquiries by mail and personal visits by parties interested to secure specific information regarding the organization. The most notable results came from a visit paid by a representative from the Agriculture Department of the University at Winnipeg, Canada.

The detailed information he secured from Mr. Halverson resulted in the organization in Canada of more than one hundred and fifty Associations that were successfully operated.

Mr. Halverson was kept busy answering inquiries relating to the Litchfield Association and addressing gatherings of farmers on Cooperative Shipping in Minnesota and bordering states.

Mr. Halverson became President about 1914 of a state wide organization of Live Stock Shipping Associations who sought thru contacts with the State Railway and Warehouse Commission and Railway Companies to further the interest of these coordinated Associations.

In speaking of this feature of his work Mr. Halverson said, "The railroads were our friends and were always accomodating and helpful."

H. L. Halverson married June 6, 1889 Mary E. Westman (daughter of Ole O. and Ingeborg Nelson-Westman).

Mrs. Halverson has proved a worthy helpmate and a deserving wife and mother.

This union was blessed with the birth of four children: Winifred V. (deceased) born April 8, 1890; Wilton L., born June 30, 1896; Glen R., born September 14, 1900 and Fern L., born December 1, 1904.

SIMONSON, JOHN ALFRED (son of Olof and Christine Anderson-Simonson) was born in Kingston township August 4, 1882. The father was a native of Varmland, Sweden, born October 17, 1836. He came to America in the late sixties and secured employment as a railroad contractor in the construction of the right-of-way for the Hastings and Dakota Railway. In 1875 he purchased 80 acres in Section 34, Kingston township and engaged in farming. He married, April 19, 1877, Mrs. Christine Anderson-Boren, a widow with two children, Emil (deceased) and August (Mrs. Edward Erickson.) They became the parents of Anna (Mrs. A. P. Johnson); Amanda (Mrs. O. J. Peterson). Both sisters are residents of Kingston township; Simon and Albert, who died in childhood, and John Alfred, the subject of this sketch.

Olof Simonson died, July 24, 1917. Mrs. Christine Simonson died May 27, 1933.

John Alfred Simonson was reared on his father's farm where he continued to reside until he reached the age of 25, giving helpful assistance in the development of the farm. The ground work of his education was acquired in the rural schools of his native township which he has expanded by a continuous program of self study.

Mr. Simonson left home in 1907 and was employed for two years by the Ives Ice Cream Company in Minneapolis. In 1909 he returned to his father's farm and took over the management of the farm. He was married June 19, 1909 to Hilma Peterson (daughter of Aaron and Mary Peterson) born in Dassel Township in 1879. In January 1915, he purchased the Lake Arvilla store in Kingston township which he continued to operate with the assistance of his wife until 1920. During his residence in the township he served for a period of three years as Township Supervisor.

John A. Simonson

In 1917 he was appointed Deputy County Auditor of Meeker County and in 1923 became the candidate, without opposition, for County Auditor. He entered upon his duties January 1, 1923 which he held until January 1, 1939 running the gauntlet of three election contests.

When the forces in opposition to the Farmer-Labor administration were seeking a sure winner candidate for State Senator in 1938 they prevailed upon Mr. Simonson to enter the list. In the primary contest he carried 21 out of 25 precincts and in the general election he was elected by a majority of 2,229.

During his service in the legislative session of 1939 he supported by his vote and influence the progressive program of legislation: Taxation, Reorganization of State Government, Labor Relations, and Civil Service. He served on the following committees: Taxes and Tax Laws, Towns and Counties, Elections and several less important committees.

Mr. Simonson's experience as County Auditor gave him a prestige with his associates that made his influence felt in the shaping of the bills enacted into law.

BAUMGARTNER, LEO L. (son of August and Dora Benway-Baumgartner) was born in Fairmont, Minnesota, April 12, 1897. He spent his boyhood days on his father's farm in Martin County. In 1910 the family established their home on a farm in Waseca County. Mr. Baumgartner was educated in the public schools and is a graduate of the Mankato Business College, Class of 1916. He enlisted in the World War in 1918 and was engaged in over seas service and was honorably discharged in July 1919 and returned to Waseca where he secured employment with a milling company. In 1920 he moved to Indianapolis, Indiana where he was employed until 1923 when he returned to Minnesota and, in partnership with his father, engaged in the operation of the H. C. Bull farm, adjoining the Collinwood townsite.

In the late winter of 1925, Mr. Baumgartner moved to Litchfield and, in partnership with W. K. Dyer, established the Litchfield Hatchery (See page 128). During the years of his residence in Litchfield he has served as President of the Community Club, Commander of the Nelsan-Horton Post of the American Legion, and Meeker County Chairman of the State Safety Council. In the spring election of 1939 he was elected mayor of Litchfield. He has taken a keen interest in the Boy Scout movement and has served as Chairman of the Litchfield District of the Boy Scout organization. Fraternally Mr. Baumgartner is a member of Golden Fleece Lodge, A. F. and A. M. of Litchfield.

L. L. Baumgartner

It is of interest to note that the Baumgartners have a common ancestry with the the author, Samuel L. Clemens (Mark Twain).

Mr. Baumgartner married, January 31, 1920, Mabel Hecht (daughter of John and Caroline Sanfferer-Hecht), born at Waseca, Minnesota, July 23, 1895. Children: Beatrice J., born November 17, 1920; Elaine, born May 9, 1925 and Bernice, who died in Childhood.

BODIN, MRS. HANNAH J., (daughter of Erick and Johanna Lusty-Johnson) was born in Nelson, Douglas County, Minnesota, May 26, 1890. She was educated in the public schools of her native county and the Ella Jones Gregg short hand school and took a course in music at the Minnesota College in Minneapolis.

Hannah J. Johnson (Mrs. Bodin) came to Meeker County in 1911 and engaged her services as assistant cashier in the Bank of Dassel, serving twelve years and was later employed for a period of six years in the Citizens State Bank and Farmers and Merchants Bank and then became Assistant Special Deputy Examiner in closing the affairs of the bank.

In January 1935 Mrs. Bodin entered the employ of the Dassel Seed Company as book keeper and remained in their employ until 1936 when she entered the employ of their successors, The Meeker County Seed Company and now serves as their office manager. Mrs. Bodin is deservedly regarded as among the most outstanding business women of Meeker County.

Hannah J. Johnson married, May 20, 1914, Victor E. Bodin (son of Nels and Karin Olson-Bodin) born April 14, 1883. He is a carpenter and farmer. They are the parents of John V. and Edith M.

WHITAKER, ALBERT J. (son of John A. and Emily Warner-Whitaker) was born at Kewanee, Carlton County, Wisconsin, March 13, 1867. In 1882 he accompanied his parents to Maple Plain, Minnesota. He was educated in the public schools and at the age of fifteen became dependent on his own resources. He took up the study of telegraphy and railroad bookkeeping and in 1883 was employed as water boy for a railroad fencing crew. In April 1884 he was employed as depot helper at Cokato, Minnesota and perfected himself in his chosen field of work. From this time forward his progress met no obstacles. He became night operator at Dassel and later was placed in charge of the Darwin station. He was only a youth and somewhat boyish in looks and action and failed to secure the necessary bonds to permit him to continue in this position and was returned to Dassel as night operator. He was later transferred to Litchfield where he served as a relief operator and assistant to O. B. Knapp. In the years that followed he served as Agent at Clontarf, Spicer, Dassel, Cokato and Marshall and was recognized by the public and railroad officials as one of the most efficient agents in the employ of the Great Northern Railway.

A. J. Whitaker

In 1898 Mr. Whitaker became permanently located as agent in charge at Litchfield. During his forty year period of service as the head of the Litchfield Office, he served two months in the spring of each year from 1900 to 1906 as an emigration agent in piloting settlers of Dunkard faith from Pennsylvania and Virginia to points in North Dakota.

Mr. Whitaker has repeatedly refused offers of advancement due to his unswerving loyalty to Litchfield and devotion to what he regarded as the best interests of his family. He is intensely interested in athletic sports and was one of the leaders in establishing the first baseball park in Litchfield. In conversation with the writer he said he owed much of his success in his early years to his wife who curbed his zeal in these activities when they might have impaired his vitality in attending to his official duties.

Albert J. Whitaker was married February 8, 1888 to Myrtle Elliott (daughter of Richard and Cyla Huntley-Elliott) born in Fillmore county, Minnesota, December 2, 1870. They are the parents of seven living children: Harry A., Montesano, Washington; Dr. Vernon D., Minneapolis, Minnesota; Philip S. and Roger B. of Litchfield, Minnesota; Mrs. Cyla Moffatt, Chokio, Minnesota; Mrs. June Bauleke, LeSueur, Minnesota and Paul D., Benson, Minnesota.

LARSON, GUY I. (son of Andrew W. and Elna Larson) was born in Atwater, Minnesota, June 27, 1890. The family moved to Meeker County in 1895 where the father had homesteaded land in Section 10, Swede Grove township. Guy was reared on the farm and educated in the public schools.

He spent the year 1909 in the employ of his brother Frans who operated a meat market at 3346 Hennepin Avenue South, Minneapolis. He returned to the farm the following year and operated a threshing machine and assisted his father on the farm. In 1924 Mr. Larson entered into partnership with his brother Nels in establishing a meat market in Atwater, Kandiyohi County, Minnesota. In 1933 he established the Larson Cash Meat Market in Litchfield in which business he has continued since that date. With the exception of eight and one-half years he has spent his entire life in Meeker County. He has taken an active interest in all matters affecting the development of Litchfield and Meeker County.

Mr. Larson married, March 12, 1919, Nellie Erickson (daughter of Nels and Anna Topp-Erickson) born August 26, 1892. They are the parents of Ardis, born January 8, 1920. She graduated from the Litchfield High School in 1937 and the Minneapolis Business College in 1938 and at present is employed as bookkeeper in the Gamble Store in her home village.

BRANDT, JOHN (son of Fritz and Henrietta Post-Brandt) was born on his father's farm in Section 30, Forest City township, July 20, 1878. Here he grew to manhood and is now the owner of the farm of 557 acres where he was born. He was educated in the public schools and attended the Litchfield High School for three terms but this constitutes only the foundation of his educational development. He has never ceased to be a student in adding to and supplementing his early education. In the school of experience he has acquired a knowledge of the problems affecting the dairy industry which has resulted in his becoming a recognized leader among the dairymen of Minnesota and neighboring states.

In 1922 Mr. Brandt organized the Land O'Lakes Creameries, Inc., and became its first president at which time headquarters were established in St. Paul and in 1925 in Minneapolis where the present plant was erected and equipped. The building is a reinforced concrete structure 600 feet long and 100 feet wide, two stories and a basement. (See page 124).

Mr. Brandt has been the governing factor in the development of the Land O'Lakes organization in manufacturing and distributing the dairy products of the northwest. He has become a nationally known character among the dairymen of the United States and is regarded by them as an authority in all matters affecting the dairy industry. He retained his residence on the farm until 1926 when he moved to Minneapolis. John Brandt married, March 11, 1908, Maud Caswell, daughter of Seth and Maud Caswell.

John Brandt

McCLELLAN, GEORGE BRUCE, was born in Clarion, Iowa, September 27, 1907. After completing the course of study in the grade schools he enrolled in the Wayzata, Minnesota High School and met his expenses by working in a restaurant. He graduated with the Class of 1926 whereupon he entered the University of Minnesota where he again met his expenses by similar work for a period of two years. From 1928 to 1931 he operated a Greyhound Bus and then obtained employment in Hart's Cafe at Wayzata. At the conclusion of this period of service Mr. and Mrs. McClellen purchased a cafe at Maple Lake, Minnesota which they operated successfully for three years. They disposed of their business at Maple Lake in 1934 and established themselves in the restaurant business at Benson and with visions of future expansion adopted as a name for their business "Mac's Coffee Bar System." Their vision became a reality with the establishment of Mac's Coffee Bars at Litchfield, Willmar, South Saint Paul and Benson.

Mr. and Mrs. McClellen have been highly successful and these Coffee Bars have become very popular with local patrons and the traveling public. The four cafes conducted by him give employment to 27 men and women. He advertises the fact that he does not serve beer in the places he operates.

Mr. McClellen married, May 2, 1928, Evelyn Paige Rome and this union has resulted in the birth of two children: Ruth, aged six and Alice Ray, aged four.

JONES, MATTHEWS KATE (daughter of Ralph and Martha Park-Matthews) was born in Wabasha, Minnesota August 7, 1865. When Kate was only two years of age her parents established their home in Kingston and seven years later moved to Litchfield. Here she attended school and graduated from the Litchfield High School with the class of 1885.

She became a teacher in the rural schools of her home county where her services were engaged for four years. She then enrolled in the Teachers' Training College at Moorhead, Minnesota and upon finishing her course of study she was thoroughly launched in the teaching profession and for a period of nine years was employed as teacher of the eighth grade in the Litchfield schools.

Mrs. Jones was elected Superintendent of Schools for Meeker County in the election of 1906 and served until 1913. During her incumbency the state had adopted a law extending aid to rural schools that met certain specified requirements. It was a period of marked growth and improvement. The old home-made wooden seats and benches were replaced with modern school furniture and other needed equipment and better methods of teaching were used by rural teachers. There were a large number of teachers who had been trained in the teachers' colleges of the state, and Meeker County kept pace with the older and more advanced counties of the state.

Kate Mathews Jones

At the conclusion of Mrs. Jones' administration, she was employed as the head of teachers' training departments in various high schools throughout the state. Mrs. Jones retired from the teaching profession in 1932 after nearly forty years of continuous interest and service in her chosen profession. Mrs. Jones resides at present in apartments at the Normandy Hotel in Minneapolis and continues to take a deep interest in world events and the social life of the community. She is a member of the Litchfield Woman's Club and Library Board and holds membership in the Molly-Stark Branham Chapter of the D. A. R. at Litchfield.

Kate Matthews was married August 29, 1888 to Elliott Jones. There was one child born of this union, Lsona (Mrs. Charles Huntoon) born in Fergus Falls, Minnesota, October 25, 1890.

ANDERSON, ALFRED (son of Olaf and Karin Nelson-Anderson), born June 25, 1882, in the parish of Mangskog, Vermland, Sweden. At fourteen years of age he came to America and joined his father at Dawson, Minnesota. He was educated in the Swedish schools of his native country but his knowledge of the English language is self-acquired. He came to Meeker County in 1897 where he found employment as a farm laborer at $8 per month, including board and lodging. It is interesting to note that he is the present owner of the farm where he was employed, 416 acres in sections 19, Litchfield township and 24 in Darwin township.

In 1904, he entered the employ of the Litchfield Cooperative Creamery Company (see page 125).

Alfred Anderson

Mr. Anderson has been active in the civic affairs of Litchfield and Meeker County, serving as mayor of the city and president of the Meeker Co-operative Light and Power Association and is at present a member of the Board of Directors.

Mr. Anderson married, April 29, 1914, Lura A. Hanson (daughter of Andrew P. and Jennie M. Hutchins-Hanson) born in Paynesville, Minnesota, January 7, 1895. They are the parents of Alfred, born March 7, 1915; Bruce, born January 23, 1918; Bonnie, born July 17, 1922; Boyd, born December 7, 1925 and Donna, born September 1, 1930.

DETERMAN, ANNA OLSON (daughter of Nels and Hannah Jonson-Olson) was born in Malmo, Sweden, January 13, 1885. Her paternal grandfather, Ole Nelson (Olson) was a land owner (Namdeman) of the province of Blekinge while the maternal grandfather, Jon Jonson, was a cabinet maker of Kyskhult. Mr. and Mrs. Nels Olson, the parents of our subject came to America with their family of nine children and arrived at Litchfield in the spring of 1888.

Anna Olson-Determan attended the Litchfield schools and graduated from high school in 1905. She supplemented her education by attendance at the Teachers Training College in Winona and the University of Minnesota. She taught school for fourteen years and later engaged her services as supervisor of high school teachers training departments.

Mrs. Determan became active in the civic and political affairs of Litchfield and Meeker County. She promoted and organized the Litchfield League of Women Voters (1921) and was its first president. At a later date she served as a member of the State Board of the League as a representative of the Sixth Congressional District. She headed the Central Parent Teachers Association of Litchfield for two years and in 1933 served as chairman of the Women's Division of the N. R. A. She has been a student of governmental affairs and became a popular speaker in support of the principles she espoused. A Minnesota weekly in commenting on her ability as a public speaker said, "Few women in Minnesota are as conversant with economic issues and few understand as well the rank and file of Minnesota citizenship."

Mrs. Anna Olson-Determan

In May 1933, Governor Floyd B. Olson appointed Mrs. Determan a member of the Board of regents of the University of Minnesota. She won national distinction while a member of the board in introducing and securing the passage of a resolution in June 1934 whereby military training at the university was made optional with the students. Minnesota was the second state in the union to take such action. The writer has seen letters from leaders in educational and religious circles which highly commend her for securing this action. In 1935 Mrs. Determan was one of two delegates that represented Minnesota at the National Conference of University Regents and Trustees held in Columbus, Ohio. Upon the expiration of her term of service in 1936 Governor Olson appointed her to membership on the Board of Control where she served until June 1939 when, by legislative enactment the Board of Control was abolished. During Mrs. Determan's occupancy of this office she furthered numerous improvements in the administration of the penal, charitable and correctional institutions of the state. She insisted on a sound and humane treatment of rehabilitation and among results achieved was the establishment of libraries in insane hospitals and the expansion of educational and recreational facilities.

Anna Olson married, June 6, 1917, Dr. Bernard S. Determan (son of Benedict and Agnes Arlington-Dettermann of Carrol, Iowa) born at Carrol, October 2, 1884.

Dr. BERNARD S. DETERMAN'S ancestors were Mr. and Mrs. Clemens Dettermann of German and Holland Dutch extraction who resided first in Pennsylvania and later at Clinton, Iowa where Benedict, father of Bernard, was born. Upon reaching his maturity Benedict established his home on a farm in Carrol County, Iowa and engaged in breeding percheron horses and shorthorn cattle.

He married Agnes Arlington, of Dubuque, Iowa, of English and German descent. Her father was a sailor and in his voyages followed the coast of South America, Europe and western United States. In 1894 Benedict established his wife and eight sons on a farm of 320 acres in Lincoln County, Minnesota and in 1914 he retired from active service and established his home at Lake Benton, Minnesota, where he died at eighty years of age. Mrs. Determan continues to reside in Lake Benton at the advanced age of 89 years.

Bernard Determan attended the public schools in this Minnesota village and continued his education at the Southern Minnesota Normal at Austin, Minnesota, the McFadden Sanitarium at Chicago, the Sanitarium at Battle Creek, Michigan and the National Chiropractic College at Chicago and became an outstanding member of his profession (drugless healing).

He located in Litchfield and practiced his profession for a period of 20 years (1918-1938).

During his residence in the county seat city he has taken an interest in public affairs and the development of the village and county. He served three terms as mayor and during this period he furthered and promoted the extension of electric service to the rural districts whereby in 1931 Corvuso, Cedar Mills, Forest City and the Washington Lake community were served from the Litchfield plant. He gave freely of his time and official influence in prevailing on the grocers of the city to cease the sale of butter substitutes, joined in the effort leading to the establishment of the Legion Park and the organizing of the drum corps.

In the early years of the present national administration he served as chairman for Meeker County of the Federal Housing Administration. Mr. Determan has served six years as a member of the Board of Education.

Mr. and Mrs. Determan are the parents of Kathryn Ann who graduated from the Litchfield High School in 1935 and from the California State College at San Jose in 1939 winning high honors in the social science department.

Dr. Bernard S. Determan

RUMSEY, ELTON K., was born in Kingston township, October 26, 1878. Upon reaching maturity he was for several years associated with his father in the operation of a threshing machine. In 1927 he introduced the raising of tobacco in the Kingston territory which for a period of ten years was the most remunerative crop raised by the farmers of that section of the county. During this period he served as president of the Kingston Tobacco Growers Association.

GAYNER, LEROY A. (son of John N. and Matilda Olson-Gayner) was born in Grove City, Minnesota where his father operated a drug store.

In 1898, his father was elected County Auditor and the family established their residence in Litchfield. LeRoy attended the public schools and graduated from the Litchfield High School. Following his graduation he attended the Minnesota Business College in Minneapolis and graduated the year following his entry as a student. He served as a postal clerk in the Litchfield post office during the period of his father's service as postmaster. He continued in this position for five years when he resigned and enrolled as a student in G. A. College at St. Peter, preparatory to his entrance in the law school of the Minnesota State University from which institution he graduated in 1929. In 1930 he was admitted to the bar and opened a law office in Litchfield, since which time he has engaged in the practice of his profession. Mr. Gayner served as city attorney of Litchfield (1932-1936).

John N. Gayner, father of LeRoy A. Gayner, was a native of Skane, Sweden, born September 27, 1860. He was 14 years of age when he came to America and shortly thereafter took up his residence in Grove City and became active in the early development of that village. He has the distinction of being the first licensed pharmacist in Minnesota. He owned and operated a drug store in Grove City and for years was the leader of the band in that village. He was a member of the Democratic party and during the administration of Ex-Governor John A. Johnson served as a member of the State Board of Equalization.

LeRoy A. Gayner

JEBB, MELVIN B. (son of Wm. and Mrs. Marietta Grignon-Pomery-Jebb) was born on the home farm in Union Grove township, June 1, 1896. He was educated in the public schools and the State Teachers College at St. Cloud. He taught school for four years, when he joined his brothers in the operation of the home farm. He has taken a keen interest in the administration of county and state affairs and has been active in cooperative movements to advance the agricultural interests of the state. He was one of the promoters of rural electrification in Meeker County and has been a director of the Meeker County Electric and Power Association from the date of its incorporation. He has served as President of the Paynesville Fair Association.

Mr. Jebb was elected and served as a member of the state legislature sessions of 1933, 1935, 1939. In the campaign of 1938 he was an active supporter of our present Governor Harold Stassen and was again elected to represent Meeker County in the legislature and during the legislative session strongly supported the legislation furthering the policies advocated by Governor Stassen during the election campaign.

Melvin B. Jebb

In the organization of the House he became a member of some of its most important committees among which was the committee on appropriations where his influence was exerted to promote economy in government. He was Chairman of the Committee on Cooperatives.

At the conclusion of the legislative session, Mr. Jebb returned to the home farm where in company with his brothers he operates the Jebb Farm of 320 acres in Section 17, Union Grove township. The brothers also conduct a trucking business.

Melvin B. Jebb was united in marriage December 7, 1934 to Miss Ruby Monson (daughter of Ole and Hilda Anderson-Monson). They have one daughter, Ardelle, born December 19, 1936.

Dr. Albert C. Nelson   Samuel G. Gandrud   Albert Earley

NELSON, ALBERT C., Dentist, (son of the territorial pioneers, James and Elizabeth Ann Caswell-Nelson) was born October 21, 1875. He spent the early part of his life on the farm where he was born in section 23, Union Grove township. He attended the rural schools and graduated from the Litchfield High School in 1898. He enlisted in the Spanish American War July 2, 1898 and upon his discharge from service, found employment as a clerk in a general merchandise store at Hancock, Minnesota. In 1901 he enrolled as a student in the University of Minnesota where he graduated in dentistry in 1904 and opened an office in partnership with Dr. E. B. Weeks and continued this partnership until 1916 when Dr. Weeks retired and Dr. Nelson continued the practice of his profession until 1939 when he disposed of his practice and accepted the position of Superintendent of the Litchfield Sewage Disposal plant. During his 35 years' residence in Litchfield Dr. Nelson has served as mayor of the city and member of the Board of Education.

Dr. Nelson married, January 31, 1905, Luella Brandt. This union resulted in the birth of a son, Milo C. born December 16, 1908, who resides at Kalamazoo, Michigan.

GANDRUD, SAMUEL G. (son of P. A. and Anna M. Gonseth-Gandrud) was born at Sunburg, Kandiyohi County, Minnesota, April 15, 1900. He was educated in the public schools and attended Luther College at Decorah, Iowa and graduated from the St. Paul College of Law in 1923 and the same year was admitted to the bar and opened a law office in the village of Litchfield. Mr. Gandrud has taken an active interest in community affairs. He has served as Village Attorney and member of the Board of Education. Fraternally he is a member of Golden Fleece Lodge A. F. and A. M., Number 89 and the I. O. O. F. Mr. Gandrud was elected County Attorney in 1926 and has successfully run the gauntlet of four successive election contests for that office in which he continues to serve.

Samuel G. Gandrud married, June 26, 1924, Olga Kvamen of Decorah, Iowa, born September 5, 1901. They are the parents of Samuel, Jr., and Thomas.

EARLEY, ALBERT (son of Walter and Elsie Ernst-Earley) was born May 5, 1898, at Niles, Ohio where his father operated a barber shop. In 1899, the family moved to Atwater, Minnesota and four years later to Litchfield, where the father opened a barber shop. Albert was educated in the public schools and, in 1918, enlisted in the World War naval service. He saw over-sea service on the cruiser Seattle. He was honorably discharged September 23, 1919. He then engaged in various lines of employment, and in 1920 became a resident of Litchfield and five years later entered the employ of the city as a member of the police force, serving as such for a period of fourteen years. He was elected sheriff of Meeker County in the campaign of 1938.

Mr. Earley married, January 19, 1920, Coral Greenfield (daughter of George and Emma Steffen-Greenfield) born March 4, 1899. They are the parents of Jerome Wallace, born August 14, 1921.

RINGDAHL, NELS (son of Per and Celia Ringdahl-Nelson) was born November 16, 1867 in Malnohualan, province of Skona, Sweden. He was left fatherless in babyhood and made his home with his mother. At the age of 13 he became a tailor's apprentice in his native village of Bjorka and later at Copenhagen, Denmark. He came to America in 1887 and found employment with his brother Ole of the merchant tailor firm of Ringdahl and Palmquist where he remained for two years and then transferred his services to Minneapolis and during the last two years of his residence operated a tailor shop at 1111 Washington Avenue. In 1897 he again entered the employment of Ringdahl and Palmquist and in the fall of that year visited his mother in Sweden and on his return resumed his former employment and purchased the interest of Andrew Palmquist and the firm became known as Ringdahl Brothers for a brief period when due to the illness of his brother he became the sole proprietor.

Mr. Ringdahl has the distinction, at the present time, of being the oldest in point of continued service of the merchants of Litchfield. During his 52 years of continued service he has taken an active interest in the civic affairs of the village having served as alderman eight years and for 35 years was a member of the volunteer fire department serving five years as chief. He is a member of the First Lutheran Church, serving several years as trustee.

Nels Ringdahl

Through self study he has acquired a good knowledge of the English language and is well informed in the current events of state and nation. Fraternally he is a member of the Masonic and A. O. U. W. orders.

Mr. Ringdahl married, October 24, 1906, Emma Larson (daughter of John and Mary Burnndotte-Larson) born November 1, 1876. They are the parents of Mildred Loaine (adopted) born March 19, 1921.

NELSON, ALFRED H. (son of Neils and Paulina Neilson) was born in the township of Lake Elizabeth, Kandiyohi County, Minnesota, September 25, 1877. He came with his parents to Meeker County in 1879 (see page 201). He was reared on the home farm and educated in the public schools and Curtis Business College (Minneapolis). In 1900 he purchased a farm of 320 acres in Sections 25 and 26, Danielson township, which he owned and operated for a period of twenty-five years.

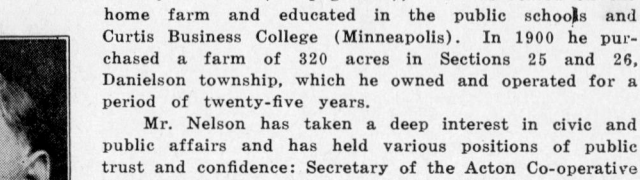

Mr. Nelson has taken a deep interest in civic and public affairs and has held various positions of public trust and confidence: Secretary of the Acton Co-operative Telephone Company; Director of the Litchfield Independent Co-operative Elevator Company; census enumerator, Danielson township (1910) and Forest City (1930). He assisted in the organization of the Meeker County Farm Bureau. Fraternally Mr. Nelson is a member of Golden Fleece Lodge A. F. and A. M., No. 89 and is a 32nd degree Mason. He is also a member of the Litchfield Lodge No. 32, I. O. O. F. and is an active member of the Litchfield Methodist Church and is a member of the Board of Trustees. Mr. Nelson was a contesting candidate for state representative in the election of 1938. He carried 12 precincts and lost the election by the narrow margin of 118 votes.

Alfred H. Nelson

Mr. Nelson married, June 1, 1903, Lydia E. Coombs (daughter of Vincent and Lydia Abbott-Coombs) born March 29, 1877. She was a graduate of the Hutchinson High School and University of Minnesota. She engaged in teaching and became one of Meeker County's most efficient and successful teachers.

Mr. and Mrs. Nelson became residents of Litchfield in 1926 and were closely identified with the social and religious life of the county seat city. Mrs. Lydia Coombs-Nelson died November 14, 1930.

WAYNE, RALPH WILLIAM (son of Anton J. and Minnie Fredericksen-Wayne) was born on a Freeborn County farm, April 20. 1907. He attended the Geneva public schools and graduated as valedictorian of his class from the Ellendale High School.

He spent one year as a student at Carleton College, Northfield, Minnesota and in 1929 graduated from the University of Minnesota College of Agriculture and was awarded a Bachlor of Science Degree with distinction and in 1931 was awarded a Master of Science degree. He spent a portion of his time in an original research of certain phases of the physiology of milk secretions and the result of his work has been widely publicised in the United States and several foreign countries.

Mr. Wayne enjoys the distinction of being numbered as one of six American students receiving a fellowship award of $1,000 for study in Scandinavian countries (1931 and 1932). He pursued his studies for one year at the Royal Veterinary and Agricultural College at Copenhagen, Denmark and also traveled through eight European countries in research work of agricultural conditions in these countries. Mr. Wayne came to Meeker County and accepted the position of agent of the County Agricultural Extension Service, entering upon his duties, December 15, 1932.

Ralph W. Wayne

Mr. Wayne is a member of the Baptist Church. During his college career he was elected a member of the following honorary fraternities: Alpha Zeta, Gamma Sigma Delta and Gamma Alpha. He is a member of the Royal Agricultural Society of Denmark and holds membership in the Litchfield Kiwanis Club, Farm Bureau and several other agricultural organizations.

Mr. Ralph W. Wayne married, June 30, 1934, Verna Charlotte Schletty (daughter of Frederick C. and Anna Wohletz-Schletty) of St. Paul, Minnesota. They are the parents of Alice Marie, born July 6, 1938.

KOERNER, ALBERT C., (son of Frederick and Otelia-Rickert-Koerner) was born in Darwin township, August 16, 1890. He was reared on a farm and at the age of 21, the family located in Harvey, Section 28, where they purchased (collectively) a farm of 320 acres. Albert was educated in the public schools, Litchfield High School and graduated from the Mankato Commercial College in 1914. He divided his time in farming and clerical work. In 1930 he was elected clerk of Court of Meeker County, a position he has continuously held since that date.

Following his graduation he engaged his services in teaching rural schools in North Dakota.

Mr. Koerner married, July 3, 1917, Jane Hatfield (daughter of Joshua and Ida May Curtis-Hatfield) born July 5, 1895. There have been four children born of this union: Karl, born June 2, 1918, is a student in electrical engineering at the University of Minnesota; Harriet, born May 23, 1920; Adelaine, born January 21, 1930 and Bruce, born September 19, 1931.

Albert C. Koerner

NORDSTROM, DAVID F. (son of John A. and Christine Borgstrom-Nordstrom) was born in St. Paul, June 22, 1887. The parents were natives of Vermland Sweden. The father came to America in 1878. David was educated in the public schools of his native city and graduated from the Mechanic Arts High School, class of 1906. He worked for several firms as an accountant and bookkeeper and from 1910 to 1916 was in the employ of the Robinson-Straus Company. From 1916-1920 he was in the employ of the state as an assistant public examiner. During a portion of these years he attended night classes at the St. Paul College of Law and in 1919 was admitted to the bar.

Mr. Nordstrom engaged in the practice of law at Olivia from June 1920 until 1926 and then accepted the position of Assistant Attorney General continuing in that service until 1931 when he entered upon the practice of law in Litchfield where he has met with marked success. Mr. Nordstrom was a member of the Draft Board during the World War and takes an active part in political activities. He directs the choir in the First Lutheran Church in Litchfield. Fraternally he is a member of the A. F. and A. M., I. O. O. F., B. P. O. E. and Kiwanis Club.

David F. Nordstrom

David F. Nordstrom married, September 12, 1911, Alexandria Carlberg (daughter of August and Ellen Swanson-Carlberg). They are the parents of Doris (Mrs. Rev. Ernest Albrecht of New Lebanon, Ohio) born June 27 1912; Harold Arthur, born November 3, 1913; Alice Mae, born December 19, 1918 and Harriet, born September 15, 1922.

SJOQUIST, BERGER N. was born in 1902 on a Marshall County, Minnesota, farm. Of poor but honest parentage he was compelled to secure the advantages of his education in High School and Gustavus Adolphus College by securing employment in varied lines of labor, janitor, druggist's assistant, waiter in a restaurant, and an assistant preacher in the churches of the Lutheran Synod.

During the period of his scholastic career he was a leader in school activities, served as valedictorian of his class in high school and at Gustavus Adolphus College was president of the senior class and also served as president of Lutheran Brotherhood, Lutheran Student's Association, Pi Kappa Delta, (honorary forensics fraternity) and National Vice President of the Lutheran Students' Association of America. He was the State Champion debater and all state football tackle.

Upon graduation from college he engaged his services as a member of the South St. Paul High School faculty and was in charge of the Department of Speech (1927-1935). He attended the night school at the St. Paul College of Law for four years at which time he served as student instructor in debate and public speaking. He graduated in 1934 and October 1, 1934 he was admitted to the bar. During the summer of 1935 he served as Assistant County Attorney of Pine County and the same year came to Meeker County and located in Dassel where he is engaged in the practice of his profession.

Berger N. Sjoquist

Mr. Sjoquist takes an active part in civic and public affairs and as a public speaker responds readily to the requests of civic, school and church organizations who desire the services of a public speaker of acknowledged ability.

KOPPLIN, EDWIN H. (son of Fred A. and Louise Manthei-Kopplin) was born in Bellingham, Minnesota, April 23, 1896. He came with his parents to Litchfield, Minnesota in 1900 where he spent the years of his boyhood and graduated from the High School in 1913. He then entered the University of Minnesota and pursued a business course which was interupted by his enlistment in June, 1917 in World War service and was attached to Base Hospital Unit No. 26, stationed at Fort McPherson, Georgia. He left for overseas service in June 1918 and was stationed at Allery-Sys-Soane, France where the hospital unit cared for casualty cases resulting from front line warfare. Following the Armistice he was sent to Berlin as a member of the Allied Commission for the care of war prisoners. He was honorably discharged in August 1919 and reentered the University and graduated in the spring of 1920. He engaged his services with George Mill in the farm machinery business at Great Falls, Montana. He returned to Litchfield the following year and joined his father in the oil business. The Kopplin Oil Company has developed into one of the largest concerns of its kind in Meeker County. Mr. Kopplin is a member of the Nelsan-Horton Post of the American Legion. He served eight years as a member of the Village Council.

Edwin H. Kopplin

Edwin H. Kopplin married, June 2, 1923, Dorothea Simons (daughter of Orlando and Effie Post-Simons) was born at Glencoe, Minnesota, March 20, 1898. They became the parents of Edwin O., born March 14, 1924 and Rose Mary who died in childhood.

ERICKSON, REUBEN C. (son of August and Mathilda Beckstrand-Erickson) was born in the village of Litchfield, September 21, 1896. He was reared from boyhood to manhood in the home of his parents and was graduated from the Litchfield High School in the year 1915. After the public schools at Litchfield he entered the University of Minnesota, where he was a student during 1915-16. At the outbreak of the World War he joined the colors and enlisted in the Seventh United States Engineers (Regulars). He was first sent to Jefferson Barracks in St. Louis and then to Fort Leavenworth, Kansas and in February 1918 went overseas with the engineering unit, Engineer Train of the Seventh Engineers, Fifth Division. Upon arrival in France he entered into active service in the Anould, St. Die and Frapelle Sectors in the Vosges Mountains. He participated in the St. Mihiel Offensive and the first and second phases of the Meuse-Argonne Offensives. The period following the Armistice his services were engaged with the Army of Occupation in France, Luxembourg and Germany and on July 14, 1919 sailed from Brest, France for the United States and was honorably discharged, Aufust 17, 1919.

Upon his return from the service he entered into the employ of Garfield Cutts, general merchant, as a grocery clerk for a number of years and in 1932 was elected to the office of Probate Judge of Meeker County, which position he has held since that date.

Reuben C. Erickson was married July 14, 1931 to Evelyn E. Gunberg (daughter of Rev. Andrew and Caroline Tour-Gunberg). Mrs. Erickson was born in Iowa, and graduated from the high school at Watertown, Minnesota and later from the Teachers College at St. Cloud, Minnesota. Prior to her marriage, Mrs. Erickson taught in the St. Peter, Hutchinson and Litchfield public schools and one year in Glasgow, Montana. Mr. and Mrs. Erickson have two sons, Robert Clarion, born October 15, 1934 and John Mark, born December 10, 1937.

RYAN, JAMES (son of Dennis and Mary Cummings-Ryan) was born in the township of Manannah July 12, 1868. He was reared from boyhood to manhood on his father's homestead in Section 18 and was educated in the public schools. With the exception of the year 1889, when he was employed in highway construction work in St. Paul, he has resided in Meeker County his entire life. He purchased an 80 acre tract adjacent to his father's farm and spent six years in its development when, his health becoming impared, he established his home in Eden Valley and engaged his services as agent and later as a salesman for farm machinery companies. He then returned to the farm for a period of two years when in partnership with E. A. Staples he engaged in the general merchandise business in the Manannah townsite.

He disposed of his interests in the business in 1907 and purchased the home he owns and occupies at the present time and entered the employ of the Standard Oil Company in the conduct of their bulk station and later became the manager of their first service station in Litchfield. He remained in their employ for a period of twenty-five years and as a side line became a dealer in real estate. The Standard Oil Company, in recognition of his long and faithful service, gave him a complimentary banquet and retired him from service on a pension.

James Ryan

During Mr. Ryan's residence in Litchfield he served four years as a member of the village council. He holds membership in the Knights of Columbus and is a devout and active member of the St. Philip's Catholic Church. He continues to own and operate the Manannah farm which has expanded to 160 acres.

In 1938 Mr. Ryan toured the countries of Europe, held audience with Pope Pius XI and visited the home of his parents in Tipperary and did not fail to stop at Blarney where he observed the custom of tourists and kissed the Blarney Stone.

James Ryan married, November 17, 1891, Mary Ann Dillon (daughter of Patrick and Mary Garvey-Dillon) born in Mount Forest, Canada, November 19, 1869. They are the parents of eight children:

James, born November 5, 1892 prepared himself to enter the Holy Priesthood by attendance at St. Thomas College and the St. Paul Seminary. He was ordained a priest, June 10, 1922 and at present is pastor of St. Peter's Parish in St. Peter, Minnesota.

Ignatius, born May 7, 1896; died May 13, 1900.

John Arthur, born December 28, 1897. He enlisted in the World War and died from disabilities incurred in service February 5, 1920.

Matthew, born July 12, 1900. He resides in Minneapolis where he is employed in the motor oil business.

Martin, born December 13, 1903.

Francis, born September 17, 1904. He resides in Merrill, Wisconsin where he is a practicing dentist.

Mary (Mrs. G. J. Sullivan) born January 9, 1908.

Veronica, born June 15, 1912.

MATSEN, J. E., a native of Finland, is an excellent representative of the Americans of Finnish birth who have contributed in a marked degree to the development of Kingston township. He was cashier of the Kingston State Bank (1902 to 1922) and president from 1922 to 1927 when the bank was moved to Dassel and the name changed to the Farmers and Merchants State Bank where he continued to serve as president until 1933. He resides at present on a farm in Kingston. In all his business relations he has preserved his reputation for honesty and efficiency and his advice, when followed, has contributed to the success of his neighbors in the Finnish settlement of Kingston township. He has served as clerk and treasurer of the town and treasurer of the local creamery.

FRIEDMANN, JOSEPH (son of Jacob and Mary Ellen Young-Friedmann was born at Cold Springs, Stearns County, March 10, 1870. He was reared on a farm, attended the public schools and later attended the State Teachers Training College at St. Cloud, Minnesota. He has enhanced his scholastic education by self study and is deeply interested in all matters pertaining to the welfare of his home community, county, state and nation.

In March 1891, he engaged in the mercantile business in Eden Valley by entering into partnership with Mathias E. Weiler. They were successful from the start and in 1913 there was a reorganization of the firm which continued the business under the firm name of Friedmann-Marx Company. Joseph Friedmann was President, J. L. Friedmann, Secretary and Frank Marx, Vice President and Treasurer. Mr. Friedmann in 1894 and 1895 operated a brick yard and the majority of the brick business buildings in Eden Valley were constructed of red brick made in the Friedmann yard. Mr. Friedmann disposed of his mercantile interests March 1, 1917.

Joseph Friedmann

Mr. Friedmann was a member of the City Council for several years, serving as mayor of the village in 1917-1918. In the election of 1906 he was elected to the lower house of the state legislature and reelected in 1908. He has the distinction of being the first native son of Stearns County to serve as a legislator from his home county.

Mr. Friedmann is a faithful member of the St. Peter's Catholic Church and was a charter member of St. Mary's Church of that denomination. He is a man of liberal views and well informed in matters pertaining to county and state history.

Mr. Friedmann was married August 3, 1897 to Ann Eliza Fournica (daughter of William and Mary O'Brien-Fournica) born December 22, 1863. They are the parents of Mary Irene born July 18, 1901.

LINQUIST, OSCAR E., was born in Dassel April 6, 1874, son of Andrew and Mary Larson-Linquist, who came to Dassel in 1869.

He was educated in the Dassel Public Schools, Emanuel Academy and Curtis Commercial College in Minneapolis. He operated a job printing office in Dassel for several years; then was employed in various business places until appointed postmaster of Dassel. He assumed the duties of that office on March 1, 1905 serving until December 31, 1934, covering a period of more than 27 years.

Mr. Linquist is reognized as one of Dassel's most public spirited citizens. He has never hesitated to join his effort to that of other citizens in every movement to advance the interests of the Village of Dassel.

In addition to his years of service as postmaster, he served as recorder 1899 to 1900; member of the Village Council, 1920 to 1923; secretary of the Dassel Free Fair for a period of 21 years; secretary of the Dassel Fire Department 25 years; manager of the Opera House 27 years. In 1935 he established himself in the restaurant business, a meeting place of the people, which he is now operating.

Oscar E. Linquist

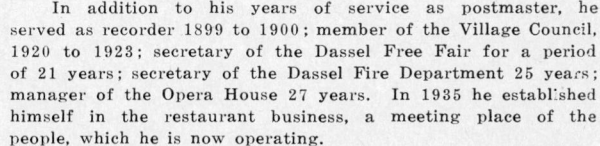

Fraternally Mr. Linquist is a member of Griswold Lodge No. 218, A. F. and A. M., Rabboni Chapter No. 39, Royal Arch Masons, and Osman Temple A. A. O. N. M. S. of St. Paul.

He was married November 8, 1899 to Alice Ellstrom, born November 28, 1880 at Fergus Falls, Minnesota, daughter of Andrew and Fredrika Abrahamson-Ellstrom. They have a daughter Lenore L. born at Dassel, Minnesota, June 3, 1903. She married Edward R. Eben, September 15, 1925. They reside in Viroqua, Wisconsin where he is employed by the Standard Oil Co. They have a son Craig E. born November 8, 1930 at Chicago, Illinois.

Edward J. Bahe, Jr.   Roderick M. Gaffney   Frank J. Coleman

BAHE, EDWARD, J., Jr. (son of E. J. and Mabel V. Thayer-Bahe) was born in Hancock, Minnesota, October 8, 1904 in the upper rooms of the Hancock Record print shop owned by his father who established this paper in February 1899 and continues as its editor and publisher.

He was educated in the Hancock grade and High School and graduated with the class of 1922. He entered Hamline University in the spring of 1924 and in 1925 he continued his education at the University. In 1925 he enrolled in the School of Jouralism of the University of Missouri from which he graduated in 1928 and the same year he leased the Hancock Record from his father and continued as editor and publisher until January 1931 when he purchased an interest in the Olivia (Renville County) Times. He disposed of his interest June 1936 and engaged in the summer resort business near Detroit Lakes, Ottertail County. He purchased the Eden Valley Journal March 1, 1939 and the first issue under his ownership was published March 3, 1939.

Mr. Bahe was married April 13, 1933 to Theresa A. Neubeiser (daughter of Joseph and Ann Weuther-Neubeiser) born August 17, 1908.

GAFFNEY, M. RODERICK (son of Henry and Mary Keeshan-Gaffney) was born in Morris, Minnesota, April 27, 1909. He spent the early years of his life in his native city. He graduated from St. Mary's High School and entered the University of Minnesota and graduated with the class of 1933, securing a B. S. degree and is doing graduate work at the University during the summer vacation periods. He was a member of the Morris High School faculty for three years and in 1936 accepted the superintendency of the Eden Valley High School in which position he continues to serve. He takes an active part in the civic affairs of the village and has served the past two years as Secretary of the Chamber of Commerce. Mr. Gaffney married, July 23, 1938, Mary Elizabeth Cameron (daughter of Samuel and Maude Kirke-Cameron) born April 26, 1909 at Jacksonville, Illinois.

COLEMAN, FRANK J., (son of John and Elizabeth Cahill-Coleman) was born on a farm in Wellington Township, Renville County, February 23, 1896. He graduated from the Fairfax, Minnesota, High School and on May 8, 1917 enlisted in the United States regular army and served two years in over sea service in the World War. He was with the American expeditionary forces where he took part in the Meuse Argonne offensive, the artillery battle on the Champagne front and the St. Mihiel and Aisne Marne offensives.

He was mustered out of service September 5, 1919 when he became an agent of the Equitable Life Insurance Company. He has been successful in this vocation, evidenced by his having received a diploma from the Company for proficiency in his work.

Mr. Coleman became a resident of Eden Valley in 1929. He has been active in community affairs, serving as Scout Master, president of the Board of Education and mayor of the village.

He is an active member of the American Legion, serving in various offices of the local post and in the county organization. He has also served as Commander of the Seventh District organization and as a member of the state executive committee.

Mr. Coleman married, June 6, 1928, Amelia Weiler (daughter of Mathias and Mary Friedmann-Weiler).

RUHLAND, JOHN L. (son of Adam and Catherine Andres-Ruhland) was born in Farmington, Washington County, Wisconsin, August 11, 1871. He was reared on a farm and educated in the public and parochial schools. At twenty years of age he entered the employ of men engaged in the meat market business and learned the butcher's trade. He was employed for a year at Jordan, Minnesota and then engaged his services with Werdick Brothers in Minneapolis.

Mr. Ruhland took up his residence in Eden Valley, June 25, 1895 and purchased the meat market owned by Gustave Fidler which he operated until 1901 when he moved to North Dakota and homesteaded 160 acres near Kenmare. Mr. Ruhland returned to Eden Valley in 1907 and engaged in the hardware and farm implement business in partnership with Henry Schoenecker. There was a division of the business in 1920. Mr. Ruhland taking over the farm implement business which he operated until 1936 when he disposed of his interest, and in company with his son, Albert, opened the Gamble Store in which business they are engaged at present.

During his long years of residence in Eden Valley, Mr. Ruhland has taken an active interest in all activities designed to promote the growth and development of the community. He has served as village councilman 23 years and 20 years of this period (1920-1940) will make a period of continuous service in this position. He has also served as a member of the Board of Education.

John L. Ruhland

Mr. Ruhland and family are devout members of the Catholic Church. He is connected fraternally with the Knights of Columbus and other organizations connected with the church.

Mr. Ruhland was married, May 30, 1898 to Amelia Schaffer (daughter of August and Dora Schaffer) born in Millwaukee, Wisconsin, September 23, 1876 and died November 20, 1904 leaving one daughter Amelia Dora, born March 15, 1904. She is a Sister of Charity of the Catholic Church and is located at Richmond, Minnesota.

Mr. Ruhland married, second, January 22, 1907 Mary A. Busch (daughter of Christian and Margaret Hoffman-Busch) born June 25, 1876. This union has been blessed with six children, all of whom are living.

Sedonia (Sister of Charity) born April 30, 1908. She is a teacher in the parochial school of St. Ann in Minneapolis.

Roman, born October 13, 1910 married Elsie Steinke. They have a daughter, Mary Antoinette.

Albert, born March 13, 1912 married Dorothy Lardy. They have a daughter, Mary Elizabeth.

Alodia, born November 27, 1913. She is a Sister of Charity at Altoona, Wisconsin.

Albin, born September 15, 1915 and Eleanor, born August 29, 1917.

NELSON. JOHN E. (son of Christian B. and Christine Hedberg-Nelson) was born in Cokato, Minnesota December 23, 1878. At three years of age the Nelson family established their home in Litchfield where the father opened a shoe store. In 1888 the family took up their residence on a farm of 109 acres in section 30, Dassel township which is owned at the present time by John E. Nelson.

John spent the years of his boyhood and early manhood in assisting his father in the labor of the farm and secured the advantages of a public school education. At the age of 21 he secured employment as an errand boy in William Fortman's General Store in Darwin. He left their employ and engaged employment with an elevator company, serving them as grain buyer and manager of elevators in succession at Mayer, Erdahl and New Germany, Minnesota, a period of nine years. In 1910 he returned to Darwin and purchased the general store owned by James Maher which he operated in connection with a farm implement business until 1927 when he disposed of the general merchandise business and continued as a dealer in farm implements. From 1910 and up to the present time Mr. Nelson has served as the village postmaster and is at present the president of the Farmers State Bank of Darwin. Prior to Mr. Nelson's entering into the business life of Darwin, the village that now exists was little better than a whistling station and it is claimed the entire townsite could have been purchased for $1,000. It has been freely stated to the writer that this thriving little village owes its present prestige to the enterprise and leadership of Mr. Nelson.

John E. Nelson married, October 16, 1902, Emma Scherdegger. They are the parents of Myrtle (Mrs. Oscar Johnson); Luella (Mrs. Ken McGhie) and Phylis.

CARLSON, GUS H., son of Anders Alfred and Elsa Johanna (Hillstrom) Carlson was born in Minneapolis July 22, 1883. In 1885 his parents established their home in Dassel township on a farm in Sections 32 and 33, bordering the east shore of Washington Lake. He was educated in the Dassel Public Schools. He spent the years of his boyhood and early manhood on his father's farm. At the age of 20 he found employment as a laborer with the Great Northern Railway and two years later entered the government service as an R.F.D. carrier from the Dassel office, on Route No. 1, and was later transferred to Route No. 2. Mr. Carlson continued in this service for twelve and one-half years and then engaged in farming for a period of four years. At the termination of this period he became a salesman for the Jones Monumental Works of St. Cloud.

From 1926 to 1931 he managed and operated an oil station in Dassel Village. Mr. Carlson was appointed to his present position as a state game warden August 15, 1931, which he fills to the satisfaction of the public. That Mr. Carlson enjoys the confidence and esteem of the citizens of his home village and county is attested by the fact that during the years of his residence he has served as deputy sheriff, village assessor and as president of the Dassel Board of Education.

Gus H. Carlson

Mr. Carlson was largely responsible for the establishment of the farmer owned and controlled Meeker County News and has served as president and as secretary of its board of directors. Fraternally he is a member of Griswold Lodge A. F. and A. M. and its auxiliary, the Eastern Star, in Dassel..

Mr. Carlson married, November 18, 1913, Agnes Evelyn Peterson, daughter of Peter and Lina (Dunn) Peterson, born January 16, 1888. They are the parents of three children born at Dassel, Minnesota: Phyllis Alene, born April 10, 1915, graduate of the St. Cloud Teachers' College; Eunice Audrey, born April 25, 1916, graduate of the Minneapolis Business College and Avis Virginia, born July 19, 1917.

C. A. Anderson   Edwin M. McGraw   Harry A. Hanson

ANDERSON, CHAS A. (son of John A. and Ida Erickson-Anderson) born at Lockridge, Iowa, September 2, 1875. He spent his childhood years on his father's farm and then accompanied his parents to St. Paul. The family established their residence in Litchfield in 1890 where Charles was educated in the public school and in 1897 he graduated in pharmacy from the Northwestern University at Evanston, Illinois. He engaged his services as a clerk in the J. B. Atkinson drug store and two years later purchased a one-half interest in the business and has been the sole proprietor since 1918. He was married, June 18, 1902 to Agnes M. Mattson.

McGRAW, EDWIN M. (son of the territorial pioneers, Martin and Maggie McGraw) was born in Greenleaf township, November 18, 1879. He continued to live on the home farm for fifty years. He was educated in the public schools and took a business course at the Metropolitan Business College in Minneapolis. During the years of his early manhood he supplemented his work on the farm in varied lines of manuel labor, lumberjack, carpentry and auto mechanics. At the age of three he was left motherless. The father remarried and at the death of his second wife again married. There were nine children of these marriages but there was harmony in the home. The father died in 1907 at which time with the aid of his good wives and children he was the owner of 373 acres and overcame the hardships and penury of his early pioneer life.

Mr. McGraw was elected Register of Deeds for Meeker County in 1930 which position he occupies at the present time.

Edwin M. McGraw married, April 18, 1918, Myrtle Hinshaw (daughter of I. M. and Ada Shaffer-Hinshaw).

HANSON, HARRY A. (son of Peter and Rachel Halverson-Hanson) was born in Litchfield, Minnesota, February 8, 1873. He spent the years of his early youth on a farm and in the village. He was educated in the public schools, Shattuck Military School and graduated from Curtis Business College. He has been engaged in various occupations, farming and office work and is at present in partnership with his wife, the proprietor of the Hanson Cafe in Litchfield.

Mr. Hanson was married September 26, 1899 to Amanda E. Birch, daughter of John and Sarah Johnson-Birch. Mrs. Birch's mother, Mrs. Ola Johnson, was a territorial pioneer of Meeker County.

SALISBURY, WALTER R. (son of J. B. and Lydia M. Weymer-Salisbury) was born on his father's home farm in Sections 18 and 19 Kingston town. Here he grew to manhood, attended the rural school and graduated from the Litchfield High School.

At the age of 18 Mr. Salisbury taught his first term of school in French Lake township, Wright County. He continued in this vocation for 34 years with few interruptions. He advanced himself in his chosen field of work by self study. He was the first principal of the Eden Valley village two room school at which time he had under his direct tutelage 144 pupils. He held this position for five years and at the end of this period there were two teachers under his direction. On or about 1901 he was employed as a teacher of the seventh and eighth grades in the village school and his tenure covered a period of three years. On his retirement from the teaching profession Mr. Salisbury's services were engaged by the Eden Valley State Bank where he served until 1920 as a cashier.

Mr. and Mrs. Walter Salisbury

Mr. Salisbury has been deeply interested in the growth and development of Eden Valley and with the exception of two years served as village recorder for thirty-five years consecutively. He also served six years as a member of the Board of Education. He retired from active public service in 1936 since which time he has represented old line insurance companies, covering all forms of liabilities with the exception of life insurance. He adopted as his business slogan: "No Insurance but the Best."

Mr. Salisbury married, May 8, 1886, Mary Myrtle Shea (daughter of Charles and Ellen Dorman-Shea) born February 7, 1869. Mrs. Salisbury's parents were among the early settlers of Meeker County. Her mother was a daughter of Nathaniel and Susannah Putnam-Dorman. The Dormans were of colonial ancestry and came from the state of Maine.

Mr. and Mrs. Walter R. Salisbury are the parents of Margaret Ellen born January 6, 1892, who is at present a teacher in the Como Harriet School in St. Paul, Minnesota and Maurice Julian born January 23, 1896 who married August 1, 1917, Grace V. Duehn by whom he is the father of five children: Walter, Eileen, Pearl, Virginia and Douglas. Mr. and Mrs. M. J. Salisbury are residents of Grand Rapids, Minnesota.

GAYNER S. N. (son of Nels and Karna Gayner) was born in Skane, Sweden, November 14, 1866. He was left fatherless in babyhood. In 1875, in company with his mother and his elder brother, John, he came to America and made his home with an older brother, Louis. At the expiration of one year, the boys (S. N. and John) left their mother behind and jumped a western bound freight train and landed at Grove City with twenty-eight cents in their pockets. They were employed by farmers and attended the public schools.

Mr. Gayner made his home on the farm of O. M. Linnell, doing farm work and attending school Later he found employment in the Lindell Hardware Store. In 1886 he went to Duluth where he worked in a jobbing shop and in 1891 he returned to Meeker County and entered the employ of Johnson and Wanvig, hardware dealers. This firm sold their business to Settergren Brothers (Gust and Frank) and Mr. Gayner, later, entered into partnership with them and they established a hardware, lumber and harness business at Eldred, Minnesota, under the firm name of S. N. Gayner and Company.

S. N. Gayner

In 1899, following the big fire that destroyed nearly all the business houses in Dassel, the interests of the firm at Eldred were sold and Mr. Gayner purchased a main street lot and erected the building on its present site.

Mr. Gayner served as County commissioner (1923-1932) and during his period of service, was successful in establishing all the main highways in the eastern part of the county. In 1923 Mr. Gayner transferred his hardware business to his sons, Karl and Bernard, who have continued to operate the same. Since that date, Mr. Gayner has spent a portion of each year in the state of Washington in supervision of his fruit ranch.

S. N. Gayner married, June 24, 1890, Emily Linnell (daughter of O. M. and Carolina S. Anderson-Linnell, of Grove City, Minnesota) born June 6, 1868. They became the parents of seven living children: Miriam E.; Karl E.; Eva E.; Hazel K.; Bernard L.; Vivian A and Seymour N.

In the sunset of Mr. Gayner's life he enjoys sitting in the shade of the apple trees at the rear of his home and while smoking a fragrant cigar view the blooming flowers in his garden. Mrs. Gayner was called to her final rest, June 21, 1934. The writer of this sketch was deeply impressed by a tribute attached to a framed photo, in Mr. Gayner's private room, which reads as follows: "She loved to give herself in faithful service to her children and others entrusted to her care. Her face and hands bore the marks of toil and sacrifice, but those rough hands and wrinkled face were emblems of a love that never failed."

SKEIM, GEORGE S. (son of John J. and Nicoline Gravin-Skeim) born, December 18, 1893 at Twin Valley, Norman County, Minnesota. He spent his boyhood on his father's farm and was educated in the public schools and Crookston Business College.

Following two years of farming experience in North Dakota, he engaged his services as a grain buyer at Tower City and Casselton, North Dakota.

In 1918 he came to Litchfield and was employed as grain buyer for the Equity Cooperative Exchange and in 1921 assisted in the organization of the Independent Livestock Shipping Association and became allied with both organizations.

In 1923 he transferred his services to the Independent Cooperative Elevator Company as

Mr. and Mrs. G. S. Skeim

bookkeeper and in 1928 became manager of the company, the position occupied by him at present. In 1934 there was a reorganization of the company under the name, Farmers Exchange Company.

Mr. Skeim married, January 28, 1916, Olive Rose Mayoue (daughter of Isaac and Rose Deranleau-Mayoue), born January 24, 1895 in Crawford, Nebraska. Children: Ethel May, born May 9, 1920 and Harold George, born February 11, 1922. Ethel May is an experienced typist and is at present employed as an operator at the local telephone office.

BIERMAN, BERNARD, son of William Bierman, a Litchfield clothing merchant, graduated from the local high school, class of 1913. He later graduated from the University of Minnesota. In high school and college he distinguished himself in athletic sports and following his graduation from the university served as football coach at Montana and Tulane Universities. In 1932 he was employed as football coach at the University of Minnesota, a position he continues to hold.

BUSINESS LEADERS—EDEN VALLEY

INDEX TO ILLUSTRATION
(Left to Right)

FIRST ROW—Frank J. Coleman, Insurance Agent; Ben Garding, Proprietor of Garding Elevator; Martin Pasche, Pasche Radio Service; Arthur Henfling, Auto Repair Shop; Joseph Wartman, Hardware and Farm Implements; W. G. Rome, President of Chamber of Commerce; Dr. F. E. Putnam, Dentist.

SECOND ROW—Joseph Steman, Duffy's Cafe; J. L. Ruhland, Gamble Store; Jacob Bischof, Bush and Bischof Garage; R. T. O'Brien, ex-Mayor and retired business man; Peter Rome, Manager of Mansard Hotel; Philip Rome, clerk; James Martin, Railroad Agent.

BACK ROW, Standing—Dr. D. C. O'Connor, Physician; C. L. Arnold, Dairyman; Arthur Hukriede, Garage; Mrs. Nicholas Stoffel, General Merchandise; Mrs. Emma O'Brien, O'Brien-Haines Drug Co.; S. J. McCarthy, Eden Valley Lumber Co.

JAMES SWISHER, who resides on the farm where he established his home in Section 16, Ellsworth township, is believed at present date, in point of years, to be the oldest continuous resident of Meeker County. His residence dates from 1867. He has reached the ripe age of 95 years, having been born in the village of Fingal, Ontario, Canada, on February 10, 1844. He married Josephine Shadomy in 1874. This union resulted in the birth of seven children, Herman and Mercy who died in infancy; Guy and Stanley (deceased); Harry who lives with his father on the home place; Grace (Mrs. Herb Curtiss), and Frank who operates a fruit ranch at Medford, Oregon.

SEDERSTROM, V. A. (son of Peter and Charlotte Anderson-Sederstrom) was born in Chippewa County, Minnesota June 24, 1885. He spent his boyhood years on a farm in his native county and received his education in the public schools at Montevideo.

At the age of 14 he entered the employ of A. C. Anderson as a clerk in a general merchandise store in Montevideo where he remained for four years. He then purchased a small grocery store in Chippewa County and disposed of the same in 1905 and then engaged in business at Brookfield from 1905 to 1920. He and his family located in Litchfield in 1920 and opened a real estate office in which business he is engaged at the present time.

During his life in Litchfield, he served six years as a member of the Board of Education and has served as secretary and member of civic organizations of Litchfield for the past 14 years. He is an active member of the First Lutheran Church of Litchfield.

V. A. Sederstrom was married February 24, 1910 to Anna Peterson (daughter of John and Emma Peterson) born in Traverse County, Minnesota. They are the parents of four children: Eva (Mrs. H. O. Norstrom) of Oakland, California; Vernon (married to Fyliss McGraw) Litchfield; Muriel (Mrs. John L. Jones) Oakland, California; and Loren who is a student at the University of Minnesota.

V. A. Sederstrom

Topical Index

PIONEER DAYS, PAGES 1 - 13: Location and Early History—First Settlers—Early Births—First Homesteaders—Citizenship—Crow River Bridge—Lost in a Blizzard—Death of Dr. Ripley—Pioneer Sources of Income—Water Power Mills—Childhood Memories of Sarah Jane Dougherty and Walter Salisbury.

THE INDIAN OUTBREAK, PAGES 13 - 29: First Blood—Acton Massacre—Battle of Acton—Locating Acton Monument—Attack on Forest City—Manannah Massacre—Killing of Little Crow—The John McKenzie Exploit.

HUMAN INTEREST STORIES, PAGES 30 - 35: The Wild Woman of Manannah—My Pioneer Grandmother.

AGRICULTURAL PROGRESS, PAGES 37 - 46: Agricultural Development—Invention of Binder Twine Knotter—Livestock Shipping Association—Agricultural Extension Service—Rural Electrification.

MEEKER COUNTY NEWSPAPERS, PAGES 48 - 57.
TOWNSHIPS AND VILLAGES, PAGES 60 - 107.
LITCHFIELD VILLAGE, PAGES 110 - 118.
MEEKER COUNTY INDUSTRIES, PAGES 121 - 132.
BANKING INSTITUTIONS, PAGES 133 - 136.
POLITICAL TREND, PAGES 137 - 139.

PATRIOTIC, PAGES 142 - 156: Meeker County War Service—Grand Army of The Republic—Forest City Home Guards—Spanish American War—World War, Financial Support—End of The World War—World War Organizations—Our Honored Dead.

SCHOOLS AND CHURCHES, PAGES 158 - 178.

BIOGRAPHIES, PAGES 179 - 188: Board of County Commissioners—Compiler of Meeker County History—The March Family—The Harvey Doughertys.

BIOGRAPHIES OF DECEASED.
BIOGRAPHIES OF LIVING.

ACCEPT THANKS

I desire to express my sincere appreciation to all individuals who have given me encouragement and assistance in the compilation of the History of Meeker County. These persons are too numerous to permit of individual mention.

Frank B. Lamson.

ERRATA

See page 42, Paragraph 2—The following line was omitted at the close of the paragraph:—attained a state wide reputation as the foremost cooperative shipping association of the northwest.

See page 134—Farmers State Bank: S. O. Ilstrup, having purchased J. W. Freer's interests the reader will substitute Ilstrup's name in lieu of Freer wherever it occurs.